B/

AUDEN: A CARNIVAL OF INTELLECT

EPISTLE TO A GODSON

For such wayfarers,
what should we write to give them the nourishment,
warmth and shelter they'll be in need of?
Nothing obscene or unpleasant: only

the unscarred overfed enjoy Calvary
as a verbal event. Nor satiric: no
scorn will ashame the Adversary.
Nor shoddily made: to give a stunning

display of concinnity and elegance
is the least we can do, and its dominant
mood should be that of a Carnival.

April 1969

Auden:
A Carnival of Intellect

Edward Callan

New York   Oxford
OXFORD UNIVERSITY PRESS
1983

Library of Congress Cataloging in Publication Data

Callan, Edward, 1917-
  Auden, a carnival of intellect.

  Bibliography: p.
  Includes index.
  1. Auden, W. H. (Wystan Hugh), 1907-1973
  2. Poets, English—20th century—Biography.
  I. Title.
  PR6001.U4Z633   821'.912   82-2167
  ISBN 0-19-503168-7   AACR2

Grateful acknowledgment is made to Random House, Inc., for permission to quote from the copyrighted works of W. H. Auden. (Individual titles appear in the list of abbreviations and the sources of all extracts are indicated parenthetically in the text.) Grateful acknowledgment is also made to Faber and Faber Ltd., for permission to quote from Auden's works and specifically for verse extracts reprinted by permission of Faber and Faber Ltd. from *Collected Poems of W. H. Auden* and *The English Auden: Poems, Essays and Dramatic Writings 1927-39* by W. H. Auden and for prose extracts from *The Dyer's Hand, Secondary Worlds, A Certain World, Forewords and Afterwords, The Enchafèd Flood, The English Auden: Poems, Essays and Dramatic Writings 1927-39, The Orators* and *Collected Poems* by W. H. Auden. Acknowledgment is also due to Viking Penguin, Inc., for permission to quote from *Poets of the English Language*, Vol. V, edited by W. H. Auden and Norman Holmes Pearson, copyright 1950 by the Viking Press, Inc., copyright renewed 1978 by Viking Penguin Inc.; from *A Certain World: A Commonplace Book*, edited by W. H. Auden, copyright © 1970 by W. H. Auden; and from *The Viking Book of Aphorisms*, selected by W. H. Auden and Louis Kronenberger, copyright © 1962, 1966 by W. H. Auden and Louis Kronenberger. Acknowledgment is due to Curtis Brown, Ltd., for permission to quote from *Elegy for Young Lovers* by W. H. Auden and Chester Kallman and to Boosey and Hawkes, Inc., for permission to quote four lines of verse from *The Rake's Progress*—Igor Stravinsky. Libretto by W. H. Auden and Chester Kallman. Copyright 1949, 1950, 1951, renewed 1976, 1977, 1979 by Boosey & Hawkes, Inc. Reprinted by permission. Grateful acknowledgment is also due to Freeman Dyson and to Harper & Row, Publishers, for permission to quote from *Disturbing the Universe* by Freeman Dyson, and to Farrar, Straus & Giroux, Inc., for permission to quote from *Christopher and His Kind* by Christopher Isherwood.

Printing (last digit): 9 8 7 6 5 4 3 2 1

Printed in the United States of America

For Claire
and
in memory of
her father
Albert Wegner

Preface

This book is about the art of W. H. Auden's poetry and the spirit that informs it. It surveys his achievement as an artist over the fifty-year period from March 1923, when at age fifteen he chose poetry as his vocation, to September 1973 when he died in a Vienna hotel within hours of his final public reading. Its aim is to enable readers to understand and enjoy the full range of Auden's poems. To this end it represents his poetry, early and late, as the work of an accomplished artist who thought deeply about the human condition, had a sharp eye for man's comic estrangement from natural innocence as well as an affinity for the physical sciences unusual among poets, and who was from the outset so accomplished a master of the craft of verse that even his earliest poems had an immediate appeal to sensitive ears. Dylan Thomas wore out his copy of Auden's *Poems*, 1930, with re-reading.

Auden was a prolific poet. On a purely quantitative basis his poetic legacy far exceeds those of Yeats and Eliot combined. On a rough calculation his *Collected Poems* contains more than 30,000 lines, Yeats's approximately 14,000 and Eliot's about 5,500. Auden may have retained much they would have discarded, and he had no Ezra Pound for friend; but putting aside such considerations and the fact that Yeats wrote more verse drama, it is immediately evident that any survey of Auden's poetry in a volume of this size must be selective.

In choosing works for close scrutiny I have, in general, given priority to longer works and to poems in sequences and cycles in

the belief that a poet's intellectual concerns may be more readily apparent in substantial works. I therefore devote separate chapters, or parts of chapters, to the consideration of *Paid On Both Sides* and *The Orators;* to his plays for the London Group Theatre in collaboration with Christopher Isherwood and to "Sonnets from China" from his final collaboration with Isherwood, *Journey to a War;* to each of his four wartime longer works in America: *New Year Letter, For the Time Being: A Christmas Oratorio, The Sea and the Mirror,* and *The Age of Anxiety;* to his later cycles of poems from Ischia and Kirchstetten in the 1950s and 1960s and to his opera libretti of that period in collaboration with Chester Kallman. In selecting shorter poems for detailed commentary I have tried to make my choice representative of each stage of his development by including some lyrics from each of his separately published volumes—from Stephen Spender's private printing, *Poems,* 1928, to the posthumous *Thank You, Fog* (1974).

Auden believed in change as a fundamental law of life. "He held it truth," as Tennyson said of Goethe, "That men may rise on stepping-stones / Of their dead selves to higher things." In his later years he modeled his thought to some degree on Goethe. He would remark, at times, on how important it was for a writer not to try to write at sixty, for example, what he might have written at thirty, and he tended to alert readers to changes in his own work. In 1964, when preparing his *Collected Shorter Poems, 1927-1957,* he arranged the poems in chronological groupings so as to indicate points of change and development; and he concluded his Foreword by saying: "This collection stops at the year nineteen-fifty-seven. In the following year I transferred my summer residence from Italy to Austria, so starting a new chapter in my life . . . ." His literary executor Edward Mendelson, respected Auden's grouping in arranging the definitive *Collected Poems* (1976).

Although not a "reader's guide" in the conventional sense, this book is arranged in some degree as an adjunct to Auden's *Collected Poems.* Twelve of its seventeen chapters roughly correspond to twelve of the thirteen divisions of *Collected Poems.* (The exception is the prose poem *"Dichtung und Warheit* (An Unwritten Poem)" that comprises Part XI of *Collected Poems.*)

Place names in the chapter titles of this book will readily identify the stage of Auden's career under review: Oxford and Berlin; Iceland, Spain, and China; America; Ischia and Kirchstetten. But this book is not wholly chronological in arrangement. The opening chapters "A Flaker of Flints" and "Three Grateful Memories" treat of Auden's general accomplishment as an artist and of early life experiences that inform his work. Chapter X, "Disenchantment with Yeats," is the focal point of the book's central theme: Auden's fear of the dangers of our intellectual inheritance from Romanticism both in politics and literature, and his rejection of its one-sided Platonist presuppositions in favor of a Christian regard for the unity and coinherence of nature and spirit.

Earlier versions of some portions of this book have appeared in a number of journals including *Southern Review, London Magazine, Twentieth Century Literature, Commonweal, University of Toronto Quarterly, The Christian Scholar, Comparative Drama* and *Journal of Modern Literature;* and in the two collections *A Tribute to Wystan Hugh Auden on His Sixtieth Birthday* (*Shenandoah,* Winter 1967) and the "Twentieth Century View" volume *Auden: A Collection of Critical Essays* (1963) edited Monroe K. Spears.

I acknowledge a special debt of gratitude to W. H. Au executor Edward Mendelson, for reading and commentin substantial draft of this book, for granting me permissio produce a previously unpublished poem of Auden's f autograph book of Maria Senese of Forio d'Ischia and else besides. In particular, I am indebted to his ex fine study, *Early Auden* (The Viking Press, 1981), whic while this book was in preparation, as did Humphre *W. H. Auden: A Biography* (George Allen and Ur which I am also indebted for a number of speci knowledge deep gratitude to Barry C. Bloomfield friend and helper whose encouragement has inc me with ordnance maps of the Pennine Lead edition of the rare *Poems,* 1928, a first edit much else. I am indebted to my colleague Seamus Cooney, and Martin Gingerich for of early drafts; to Auden's friends Luigi

Maresca, of Forio d'Ischia for showing me through the houses
Auden had lived in; to Maria Senese for a copy of Auden's autograph poem; to the late Chester Kallman for showing me the
house at Kirchstetten and sharing his reminiscences of Auden;
to the curators of the Berg Collection, New York Public Library,
for making typescripts and manuscripts available to me, and to
the Faculty Research Committee of Western Michigan University
for grants in support of my research.

June 1982   E.C.

Contents

ABBREVIATIONS

ABH	*About the House* (1965)	LI	*Letters from Iceland* (1937)
ACW	*A Certain World* (1970)	NYL	*New Year Letter* (London, Faber, 1965)
CP	*Collected Poems* (1976)		
CWW	*City Without Walls* (1969)	O	*The Orators* (1932)
DBS	*The Dog Beneath the Skin* (1935)	O2	*The Orators* (1st American ed. 1967)
DD	*The Dance of Death* (1933)	OF	*On the Frontier* (1938)
DH	*The Dyer's Hand* (1962)	P	*Poems* (1930)
DM	*The Double Man* (1941)	P1928	*Poems* (1928). Printed by Stephen Spender
EA	*The English Auden* (1977)	PEL	*Poets of the English Language* (5 vols. 1950)
EF	*The Enchafèd Flood* (1950)	PT	*The Poet's Tongue* (1935)
EYL	*Elegy for Young Lovers* (1961)	RP	*The Rake's Progress* (1949)
F6	*The Ascent of F6* (1936)	S	*Spain* (1937)
F&A	*Forewords & Afterwords* (1973)	SW	*Secondary Worlds* (1968)
JW	*Journey to a War* (1939)	TYF	*Thank You, Fog!* (1973)

AUDEN: A CARNIVAL OF INTELLECT

I

A Flaker of Flints

> *"The 'laurel leaf' flint 'tool' tells us, as do the cave paintings, that Cro-Magnon Man was possessed of great artistic skill. Because it is so delicate it is probable that it served no useful purpose, but is an expression of fine craftsmanship and a sense of form."*
>
> Richard E. Leakey,
> *Origins,* 1977

> *"For poetry makes nothing happen: it survives*
> *In the valley of its making where executives*
> *Would never want to tamper, flows on south . . ."*
> W. H. Auden,
> "In Memory of W. B. Yeats."

1

In the forty-four years between his first volume, *Poems,* 1930, and his final collection, *Thank You, Fog!,* published some months after his sudden death in September 1973, W. H. Auden produced a body of poems, plays, opera libretti, and criticism unmatched in the twentieth century. He wrote rapidly, and sometimes he was slipshod; but his best and most characteristic work achieved what good artists are commonly remembered for: the highlighting of some facet of truth that was always there, but outside the circle of our recognition until brought into focus by their art.

At one time or another Auden sought to reach a variety of audiences and tastes, from popular to highbrow. He could range widely in tone from shrill name-calling in a political broadside—

"Beethameer, Beethameer, bully of Britain, / With your face as fat as a farmer's bum" (EA, 86)—to erudite bookish allusion that assumed everyone who read Auden had also read Freud (and as time went on, Goethe and Kierkegaard, too). As his choices for *The Oxford Book of Light Verse* (1937) attest, he liked all sorts of light verse, and his own includes ballads, blues, limericks, clerihews, and cabaret songs—forms attuned in some degree to the tinselled social atmosphere of the twenties in which he grew up. But the things that most excited his imagination had an intellectual reach; and if the term *intellectual* implies an aptitude for thought coupled with a well-stocked, witty, and logical mind, Auden was an intellectual. He particularly respected books by "thinkers"—R. G. Collingwood and A. N. Whitehead as well as Freud, Jung, and Groddeck in his earlier years in England where his reputation as a poet was first established in the 1930s; and Paul Tillich, Reinhold Neibuhr, Simone Weil, and Hannah Arendt, as well as Kierkegaard and other existentialists in his later years in America.

He valued books for their language as well as for their ideas, and he had a special passion that increased with age for dictionaries, crossword puzzles, and linguistic oddities of all sorts. He was pleased when his usage was cited in dictionaries—a pleasure given him by several entries in the unabridged *Webster's Third* (1961) where, for example, the instance cited for *egoist* in the sense of *egocentric* is his, and the instance given of *abrupt* as a verb is "let brazen bands abrupt their din" from *The Age of Anxiety* (1947). His playful late poem "A Bad Night: A Lexical Exercise" exhumes gnarled dialect words like *hirple, glunch,* and *sloomy;* but even his earliest verse employed unusual words—typically with the clinical air of a detached observer. At nineteen, for example, he wrote a poem on lovers' partings ("Consider if you will how lovers stand") that brought surprise to this genre with words like *suction, heartburn, clinically-minded,* and *ligatured*—this last in a laconic phrase of the kind that became his early hallmark: "Have ligatured the ends of a farewell." (EA, 438)

Although it may have become so in old age, Auden's youthful fascination with words was not a sterile one. The first quality in his work that proclaims him an artist—the marked ability to

give to "airy nothing / A local habitation and a name"—is manifest in his effective figurative use of clinical terms like "ligatured"; and in the comic extravagance of a metaphorical line
like: "Or hum of printing presses turning forests into lies," to
depict the partisan slant of mass-circulation English dailies in
the thirties. But his gift for imaginative "naming" went beyond
verbal marksmanship. It enabled him to discover a poetic
mythology for the times.

Born into an Age of Psychology, he invented an allegorized
poetic landscape of the psyche—peopled with explorers, spies,
and frontier guards—for Freud's description of the transforma-
tions and exchanges of energy within the psychic personality.
As a schoolboy he had read the standard psychological works
of the day, many of them available to him in his father's library.
Freud was then including in his writings topographical diagrams
of the psyche that accorded separate territories to *id, ego,* and
super-ego, and he tended to speak of these psychic energies as
of actors in a medieval morality play:

> The id . . . cannot say what it wants; it has achieved no
> unified will. Eros and the death instinct struggle within
> it; we have seen with what weapons the one group of
> instincts defends itself against the other. It would be
> possible to picture the id as under the domination of the
> mute but powerful death instincts, which desire to be at
> peace and (prompted by the pleasure principle) to put
> Eros, the mischief-maker, to rest; but perhaps that might
> be to undervalue the part played by Eros.[1]

Auden's poetry does not undervalue either the part played
by Eros or the atrophic power of the death instincts in their
desire to be at peace. The closing lines of "In Memory of Sigmund Freud," for example, find a metaphor for the creative
energies of Eros:

> sad is Eros, builder of cities,
> and weeping anarchic Aphrodite;   (CP, 218)

and in "Kairos and Logos" he speaks of the destructive power of
the opposing anarchic instincts:

Night and the rivers sang a chthonic love,
Destroyer of cities and of daylight order.   (CP, 238)

But what we find, characteristically, in Auden's early poems—
Paid on Both Sides, "The Secret Agent," "The Watershed," for
example—are not simply *statements* of this kind, but lively
dramas in which the conflict between the opposing psychic
energies is staged on an allegorical landscape. Freud supplied a
cast of characters and suggested a scenario; Auden invented a
poetic vehicle. There are recurring images in his early poems
for the natural desire to be at rest (the Pleasure Principle) and,
from the viewpoint of that desire, Eros is seen as a mischief-
maker as, for example, in "The Secret Agent." Freud's description of the ego as a "frontier-creature" who "tries to mediate
between the world and the id" also fits Auden's allegorical
method; and much of the dramatic action in these poems occurs
on the frontiers separating aspects of the psyche, and particularly
on the ultimate frontier between the unanxious realm of pre-
conscious nature and the world of human consciousness, where
the ego's anxiety in time finally begins. In the course of a summary of "the essence of Freud's teaching" in a 1935 essay, Auden
said of man's evolutionary heritage: "The introduction of self-
consciousness was a complete break in development, and all that
we recognize as evil or sin is its consequence. Freud differs both
from Rousseau who denied the Fall . . . and also from the
theological doctrine which makes the Fall the result of a deliberate
choice, man being therefore morally responsible." (EA, 339)
     In the course of time Auden's attitude toward the moment
when man "faulted into consciousness" changed more than once;
and these changes mark the successive stages of his philosophical
development. The signposts are already apparent in his 1935
summary of the essence of Freud's teaching. By the late 1930s
he becomes preoccupied with the dangers of the intellectual
legacy of Rousseau's Romantic notion of inherent natural innocence—an outlook he considered to have contributed to the
failure of German liberal humanism when faced by the manifest
evil of Nazism. In the early 1940s—notably in "The Meditation of
Simeon" in *For the Time Being* (1944)—he seeks figurative
equivalents for the Christian doctrine of the Fall and the Re-

demption: ". . . as long as there remained the least understanding between Adam and the stars, rivers and horses with whom he had once known complete intimacy, as long as Eve could share in any way with the moods of the rose or the ambitions of the swallow, there was still a hope . . . that the exile from Paradise was only a bad dream, that the Fall had not occurred in fact." (CP, 297)

At the outset, psychological theory was Auden's imaginative mother lode but not his only resource. He had an affinity for the natural sciences, particularly chemistry. He defined each personal life as "an isomorph of the general human condition," and he versified this as:

> We need to love all since we are
> Each a unique particular
> That is no giant, god, or dwarf,
> But one odd human isomorph;   (CP, 192)

and he also readily found useful metaphors for human experience in the worlds of relativity and quantum mechanics:

> A particle, I must not yield
> To particles who claim the field,
> Nor trust the demagogue who raves,
> A quantum speaking for the waves,
> Nor worship blindly the ornate
> *Grandezza* of the Sovereign State.   (CP, 180)

The range of Auden's poetic imagery, and the scope of the several technical vocabularies he from time to time employed show him remarkably aware of twentieth-century intellectual trends, and more attuned to discoveries in the natural sciences than either Eliot or Yeats. One may encounter in his poetry, on the one hand, technical terms from the specialized vocabularies of existentialist thinkers like Jaspers, Heidegger, Kierkegaard, and Buber; and on the other, precise images from various natural sciences—from the chemistry of cellular division, for example, in "Meiosis"; from paleontology in "Winds"; and from microbiology in "A New Year Greeting" (a humorous *tour de force* first published in *Scientific American*). Given the wide range of his interests, there is little to be gained from approaching Auden's art—as was once commonly done—by comparing it with the work of his Oxford contemporaries in "The Auden Group": Louis MacNiece, Cecil Day Lewis, and Stephen Spender, none of whom grew and changed to the extent that he did, or continued to deploy new technical equipment to meet the challenge of new themes. Auden is more aptly classed in the company of Pope and Wren whose names recall an age.

2

Much as the art of Pope and Wren mirrored eighteenth-century trust in the logic of Newton's universe—a universe in which set-squares and clocks could reliably answer all questions of space and time—the imaginative range of Auden's poetry accords more nearly with twentieth-century intellectual experience, particularly its psychological and scientific discoveries. Wren, in answer to whose questions on aesthetic form Newton wrote the *Principia,* set out an eighteenth-century credo in *Parentalia:*

> Geometrical Figures are naturally more beautiful than other irregular; in this all consent as to a Law of Nature. Of geometrical Figures, the Square and the Circle are most beautiful; next, the Parallelogram and the Oval. Strait lines are more beautiful than curve. . . .[2]

This credo of the Age of Reason points up, by contrast, the revolutionary character of the age in which Auden began to write: an age in which reason, deified in the age of Pope, was being forced to seek accommodation with unreason and uncertainty; an age, too, in which the metaphor for *mind* could no longer be *tabula rasa,* but something more like an ancestral cellar haunted by "family ghosts":

> Before this loved one
> Was that one and that one,

> A family
> And history
> And ghost's adversity . . .   (CP, 44)

And as with mind, so also with the material universe. Where Wren, like Pope, envisioned a universe respectful of law and order, Auden, in his later poetry, contemplated an unstable universe as much inclined to riot as wilful man:

> . . . if galaxies
> bolt like panicking mobs, if mesons
> riot like fish in a feeding-frenzy,
>
> it sounds too like Political History
> to boost civil morale, too symbolic of
> the crimes and strikes and demonstrations
> we are supposed to gloat on at breakfast.   (CP, 608)

But, as masters of the art of verse, Pope and Auden have in common a substantial artistic accomplishment that responds imaginatively to the *Weltanschauung* of their times. If not pre-eminent, each was at least a representative journeyman of his age. Also, to the casual eye, the poetic methods of Pope and Auden may seem very much alike; and as professionals of the craft of verse they certainly have qualities in common. Auden had in good measure Pope's ability to strike sparkles of wit from some technical detail of versification: an improbable rhyme, an unexpected counter-turn, or a skillful effect of syntax. Both were gifted satirists, but their visions of the ideal nature of society differed. Each, although admired and befriended, was in some degree cut off from normal family life and marriage by a personal circumstance corresponding to the wound of the mythical bowman Philoctetes—a God-given unpleasant defect to balance a great gift (the allusion in Edmund Wilson's title *The Wound and the Bow*)—Pope by a diseased spine that stunted his growth and caused him a life of pain, Auden by the psychological wound of his homosexuality.

Whatever their deeper differences, both Pope and Auden were committed to their craft; and both were primarily occasional poets. Pope wrote *The Rape of the Lock* in the hope of mend-ing a family quarrel, and his other more memorable works are in such traditional occasional forms as the verse essay and the epistle. Auden also wrote many letters in verse, including the two long works *Letter to Lord Byron* and *New Year Letter,* a number of shorter verse letters in *Letters from Iceland,* and the title poem in *Epistle to a Godson.* Pope wrote few elegies and a great number of epitaphs. Auden wrote few epitaphs: one of them for a favorite cat, Lucinda, that he and Chester Kallman owned in Ischia, but none of them for specific people. However, he often turned to the elegy as an occasional form. A remarkable proportion of the poetry of his later years is elegaic including memorial poems for his housekeeper at Kirchstetten, Frau Emma Eiermann, and for his New York doctor, David Protetch, M.D. Several of his elegies, including "In Memory of W. B. Yeats," "At the Grave of Henry James," and "In Memory of Sigmund Freud," are among his better known occasional poems.

Auden represented himself not in the high Romantic manner as a lover of the Muse—an *amateur*—but as a professional who could produce verse for a play, a libretto, an epistle, or an elegy as the occasion demanded. In the English cricketing terms of his day he was a "Player," as professionals were then called, not one of the amateur "Gentlemen." At a time when some literary theorists found traditional forms suspect, he preferred to believe that a poet's first duty was to master the technical elements of his craft. For more than forty years he commanded a greater variety of poetic forms than any poet writing in English. Readers who have sampled his poetry from time to time may well recall a cluster of ballads; various sonnets and sonnet sequences; instances of the villanelle, ballade, and canzone; a number of sestinas—four of them in "Kairos and Logos"; and sustained passages of terza rima and of alliterative verse. Some of the more complex stanza forms in the poems of his middle years—those employed in "Streams" and "In Transit," for example—are derived from elaborate courtly metrical forms whose names he brought back into the general vocabulary: the Welsh englyn, and the Skaldic drott-kvaett; and in his sixties he perfected other syllabic forms, derived ultimately from Greek prosody, but more immediately based on Goethe's hexameters and Horace's Sapphics and Alcaics. He imposed on himself even stricter limitations than those inherent in the traditional forms he adopted. He would add for example—even in sonnets—a pattern of internal rhyming syllables, or of counterpointed rhymes crossing over the lines. The opening quatrain of "Streams," the seventh poem in the cycle *Bucolics,* runs as follows:

> Dear water, clear water, playful in all your streams,
> as you dash or loiter through life who does not love
>   to sit beside you, to hear you and see you,
>   pure being, perfect in music and movement?

(CP, 433)

Syntactically this may read like prose, but it is far from prosy. Here, from a Caedmon record sleeve, is Auden's description of the form he employed: *"Streams.* In each quatrain, lines 1 and 2 have twelve syllables each and masculine endings, line 3 has nine syllables and a feminine ending. A syllable within line 1 rhymes with a syllable within line 3, the final syllable of line 2 rhymes with the penultimate syllable of line 4, and the penultimate syllable of line 3 rhymes with a syllable within line 4."[3] Auden does not hold rigidily to the pattern either in print or in his reading. In print he occasionally allows himself a variance of one syllable, and as in French verse the syllable count requires elision of contiguous vowels. The third quoted line is unusual in having two such elisions: "t'hear" and "you'nd." But in Auden's reading "to hear" is not elided and the line is heard as ten syllables. Nor is the rhyme linking stressed syllables necessarily strict as in *love* and *move*ment in lines 2 and 4—for the aim is not a mechanical pattern but an intensified texture of sound to which, as in Hopkins, imperfect rhyme and assonance may contribute more subtly than perfect rhyme. This demanding pattern, superimposed on a modified Alcaic stanza (line 4 has ten syllables) and sustained through the poem's eighteen quatrains, shows that Auden disdained to carve in soapstone. He preferred to be a flaker of flints. And what enabled him to transform rigid formal restrictions into unobtrusive background music was his mastery of subtle syntax and his great lexical range.

As one might expect from such a poet, his critical writings, and even his conversations, reveal a constant preoccupation

with questions of technique. Igor Stravinsky, recalling his collaboration with Auden on *The Rake's Progress,* said: "When
we were not working he would explain verse forms to me, and
almost as quickly as he could write, compose examples. I still
have a specimen sestina . . . that he scribbled off for my wife;
and any technical questions of versification, for example, put
him in a passion; he was even eloquent on such matters."[4] Auden himself said in "The Dyer's Hand" that if he were to run a
training school for poets, "the technical side would consist of
learning thirty lines of poetry a day by heart, and instruction in
prosody, rhetoric, and the history of language";[5] and he claimed
to distrust literary critics who did not really like "Complicated
verse forms of great technical difficulty, such as Englyns, Drott-
Kvaetts, Sestinas, even if their content is trivial." (DH, 47) On
one occasion he said, "Every poet has his dream reader: mine
keeps a look-out for curious prosodic forms like bacchics and
choriambs."[6] (He once told me—at a luncheon meeting in 1959—
that he had spent the morning making lists of amphisbaenic
rhymes.)

His response to the general view of "natural" form espoused
by contemporary critics like Sir Herbert Read appears satirically
in the poem "The Truest Poetry Is the Most Feigning":

> Be subtle, various, ornamental, clever,
> And do not listen to those critics ever
> Whose crude provincial gullets crave in books
> Plain cooking made still plainer by plain cooks.

(CP, 470)

Also, while acknowledging that some poets—notably D. H. Lawrence and T. S. Eliot—could handle free verse effectively, he was
forthright in asserting that "Those who confine themselves to
free verse because they imagine that strict forms must of necessity lead to dishonesty, do not understand the nature of art, how
little the conscious artist can do and what large and mysterious
beauties are the gift of language, tradition, and pure accident."[7]
He agreed with Paul Valéry's view that "a poem ought to be a
festival of the intellect, that is, a game, but a solemn, ordered,
and significant game" (F&A, 363), and he once remarked: "What-

ever else it may be, I want every poem I write to be a hymn in praise of the English language."[8]

3

No writer of occasional verse can feel completely comfortable with Wordsworth's dictum: "For all good poetry is the spontaneous overflow of powerful feelings," to the extent that it suggests an upsurge from prophetic or oracular depths. Although tempted at times to think he could fill either role, Auden, as poet, was neither oracle nor prophet. He had no new truth to tell. There were some who thought his voice prophetic in the early 1930s when Fascism threatened European democracy; and, indeed, Auden was then more alert than some of his contemporaries to the signs of impending cataclysm in Europe; for just turned twenty-one and fresh from Oxford, he lived in Berlin during 1928-29. As a frequenter, with Christopher Isherwood, of sleazy homosexual bars, he saw, and shared in some remote degree, the plight of workers and laborers faced simultaneously with unemployment and unprecedented inflation. There is no indication that he then read Hitler's *Mein Kampf* (published in two parts in 1925-26), although he does refer to it later. Neither is there any indication that he took an interest in German politics; but he did recognize while there that the prewar Edwardian society into which he had been born was gone beyond recovery.

On returning to England in 1929 he did not immediately identify himself with those who eventually formed the Popular Front against Fascism in the mid-1930s; but the vaguely utopian promise of his early volumes, and the Byronic zest of his satirical thrusts against conventional society, made him seem their natural ally. It was Michael Roberts, editor of two popular left-wing anthologies in the early 1930s, *New Signatures* (1931) and *New Country* (1933), who proclaimed him a leader of the left-wing cause. His plays for the Group Theatre from 1933 to 1938 lent substance to his anti-fascist reputation; and in private life he shared with his parents, who sheltered a succession of refugees, a revulsion against Fascist excesses, particularly Hitler's

persecution of Jews. In so far as he was to develop his own measure of fanaticism for anything in later life, it took the form of
constant preoccupation with the threat posed to society by self-
obsessed mystics like Hitler who thought the truth private to
themselves. Even his use of the term *egoist* cited in *Webster's
Third* points to his concern with the self-obsessed: "To a selfish
or a proud man, triumph is pleasant and defeat painful, but to
an egoist both are equally interesting, for what matters is not
the content of the experience but the fact that it is his." This
concern with the narcissistic personality becomes, at a later
point, the theme of his opera libretti: *The Rake's Progress* (with
Igor Stravinsky) and *Elegy for Young Lovers* (with Hans Werner
Henze).

Yet there was a strong utopian strain in Auden's work of the
early 1930s welcomed by a generation struggling out from the
quagmire of war and depression. Many among his contemporaries nursing a sense of betrayal by their elders whose policies
had led to the mass slaughter of the 1914-18 war were delighted
by the irreverent vision he set before them of England's ruling
caste beguiled by its native forms of oratory: the lies of press
lords; the dubious rhetoric of pulpit and political platform; and
the vapid talk above the old school tie. The poetry of Wilfred
Owen had linked the patrician rhetoric of these elders—*Dulce
et decorum est pro patria mori*—to the slaughter in the trenches,
and it was to Owen's banner that Auden rallied with lines like
the one about "printing presses turning forests into lies." Many
among Auden's contemporaries also welcomed the fresh combination of qualities in his verse that gave rise to the term *Au-
denesque:* a clinical air, clipped phrase, sharp ironical eye, and
deft control of line and rhythm. Such verse seemed designed to
probe the infected spots on the body politic like a surgical scal-
pel. Auden was soon a newspaper celebrity in England at a time
when the growing Fascist power in Germany, Italy, and Spain
seemed to outweigh all other dangers, so much so that from
1931 onward it brought socialists and liberals into an alliance
with the Communist Party in a Popular Front against Fascism.

The Popular Front rallied to the Republican cause during the
Spanish Civil War—a war that presented intellectuals in the
West with a crisis of conscience comparable to that faced by

Americans during the Vietnam War thirty years later—and Auden's widely heralded intention to serve in an ambulance unit that resulted in a short visit to the Spanish war zone in 1937, together with his subsequent journey, in 1938, to the Sino-Japanese war front, seemed to set him on the high road to a poetry grafted to political Romanticism. In retrospect, Auden saw in his politically oriented poetry of the mid-thirties a departure from the true line of his poetic development. He also felt on looking back that the public acclaim given him and his fellow poets in the thirties was undeserved. In the second half of life he turned the searchlight of his art on the Romantic obsession with oracular truth within, not only in the realm of politics but in the realm of poetry, where so many of the Romantic poets, including some older contemporaries he had admired, like W. B. Yeats and D. H. Lawrence, had fancied that they had discovered truth anew within themselves.

Auden's misgivings about the Romantic imagination were not apparent in his writings until 1937-38, when he was thirty years old and already fairly widely acclaimed as the leader of a new and politically oriented poetic movement, consisting mainly of his friends C. Day Lewis, Stephen Spender, and Louis MacNeice. Then, partly through a re-examination of his own personal values and of his public role as a poet, he began to question the conventional Romantic assumption that the artist-genius was more than commonly privy to the truth and that his creative imagination was geared exclusively to the service of freedom. This questioning first becomes evident in his sonnet sequence from China in *Journey to a War* (1938). His later American work expresses a conviction that Romanticism's deification of the imaginative original genius spawned the modern totalitarian dictator, whether of the Left or of the Right.

By 1940 he had come to recognize, perhaps with the aid of Kierkegaard's categories, that an analogous urge for the creation of perfect order marked both artist and tyrant—the one in the aesthetic sphere, the other in the political. He felt that the artist, habituated to shaping or discarding his materials at will, was by cast of mind inclined to seek tyrannical solutions in civil affairs—a weakness he had begun to diagnose in himself. Conversely, he felt that tyrants like Hitler or Stalin who sought to

mould human societies to utopian ideals were artists out of their
spheres. For, in pursuit of civil order, tyrants display the quality
of ruthlessness with which the poet, for aesthetic reasons, liqui-
dates unsound rhymes or removes whole stanzas to some other
part of his design.

Hitler's dream of a racially pure Nordic state was but one
such twentieth-century "aesthetic" Utopia; apartheid was to be
another; and the Marxist dream of pure Communism, a third.
As Auden put it in *The Dyer's Hand:* "A society which was really
like a good poem, embodying the aesthetic virtues of beauty,
order, economy and subordination of detail to the whole,
would be a nightmare of horror." (DH, 85) And he presented a
brilliant metaphor for this nightmare of horror in "The Shield
of Achilles"—the title poem of his best volume of the 1950s—
where what the aesthetic god, Haephestus, wrought was not
the ideal Thetis envisioned: "Marble, well-governed cities, / And
ships upon untamed seas"; but the utopian reality: "A million
eyes, a million boots in line, / Without expression, waiting for a
sign." (CP, 454) Auden also warned in a note to his *New Year
Letter* (1940) that inside every would-be artist a petty tyrant is
waiting to step out and tidy up the world, and his later work
strongly discouraged looking to art for salvation.

Now that Auden's work is complete it can be seen that his
long identification with the *avant garde* of the thirties is not the
whole measure of his art. His perspective changed with time,
but he continued to illuminate in his poetry obscure areas of individual human freedom necessarily circumscribed in each life
by ties to nature and to history; and he scorned W. B. Yeats for
reviving outmoded cyclic theories in which, as in Greek religion, nature and history were confused. He regarded formal
restrictions in art and natural limitations in life as both circum-
scribing and nurturing liberty by contributing to creative in-
genuity. As he put it in an essay on Valéry where he also says it
is more becoming in poets to talk of versification than of mysterious voices: "The formal restrictions of poetry teach us that
the thoughts which arise from our needs, feelings, and experiences
are only a small part of the thoughts of which we are capable."
(F&A, 364) This is the theme of his "Ode to Terminus" honor-
ing the Roman god of limits and boundaries whom he thanks

"for giving us games and grammar and metres." (CP, 609) The couplet from his "In Memory of W. B. Yeats," now inscribed on Auden's memorial in the Poets' Corner of Westminster Abbey,

> In the prison of his days
> Teach the free man how to praise,   (CP, 198)

is but one instance of the type of analogy he liked to draw between vitality arising from imposed restraint in the making of a poem and from natural limitations in the life of a free man.

Some of Auden's later poems draw a fine distinction between vocation and fate, identifying the one as a prime instrument of freedom and the other as a projection of natural necessity. Many poets have written solemnly about Good Friday, but only Auden—who like Kierkegaard thought humor a better companion than reason at the moment of the absurd leap of faith—found Good Friday an occasion for celebrating in witty metaphor the transformation of a sense of fate into a sense of vocation that includes the freedom to choose:

> To ignore the appetitive goddesses,
> to desert the formidable shrines
>
> of Rhea, Aphrodite, Demeter, Diana,
> to pray instead to St. Phocas,
>
> St. Barbara, San Saturnino,
> or whoever one's patron is,
>
> that one may be worthy of their mystery,
> what a prodigious step to have taken.
>
> There should be monuments, there should be odes,
> to the nameless heroes who took it first,
>
> to the first flaker of flints
> who forgot his dinner,
>
> the first collector of sea-shells
> to remain celibate.
>
> Where should we be but for them?
> Feral still, un-housetrained, still

wandering through forests without
a consonant to our names,

slaves of Dame Kind, lacking
all notion of a city,

and, at this noon, for this death,
there would be no agents.　　　　(CP, 477-78)

The stone and shell as symbols for the origins of science and art
in these lines may be drawn from the passage with which Auden begins his account of Romanticism in *The Enchafèd Flood*—
Wordsworth's portentous dream of the Arab on a dromedary in
The Prelude:

　　　　　　　　　　. . . the Stone
　　To give it in the language of the Dream,
　　Was Euclid's Elements: "and this," said he,
　　"This other," pointing to the Shell, "this Book
　　Is something of more worth."[9]

But unlike Wordsworth and his fellow nineteenth-century Romantics who distrusted science, Auden regarded art and science
as of equal worth, and the artist and scientist, through their
conscious commitment to a vocation, as equally bearing witness
to the necessity of human freedom for Mother Nature's sake.

　Like the First Wise Man in the Christmas Oratorio, *For the
Time Being,* Auden came to understand that science in the
Quantum Age postulates a reciprocity, or mutual bond of partnership, between man and nature. His First Wise Man, who had
previously relied on Bacon's definition of science—"Putting nature to the question"—has come, like the quantum physicist, to
accept ambiguous answers:

　　With rack and screw I put Nature through
　　　　A thorough inquisition:
　　But She was so afraid that if I were disappointed
　　I should hurt Her more that Her answers were disjointed—
　　　　I did. I didn't. I will. I won't.

> She is just as big a liar, in fact, as we are.
>   To discover how to be truthful now
>   Is the reason I follow this star.   (CP, 285)

Auden further warned in his Commonplace Book that we en-
slave Nature at the risk of enslaving ourselves when, in fact, our
task is "to discover what everything in the universe, from elec-
trons upwards, could, to its betterment, become, but cannot become without our help." (ACW, 282) His notion of man's obligation to share his freedom so that Nature might fulfill her potential
presumes that something unique occurred in the long process of
evolution when, as he put it in a geological metaphor, man
"faulted into consciousness." Specifically, his notion of man's
responsibility toward Nature presumes that when in the course
of the evolutionary process Nature produced a conscious crea-
ture capable of voluntary choice, the old involuntary order of
the world of Dame Kind (in which Nature decided the destiny
of all her offspring) was replaced by an era of partnership in
which we, as Nature's conscious children—like the daughters of
Oedipus—must lead our maimed parent to a mutual denoue-
ment. An early expression of the reliance of the natural and instinctive world of Mother Nature on our conscious regard may
be found in his magnificent elegy, "In Memory of Sigmund
Freud (d. September 1939)":

> but he would have us remember most of all
> to be enthusiastic over the night,
>   not only for the sense of wonder
>   it alone has to offer, but also
>
> because it needs our love. With large sad eyes
> its delectable creatures look up and beg
>   us dumbly to ask them to follow:
>   they are exiles who long for the future
>
> that lies in our power, they too would rejoice
> if allowed to serve enlightenment like him. . . .
>   (CP, 217-18)

(While celebrating his genius, these Alcaic stanzas—wrought as
carefully as those of "Streams"—implicitly criticize Freud's ten-

dency to overlook the conscious shaping that distinguishes poetic creativity from dreaming.)

Auden's conception of man's responsibility for Nature's freedom—less common perhaps among poets than among physicists —sets him apart from those poets among his contemporaries more immediately concerned with social and political ideologies, and as we shall see, it certainly set him apart from W. B. Yeats. The difference is fundamental. Therefore simplistic charts of his changes of attitude toward questions of politics or religion help little toward the enjoyment of his later, more philosophical, poems that are so frequently concerned with the nature of man and the origins of creativity. Having thought as a schoolboy that his future lay in mining engineering, in time he came to regard his choice of a poetic vocation as providential—given his life circumstances.

II

Three Grateful Memories

1

On the evening of Friday, September 28, 1973, at the Palais Palffy in Vienna, Auden read a selection of his poems for the Austrian Society for Literature. Ordinarily, he would have returned after such a reading to his house in the village of Kirchstetten, twenty-five miles away, where he and Chester Kallman had spent each spring and summer for fifteen years. But he had closed up the Kirchstetten house on finishing their last collaboration—the libretto for *The Entertainment of the Senses*—a day or two earlier and arranged to stay for the weekend in a Vienna hotel before returning to his retirement cottage at Christ Church, Oxford, for the winter. He declined supper after that final reading and asked to be driven to his hotel. Next morning Kallman, who called for him at the hotel, had the room opened by the hotel management and found that Auden had died during the night.

A burial site at Westminster Abbey was offered to his family, but Auden was buried according to his wishes in the graveyard of the Lower Austrian village church where, although an Anglican "obedient to Canterbury," he had regularly attended Sunday Mass. In keeping with local custom his "grave of honour" near the cemetery gate was marked, temporarily, by a picture frame with his photograph and the simple inscription: "W. H. Auden, *Dichter und Kritiker.*"

Poet and critic, as this inscription asserted, were Auden's true

vocations; but as is common in a full life—and even more common among twentieth-century poets writing in English who
find what employment they can to support their art—he filled
a variety of roles. He was a schoolmaster at a number of private
schools in England and Scotland between 1930 and 1935; and
after emigrating to America in 1939 he again became a teacher,
this time in colleges and universities, until fame and popularity
brought him good fees for the poetry readings he describes in
"On the Circuit" (1963), which concludes with an ironic salute
to his audiences:

> God bless the lot of them, although
> I don't remember which was which:
> God bless the U.S.A., so large,
> So friendly, and so rich.   (CP, 549)

Although reclusive to the degree necessary for any writer as
productive as he was, Auden was anything but an ivory tower
poet. He was a professional writer with an active interest in the
arts of music, opera, and drama; and he was alert to intellectual
trends and the significance of political events. He was not a
stretcher-bearer in the Spanish Civil War as was so frequently
said of him (although he had intended going there to drive an
ambulance, or even to fight), but he did go to Spain for several
weeks early in 1937 and out of his experience came the long
poem *Spain*. In 1938, as an unconventional war-correspondent,
he took photographs of the Sino-Japanese war front for his
collaboration with Christopher Isherwood on *Journay to a War*,
and in this capacity met and photographed Chou En-lai. He
appeared in American uniform in 1945, with the substantive
rank of major in the U.S. Strategic Bombing Survey, to collaborate with John Kenneth Galbraith and others in studying
the effects of bombing on the morale of German civilians. (Their
report that strategic bombing often stiffened resistance did not
please military chiefs.)

The variety of these temporary occupations, and the om-
nipresence of war, reflects the century Auden was born in. It
could have been otherwise. Had he been born a generation
earlier—given his family background—he might have become the

kind of Anglican cleric met with in Trollope. Both of his Victorian grandfathers were clergymen of the Church of England, and each fathered seven children; and four of his uncles became Anglican priests. But his father, George Augustus Auden, studied medicine, and Wystan was born into the Edwardian professional middle class, in York, in 1907—with "a coachman who did not live in, as well as a cook and two maids who slept in the attic."[1]

Before Wystan was a year old the family moved to Birmingham, and his first memories were of "Apsley House," Lode Lane, in suburban Solihull:

> My earliest recollection to stay put
>   Is of a white stone doorstep and a spot
> Of pus where father lanced the terrier's foot;
>   Next, stuffing shag into the coffee pot
>   Which nearly killed my mother, but did not;
> Both psychoanalyst and Christian minister
> Will think these incidents extremely sinister. (CP, 95)

In an earlier poem, "Through the Looking-Glass" (1933), he had offered a "transfigured" scene of Edwardian-Georgian childhood (George V succeeded Edward VII in 1910 when Auden was three years old):

> My father as an Airedale and a gardener,
> My mother chasing letters with a knife.   (CP, 107)

And more prosaically, in an unpublished book he worked on after emigrating to America in 1939: "My father was a doctor, my mother had a university degree. The study was full of books on medicine, archaeology, the classics. There was a rain-gauge on the lawn and a family dog." (EA, 397) More than a decade later in "Winds" (1953), in search of an image for "our Authentic City"—a symbol of peace restored that haunts his poetry in various forms from beginning to end—he recalls the lost Eden of a middle-class Edwardian-Georgian childhood, an era that ended with World War I and the Great Depression (and, in the details of this scene, with the advent of radio weather reports):

> When I seek an image
> For our Authentic City
>   (Across what brigs of dread,
> Down what gloomy galleries,
>   Must we stagger or crawl
> Before we may cry—O look!?),
>   I see old men in hall-ways
> Tapping their barometers,
>   Or a lawn over which
> The first thing after breakfast,
>   A paterfamilias
> Hurries to inspect his rain-gauge.   (CP, 426)

Auden envied Shakespeare his luck—or foresight—in leaving behind nothing of much value to biographers; and he leaned toward the view that successful poems, like other successful works of art, acquire an existence largely independent of their makers. In 1937 when, with John Garrett, he edited the school anthology *The Poet's Tongue,* they arranged the poems in "an alphabetical anonymous order" on the reasonable grounds that young readers should first approach poems "free from the bias of great names." But however often Auden insisted that the poems and not the poet should be the object of our curiosity, he incorporated much that was personal into both his poetry and his criticism; for the portrait of the poet as a young man in "Making, Knowing, and Judging" (DH, 31-60)—his Inaugural Lecture as Professor of Poetry at Oxford—is a self-portrait.

Always alert for a critic's fundamental bias, which he felt should be openly declared, he was careful to label his own collected criticism as a poet's criticism; and to indicate its bias— the coloration of one steeped in his trade—he chose its title, *The Dyer's Hand,* from Shakespeare's Sonnet 111:

> O, for my sake do you with Fortune chide,
> The guilty goddess of my harmful deeds,
> That did not better for my life provide
> Than public means which public manners breeds,
> Thence comes it that my name receives a brand,

And almost thence my nature is subdu'd
To what it works in, like the dyer's hand . . .

This personal element in his criticism, and also such auto-biographical poems as *Letter to Lord Byron,* "Good-Bye to the Mezzogiorno," and the cycle, "Thanksgiving for a Habitat," in-vites some consideration of the relation of Auden's life and ideas to his poetry. His dedication of *The Dyer's Hand* to his Irish-born Oxford tutor, Nevill Coghill—in the form of an Irish triad—offers a plausible starting point:

> Three grateful memories:
> a home full of books,
> a childhood spent in country provinces,
> a tutor in whom one could confide.   (DH, vii)

2

Auden owed the first of his three grateful memories to his father, of whose library he once said: "In my father's library, scientific books stood side by side with works of poetry and fic-tion, and it never occurred to me to think of one as being less or more 'humane' than the other." (F&A, 497)

George Augustus (born August 27, 1872, the son of the Rev. John Auden, of Horninglow, Burton-on-Trent) was a man of great personal charm and exceptionally wide human interests. He attended Repton School, and afterwards had a brilliant career at Cambridge where, in 1893, he was awarded the Porteus gold medal and a First in Natural Sciences. He went on to study medicine at St. Bartholomew's Hospital, London. There he was Kirkes Scholar and gold medalist in 1896, and Lawrence Scholar and gold medalist in 1897. While at St. Bartholomew's he met Constance Rosalie Bicknell (b. 1869), one of the first women to win an Honors degree in French at London University, who was studying to be a missionary nurse. They were married in 1898.

Miss Bicknell, whose father was the Rev. R. H. Bicknell of Wroxham in Norfolk, came from what would now be considered an unbearably class-conscious family. Her mother, whose family name was Birch, was a relative of the Rev. Dr. Birch sometime tutor to the Prince of Wales who in 1901 became Edward VII. John Constable's wife, Mary Bicknell, was another distant relative. Her marriage to the landscape painter was long delayed by a storm of protest from the Bicknell family who felt she was marrying beneath her. This Bicknell consciousness of class remained strong; for when Auden's mother became engaged to a young physician, one of her sisters, the wife of an Anglican clergyman, warned her: "If you marry this man, you know nobody will call on you." (F&A, 496)

In the year following his marriage, Dr. G. A. Auden set up practice in York, where the couple's three sons were born. Their first son, Bernard, born in 1900, was old enough to be called up for military service in the closing months of the first World War. He emigrated to Canada shortly afterwards to become a farmer. The second son, John Bicknell, born in 1903, was to make his reputation as a geologist and mountaineer in the Himalayas. The third and youngest son, born in 1907, was Wystan Hugh, the poet. The year after Wystan's birth, Dr. Auden gave up his lucrative private practice in York and took a post as School Medical Officer in Birmingham, where he also acted as honorary psychologist to the Birmingham Children's Hospital and as Sanitary Adviser to the Governors of Rugby School. (His motives appear to have included a strong sense of dedication to public health, but his children's legend was that his wife "slightly disapproved of his proficiency in gynecology.")[2] In 1941 he was appointed Professor of Public Health at the University of Birmingham, where for many years he had lectured on this subject. His professional reputation was by no means local; for he held appointments, at various times, as a Visiting Lecturer in Public Health with the Ontario Board of Education; at Columbia University, New York; and at the University of Michigan, where he was preceded by his son, Wystan, who taught courses in literature there in 1941.

Dr. G. A. Auden had a range of intellectual interests almost as wide as Wystan was later to develop. One finds from him, for example, a letter to *The Times* supplying for a correspondent who had offered a phrase from Juvenal as the origin of Keir Hardie's favorite metaphor, "cauld kale het again" (cold cabbage warmed over), a still earlier proverb in Greek to describe "the sorry effects of re-dishing up stale stuff, of considerable antiquity when Juvenal found it apt application in his satire." (Keir Hardie, 1856-1915, an Ayrshire miner, founded the Independent Labour Party in 1892.) Another of Dr. Auden's letters to *The Times* supplements an article on Malthus with the precise reference to the passage where Darwin credits Malthus, whom he happened "to be reading for amusement," for triggering in his mind the idea of the origin of the species.[3] From his schooldays on, Dr. Auden had a keen interest in classical literature: he published papers on its medical aspects; and was for many years Honorary Secretary of the Birmingham branch of the Classical Association. Even more active as a local historian and as an antiquarian than as a classicist, Dr. Auden edited a handbook on York in 1906, and another on Birmingham in 1913, for the British Association;[4] and as a Fellow of the Society of Antiquaries with a special interest in Iceland and Scandinavia, he translated into English both Rathgen's *The Preservation of Antiquities* and the official *Guide to the Prehistoric Collection* of the National Museum of Copenhagen. He believed himself to be of Icelandic descent, and he read the Norse myths and folk tales to his children—and this, Wystan admits, is what attracted him to Iceland and to the sagas. Wystan recalls this interest of his father's in *Letters from Iceland:* "Few English people take an interest in Iceland, but in those few the interest is passionate. My father, for example, is such a one, and some of the most vivid recollections of my childhood are hearing him read to me Icelandic folk-tales and sagas, and I know more about Northern mythology than Greek." (LI, 214)

As a young boy, Wystan Auden made precocious use of his "home full of books." Christopher Isherwood recalls in *Lions and Shadows* that Auden, not yet twelve, gained a certain fame among his schoolfellows for knowledge derived from his father's books on anatomy;[5] and Auden himself recalls in one of his autobiographical "Shorts" in *City Without Walls* (1970):

> Father at the wars,
> Mother, tongue-tied with shyness,
> struggling to tell him
> the Facts of Life he dared not
> tell her he knew already.   (CP, 602)

Since Auden went off to boarding school at seven, he was, by his own account, very precocious indeed:

> I must admit that I was most precocious
>   (Precocious children rarely grow up good).
> My aunts and uncles thought me quite atrocious
>   For using words more adult than I should;
>   My first remark at school did all it could
> To shake a matron's monumental poise;
> "I like to see the various types of boys."   (CP, 95)

3

For the second of his "three grateful memories"—"a childhood spent in country provinces"—Auden was indebted in good measure to his mother, but perhaps even more to chance, and to unusual circumstances related to the first World War. Yet he felt that these circumstances contributed, in an exceptional degree, to his mature ability to create poems where the imaginative and the real were wedded and fulfilled—poems of the sort that would fit Marianne Moore's definition: "imaginary gardens with real toads in them." In his Inaugural Lecture at Oxford in 1956, he said that apart from a few stories like George Macdonald's *The Princess and the Goblin,* and Jules Verne's *The Child of the Cavern,* "which touched upon my obsessions," his favorite childhood books bore such titles as *Underground Life, Machinery for Metalliferous Mines,* and *Lead and Zinc Ores of Northumberland and Alston Moor* (DH, 34); and in his Commonplace Book he adds to these, Thomas Sopwith's *A Visit to Alston Moor.* (ACW, 292)

Unusual childhood circumstances contributed to Auden's

absorption in a private imaginary world to a degree beyond the ordinary. As the youngest of three brothers he remained at home alone with his mother, at Solihull near Birmingham, when the two older boys went off to boarding school. Then, between the ages of seven and thirteen, he was himself away from home at St. Edmund's School at Greyshott in Surrey, where he first met Christopher Isherwood. At this time also his father was serving abroad with the Medical Corps, in Egypt, Gallipoli, and France, from 1914 to 1918; and his mother decided not to keep the Solihull house and live there alone. During the war years, therefore, Wystan and his brothers, deprived of a father's influence, had no settled home in familiar surroundings, but only a succession of resort boarding houses where they joined their mother during school vacations. These vacations included, in particular, visits to parts of central Wales where the whole family had holidayed before the war, and also to Cleeve Hill in the Cotswolds, Clithero in Lancashire, and Totland Bay on the Isle of Wight as well as to the home of maternal grandparents in Norfolk. According to his brother John, Wystan's passion for limestone landscapes originated during one such vacation at Bradwell in Derbyshire.[6] Possibly, at Bradwell, the Bagshaw Cavern and its stalagtites first opened to him the hidden mystery of limestone caves and conduits that became his symbol for primordial innocence:

> Dear, I know nothing of
> Either, but when I try to imagine a faultless love
> Or the life to come, what I hear is the murmur
> Of underground streams, what I see is a limestone landscape.
>
> (CP, 415)

In time he transferred the focus of his passion for limestone landscape to Alston Moor in Cumberland—a Pennine watershed on which the counties of Durham, Westmorland, Northumberland, and Yorkshire also abut:

> Always my boy of wish returns
> To those peat-stained deserted burns
> That feed the WEAR and TYNE and TEES,

> And, turning states to strata, sees
> How basalt long oppressed broke out
> In wild revolt at CAULDRON SNOUT.   (CP, 182)

In later years, when speaking of the creative imagination, Auden frequently drew a parable of authentic creativity from his early imaginative experience. The theme of this parable is the balance struck, in his case, between fascination with an imaginary world of lead mines, and ready access to real objects like winches and pumping-engines related to it. These latter also included ore specimens and crystals; maps and technical books; and, above all, occasional visits to the Lead Dales near Alston Moor, where the rural landscape was dotted with both active and abandoned lead-mine shafts and smelting mills, and even, on occasion, offered such special wonders as the great undershot water-wheel (still preserved in the 1980s) on an old mill between Alston and Rookhope, or the no longer evident landmark above Rookhope of which he wrote in 1940:

> The derelict lead-smelting mill,
> Flued to its chimney up the hill,
> That smokes no answer any more
> But points, a landmark on BOLTS LAW,
> The finger of all questions.   (CP, 182)

The game of integrating these "sacred objects" from the real world into the secondary world of his imagination taught him, he says, to balance the claims of the real and the imaginary and to understand that there were realistic bounds to imaginative freedom. "In constructing my private world," he says in his Commonplace Book, "I discovered that though this was a game . . . something I was free to do or not as I chose, not a necessity like eating or sleeping, no game can be played without rules." (ACW, 424) He became aware, instinctively, of the need for restrictions to limit fantasy.

    Auden felt that in the course of this childhood play he acquired certain insights—either intuitively or providentially—that had important consequences when he came to write poetry. Looking back, in the second half of life, he realized that when

fabricating his imaginary world of lead-mining he had not only reined-in fantasy but, voluntarily, had set certain realistic limitations on imaginative possibility. Auden recalls that when he introduced a machine into his imaginative childhood play, he felt an obscure obligation to respect its integrity. If he wanted a water-turbine, for example, he could choose among actual turbines he found illustrated in textbooks or catalogues, but he could not invent one *ex nihilo*. He felt similarly bound, in the imaginary functionings of his mines, to choose among practical possibilities. He says he felt that an imaginary mine could be "drained either by an adit or a pump—but physical impossibilities and magic means were forbidden"; and he adds: "When I say forbidden, I mean that I felt, in some obscure way, that they were morally forbidden." (ACW, 424) As a consequence of this apprenticeship in shaping imaginary worlds to accommodate the real, when he came to write poetry he felt the same sense of obligation to the actual world. From this he eventually derived a theory of imagination rooted in a recognition of moral obligation: "What the poet has to convey" he says, "is not 'self-expression,' but a view of reality common to all, seen from a unique perspective, which it is his duty as well as his pleasure to share with others." In support of this he calls on a statement of St. Augustine: "The truth is neither mine nor his nor another's; but belongs to us all whom Thou callest to partake of it, warning us terribly, not to account it private to ourselves, lest we be deprived of it." (ACW, 425)

Auden's several accounts of his childhood insight into the workings of the imagination and of the significance of this for poetry may seem disarmingly simple, but all are indirect and diffident efforts to focus attention on one of his own singular intellectual accomplishments: his reassessment of the Platonic theories on art and the artistic imagination that have long dominated literary theory, and his proposal to replace these by a more "realistic" theory of imagination not based on a philosophical abstraction "like the Good," but on the Christian doctrine of the union of the material and the divine in the Word made Flesh.[7]

Auden speaks of this discovery made during "a childhood spent in country provinces" only late in life when his attitude

toward the creative process was rooted in a theological understanding he first explored in a suite of four sestinas, "Kairos
and Logos," composed about the time of his return to Christianity over a period in 1939-40. In "Words and the Word," the
fourth of his T. S. Eliot Memorial Lectures, 1967, he put it this
way:

> Man was created by God as a culture-making creature,
> endowed with imagination and reason, and capable of
> artistic fabrication and scientific investigation, so that to
> say that Christ calls art into question does not mean that
> it is forbidden to a Christian as it is forbidden to a
> Platonist, only that the nature of the imagination and
> the function of the artist are seen otherwise than they
> were in pre-Christian times. In a magico-polytheistic cul-
> ture all events are believed to be caused by personal
> powers . . . and the nearest that men can come to the
> concept of necessity is in the myth of the Fates who deter-
> mine events by whim. . . . (SW, 137)

To reveal how Auden arrived at this standpoint after initial
periods of dependence on the thought of Freud as well as Darwin and Marx—whom he later numbers among the "prophets of
Victorian monism" who see only one side of the truth—is in part
the task of subsequent chapters in this book. For the moment
his intellectual odyssey concerns us only to the extent that it was
nurtured by his memories of "a home full of books" and "a
childhood spent in country provinces."

4

On the third grateful memory, "a tutor in whom one
could confide," only Auden himself or his Oxford tutor Nevill
Coghill, neither of them now alive, could have anything valuable or interesting to say. Coghill recalled that in the course
of his first conference with Auden, who had switched to English
in his second year, he asked the conventional question, "What

are you going to do, Mr. Auden, when you leave the university?"
Auden replied, "I am going to be a poet." Of his response to
this Coghill wrote more than forty years later: " 'Ah yes!' I said
in my lordly way—one is capable of every blunder at twenty-
seven—'that's the right way to start reading English. It will give
you insight into the technical side of your subject if you try to
write poetry; there's more in it than just *O Altitudo!* Besides,
writing your poems will improve your prose.' I felt rather
pleased with that. But the scowl returned. 'You don't understand at all,' he said. 'I mean a great poet.' "[8] Even allowing for
an impish intention in this response, we may presume that having seriously chosen poetry as his vocation, Auden did not
intend to be a mere coterie poet. But in his case, because of his
homosexuality, the task of avoiding one kind of coterie influence was not an easy one.

To pursue this point I take my cue from the autobiographical stanza in *Letter to Lord Byron* where Auden moves on from
an account of his childhood and schooldays to his university
years:

> Without a bridge passage this leads me straight
>   Into the theme marked "Oxford" on my score
> From pages twenty-five to twenty-eight.
>   Aesthetic trills I'd never heard before
>   Rose from the strings, shrill poses from the cor;
> The woodwind chattered like a pre-war Russian,
> "Art" boomed the brass, and "Life" thumped the
>   percussion.   (CP, 98)

Dacre Balsdon begins a chapter in *Oxford Now and Then*
(1970), "Homosexuality: The Sublimely Silly Twenties," with
the remark: "A vice from which present-day Oxford does not
suffer is homosexuality. There have been times—after the 1914
war, for instance—when, if you believed what you were told, it
was Oxford's single but overpowering weakness. Headmasters
took you aside and whispered their hoarse enquiries, 'Tell me
how much truth there is in what people are saying about Oxford?' "[9] Auden, who was at Oxford from 1925 to 1928, recalls
this era in *Letter to Lord Byron:*

We were the tail, a sort of poor relation
To that debauched, eccentric generation
That grew up with their fathers at the War,
And made new glosses on the noun Amor.   (CP, 98)

That was the Oxford generation later described in Evelyn
Waugh's *Brideshead Revisited* (1944) where Anthony Blanche—
the "aesthete" par excellence—lisps lines from Eliot's *Waste Land*
through a megaphone to hearty oarsmen passing toward the
river: "And I Tiresias have foresuffered all. . . ." (Waugh's
characterization of Blanche drew on his Oxford contemporary
Brian Howard, to whom Auden's poem "Ischia" is dedicated.)
Louis MacNeice says that when he arrived there in 1926, Oxford
was just at the end of its postwar deliberate decadence: "At the
first party I went to there was no drink but champagne . . . and
the air was full of the pansy phrase 'my dear.' I discovered that
in Oxford homosexuality and 'intelligence'; heterosexuality and
brawn, were almost inexorably paired."[10]

While still at school Auden became aware that his emotional
attachments tended to be homosexual. He has hinted at possible
contributing causes in various essays where he points, for example, to the eleven years he spent away from home and parents
between the ages of seven and eighteen at boarding schools for
boys, and also to the fact that between his seventh and twelfth
years his father was absent on war service in France and Egypt.
Besides being deprived by circumstances of his father's influence,
the young Auden had an overly possessive mother who could, he
says, "be very odd indeed": "When I was eight years old, she
taught me the words and music of the love-potion scene in *Tristan,* and we used to sing it together." (F&A, 501) (According to
his brother John, Wystan's was the Isolde role in this scene.)

The body of Auden's mature work—particularly after 1937—
does not parade his sexual concerns. Some of his earlier volumes—*The Orators* (1932) is the most obvious example—indulge
in coterie jokes and covert homosexual allusion. Several poems
dating from 1939 celebrate the beginning of his relationship
with Chester Kallman, but without naming their subject; and
there are occasional subsequent pieces of satirical light verse like
"Pleasure Island" (1947) and "The Love Feast" (1948), on holi-

day scenes in a generally homosexual ambience. There are also in *Collected Poems* (1976) the "Three Posthumous Poems," frank to the point of banality, that record, but do not celebrate, late liaisons. The early literary record is supplied by Christopher Isherwood in his fictionalized autobiography *Lions and Shadows* (1938), and in his more directly confessional *Christopher and His Kind* (1976). (They had first met and become friends at boarding school when Auden was seven and Isherwood ten.)

In general, Isherwood represents himself in these books as committed to a struggle between an "Us"—an inner circle of homosexual loyalists—and a "Them"—the enemy without. This ubiquitous "enemy" included at times his own mother as well as England and England's laws, her police, and her immigration authorities (who once refused to admit a German friend of Isherwood's even though both he and Auden were at the dockside to intercede for him). By extension the enemy included established officialdom everywhere, and Isherwood notes—and this is the significant point here—that his political convictions were influenced by his test of loyalty to a homosexual cause. In the twenties he tended to share the Communist sympathies fashionable among his group at the time, and he says that he admired the Soviet government because on coming to power in 1917 it "had declared that all forms of sexual intercourse between consenting individuals are a private matter, outside the law";[11] and he also says that while living in Germany he identified himself with the German Communists because of their support, in 1929, for a proposal to revise Paragraph 175 of the German Criminal Code so as to decriminalize homosexual acts. The Nazis opposed this. When they came to power in 1933 they denounced homosexuality as a form of treason to the state; and the Soviets, in turn, came close to duplicating this in 1934 when Stalin's administration made all homosexual acts punishable by heavy prison sentences. It was this approximation to the Nazis, Isherwood says, that in 1939 disillusioned him and caused him to realize that "he must dissociate himself from the Communists, even as a fellow traveler."[12] In his case, at least, homosexuality rather than class origins influenced political loyalties.

Isherwood represents Auden in these books as a fellow homosexual who introduced him to "boy bars" in Berlin, but less obsessed than he was with "Them": "Wystan was much more apologetic about his homosexuality than Christopher was, and much less aggressive. His religion condemned it and he agreed that it was sinful, though he fully intended to go on sinning."[13]

The prevailing metaphor in Auden's early poetry is the malaise of man endowed with consciousness and at odds with his instinctive nature. In a mind otherwise convinced of its genius, such an obsessive concern with man's self-estrangement could arise from a more than ordinary personal sense of conflict between instinctive life and the life of the mind. At least in private, according to Isherwood, Auden spoke ill of homosexuality, and he inscribed a copy of Robert Bridges's *The Testament of Beauty:*

> He isn't like us
> He isn't a crook
> The man is a heter
> Who wrote this book.[14]

And there was a time when he sought help, apparently in anticipation of conventional marriage. To this end he spent some weeks with a psychologist at Spa, in Belgium, in 1927. In 1928 he became engaged to a Birmingham nurse, and may have journeyed to Berlin that year with some hope for change;[15] but he shortly broke off the engagement (influenced, possibly, by Homer Lane's theories). In Berlin he indulged his sexual proclivities with delinquent boys in impoverished quarters of the city. On returning to England he assumed the responsibilities of a teacher in private schools for the wealthy. The inevitable tension, long endured, has consequences in Auden's poetry at its best as well as at its worst. There is in his work, at times a sophomore humor and, at times, a touch of the agony of a Lear, wracked by the storm in his mind.

Most of Auden's published work may be read for its artistic, psychological, or philosophical interest as one might read E. M. Forster's masterpiece, *A Passage to India,* without any awareness of its author's homosexuality. In most of his work Auden seems to subscribe to William Plomer's summing up of the homosex-

ual writer's situation: "Although as we know, it is now possible
and customary to be much more candid than it was when I was
young, I never feel that candour is a constant necessity, if only
because people who keep telling one all about themselves, in
print or *viva voce,* are apt to be unduly self-centered . . . and
therefore to be extremely boring. I think blatant homosexuality, like other forms of blatancy, can be tiresome and uncivi-
lized."[16] In middle life Auden was capable of writing with both
wisdom and detachment on the problems of the homosexual
artist, as he did, for example, on Oscar Wilde in "An Improbable Life." (F&A, 302)

In later life Auden disciplined his daily life with somewhat
the same rigor as his verse. This may possibly point to an obses-
sive-compulsive orderliness of a kind sometimes associated with
an Oedipus complex. However, anyone intent on searching Auden's poems for signs of his psychological make-up should look
beyond his subject-matter to the technical qualities of his craft.
On one occasion while comparing the verse techniques of Tennyson and Baudelaire, he remarked on how both these poets
displayed the same musical ear and love of "line," and he added
a footnote that may throw light on his own emotional need for
strictness: "It is interesting to speculate on the relation between
the strictness and musicality of a poet's form and his own anxiety. It may well be, I think, that the more he is conscious of an
inner disorder and dread, the more value he will place on tidi-
ness in the work as a *defense,* as if he hoped that through his
control of the means of expressing his emotions, the emotions
themselves, which he cannot master directly, might be brought
to order." (F&A, 230)

In any assessment of Auden's artistic achievement, or of the
emotional, intellectual, or moral stature of his work, the question of his homosexuality—while in some ways pertinent—is not
the overriding one. With Auden—whose *Age of Anxiety* makes
him uniquely the poet of the psyche—it seems hardly necessary
to recall that he had studied psychoanalysis far beyond the needs
of immediate personal concern, and that he had mastered a variety of psychological theories. His father, a student of child psychology, was particularly interested in the psychic sources of

ill-health, and an advocate of the treatment of the "whole" personality of the patient. He would have had a good range of psychology texts in his library and therefore available to the young Auden. Michael Davidson speaks of Auden, while still a schoolboy, as having "schooled himself in Freud and Jung" and as "having the entire psychological pentateuch at his fingertips."[17] He read Freud closely, but he did so at first in the period when Freud was still changing or modifying his own earlier theories. Much of Auden's early poetry is concerned with the conflict between Eros and death. His 1929 Journal discusses Freud's theories and sometimes takes issue with them, and his 1935 essay "Psychology and Art Today" presents an elaborate summary of "the essence of Freud's teaching," which becomes, as it develops, a summary of Auden's teachings. On Freud's death, in 1939, he composed "In Memory of Sigmund Freud"—an even greater elegy than the better known one on Yeats; and in the 1950s he wrote quite extensively on Freud's works.[18]

Auden's three grateful memories point to characteristic qualities in his poetry. "A home full of books" sparked his lifelong interest in language and things of the mind. His "childhood spent in country provinces" nurtured a creative imagination that was not self-obsessed, but disposed to reshape common human experience with due regard for the actualities of life. And who but someone whose feet were on the earth even when his head was in the clouds could have written into the official anthem of the United Nations the lines:

> Let mortals beware
> Of words, for
> With words we lie,
> Can say peace
> When we mean war,
>
> . . .
>
> Let music for peace
> Be the paradigm,
> For peace means to change
> At the right time . . .   (CP, 621)

The process, in his case, began at Oxford.

III

Oxford Poems:
Beyond the Pleasure Principle

1

Moments of revelation occur in odd places. "Revelation came to Luther in a privy," Auden wrote in "Thanksgiving for a Habitat," and revelation came to Auden himself, aged fifteen, in a ploughed field "one afternoon in March at half-past three"; for having previously thought of himself as a potential mining-engineer, the chance remark of a schoolfriend caused him that spring afternoon in 1922 to entertain the novel notion of poetry as a vocation:

> But indecision broke off with a clean cut end
>   One afternoon in March at half past three
> When walking in a ploughed field with a friend;
>   Kicking a little stone, he turned to me
>   And said, "Tell me, do you write poetry?"
> I never had, and said so, but I knew
> That very moment what I wished to do.   (CP, 98)

The friend, Robert Medley, who was Auden's senior by a year at Gresham's School, had his own memory of this moment of revelation: "Walking one afternoon towards the woods . . . on the far side of Sheringham Road, I made an attack on the Church and discovered to my surprise that Wystan was devout. An argument followed, and to soften what I feared might become a serious breach, after a pause I asked him if he wrote poetry, confessing by way of exchange, that I did. I was a little surprised that he had not tried and suggested that he might do so."[1]

Auden wrote some verse later that year during his summer holidays in the Lake District, where his parents had a cottage in the shadow of Blencathra, a Cumberland hill that rises east of Derwent Water between Keswick and Penrith. The Auden cottage was reached in those days by taking a little local train from Penrith junction to the village of Threlkeld. About a mile from Threlkeld along a narrow country lane two or three clustered farmhouses form the hamlet of Wescoe. Set a little apart, and called "Far Wescoe," is a separate cluster consisting of a farmhouse with barnyard and byres, the stone cottage the Audens owned, and a Post Office letter-box set into a stable wall.

Wescoe remains untouched by the bustle generated in Grasmere, Ambleside, and Keswick by the fame of Wordsworth and the Lake Poets. Its surroundings, described in the third part of the poem "1929," are pastoral still. Sheep graze on the nearby slopes of Blencathra. Off to the north, the dark rocky face of Skiddaw looms higher and somewhat menacing. Westward, beyond Derwent Water, the fells and pikes of the central Lake District crowd the horizon. Scafell Pike is prominent twelve miles off, and near it is Pillar Rock, the setting used by Auden and Christopher Isherwood for the opening scene of their play *The Ascent of F6*. A mountain-bred stream, St. John's Beck, flows south from the vicinity of Wescoe for about five miles though a green valley until it broadens into the long narrow water called Thirlmere. Among the crags above Thirlmere there are a number of deep tarns, plucked out by the retreating glacier. One of these, situated about seven miles south of Wescoe, is Blea Tarn. The first poem that Auden could recall having written—at age fifteen in 1922—was, by his own description, a Wordsworthian sonnet on Blea Tarn. More than forty years later he remembered its last line and a half for his bibliographer, Barry Bloomfield:

> . . . and in the quiet
> Oblivion of thy waters let them stay.

But he could not recall "who or what *They* were," consigned by this youthful sonnet to such deep oblivion.[2]

Nevill Coghill recalled that Auden, after reading T. S. Eliot at Oxford, tore up all his early poems because they were based on Wordsworth and "wouldn't do nowadays"; and at thirty, he made Wordsworth his comic butt in *Letter to Lord Byron* (1937):

> I'm also glad to find I've your authority
>   For finding Wordsworth a most bleak old bore,
> Though I'm afraid we're in a sad minority
>   For every year his followers get more,
>   Their number must have doubled since the war.
> They come in train-loads to the Lakes, and swarms
> Of pupil-teachers study him in *Storm's*.[3]   (CP, 89)

When he wrote this, Auden had discovered his own symbolic landscape in the Pennine Lead Dales near the Roman Wall where mining and other industrial activity—in contrast to the Lake District's lonely crags and tarns—offered evidence of man the conscious maker. It is only half-jokingly, therefore, that elsewhere in the same poem he chooses the urban industrial sprawl surrounding the family home near Birmingham over the Lake District view from the Far Wescoe cottage:

> Clearer than Scafell Pike, my heart has stamped on
> The view from Birmingham to Wolverhampton.   (CP, 82)

But poking fun at Wordsworth or at the cult of Lake District in a Byronic satire is not a revolt against Romanticism. That revolt, in Auden's case, came later; and with such zeal that had he written a poem on Blea Tarn after 1940, the *They* consigned to the oblivion of its waters might well include some followers of the famed Romantic poets to whom the Lake District was holy ground.

His surviving schoolboy poems appear to be fairly conventional imitations of Wordsworth (with some echoes of Robert Frost and Thomas Hardy). His first printed poem, "Woods in Rain," beginning "It is a lovely sight and good / To see rain falling in a wood," was probably written when he was between the ages of fifteen and sixteen. Submitted for him by a friend, it appeared in *Public Schools Verse, 1923-24,* with the author's name misprinted as "W. H. Arden."

Even though he turned to writing verse as a schoolboy, Auden's formal school studies remained primarily scientific. He had first set out to be a scientist; he spent his last two years at Gresham's School in the exclusive study of chemistry, zoology, and botany; and in 1925, aged nineteen, he entered Christ Church, Oxford, as a Natural Science exhibitioner. His school science paper "Enzyme Action" was read to the School Natural History Society earlier in 1925, and he retained an interest in new scientific discoveries throughout his life, relying on fairly popular accounts written by scientists for the common reader. In the thirties he studied Professor Hyman Levy's Marxist-oriented *Modern Science,* a work he drew on in both prose and poetry, including *New Year Letter* (1941). In his later years he read books on more recent developments in physics by writers like Werner Heisenberg, who formulated the uncertainty principle in quantum physics.[4] For many years he was an avid reader of *Scientific American,* whose editors were happy to print—and to reprint in an illustrated booklet as a Christmas card—his ode to the microorganisms inhabiting his skin, "New Year Greeting" (1969), which he based on an article in its January 1969 issue, "Life on the Human Skin" by Mary J. Marples. While not a trained scientist, Auden acquired the knowledge of science on which to base a poetic imagery drawn from nature in this century, and he had it from his schooldays.

As an undergraduate at Oxford from October 1925 to June 1928 Auden was not a model student. He had entered the university on a science scholarship, but switched in his second year to the school of English language and literature; and he followed the required curriculum just enough to achieve an undistinguished pass degree (third class). By his own standards for young poets, whose first duty he said in his 1956 Inaugural Lecture as Professor of Poetry was to store all kinds of experiences in the memory, he assiduously prepared himself to be a poet: he read a great deal, played the piano, and wrote poetry. Among the lectures he attended was one by J. R. R. Tolkien that sparked his interest in Anglo-Saxon poetry: "I do not remember a single word he said, but at a certain point he recited, and magnificently, a long passage of *Beowulf.* I was spellbound. This po-

etry, I knew, was going to be my dish." (DH, 41) John Betjeman—a fellow undergraduate who forty-six years later as Poet
Laureate unveiled the Auden memorial in Westminster Abbey—
was astonished at the range of Auden's reading, his knowledge
of Anglo-Saxon poetry, and his familiarity with the works of little known poets.[5] Others among his contemporaries obviously
respected Auden's aspiration to be a poet, for he was twice in
his three years editor of *Oxford Poetry:* in 1926 with Charles
Plumb, and in 1927 with C. Day Lewis. The preface to the 1927
volume declared—in what may be the first manifesto Auden put
his hand to—that "the emergent evolution of mind" was "the
prime development of this century."

Stephen Spender, two years Auden's junior, was among Auden's admirers at Oxford, and his admiration led him to privately printing a group of Auden's undergraduate poems, few
of which might have otherwise survived. Spender recalls in
World Within World that in 1928 he spent part of the summer
vacation "printing a little volume of the *Poems* of W. H. Auden, an edition of thirty copies that is much sought after to-
day."[6] This volume—begun by Spender on a small Adana printing set for chemist's labels and when this press broke down
completed by the Holywell Press, Oxford—is indeed a "little"
volume (hardly bigger than the palm of a hand). Eleven num-
bered copies and four unnumbered copies survive. One of the
latter was sold at Sotheby Parke Bernet in 1973 for $8500.

Spender's little volume helps to identify a fairly substantial
group of poems Auden wrote before going to Berlin in the summer of 1928 to spend a year there, in the course of which he assembled most of the poems in his first conventionally published
volume, *Poems,* 1930. The twenty poems in Spender's private
printing show that Auden's cast of mind from the start was scientific. They draw their images primarily from anthropology,
geology, and psychology. The psychological images are characteristically of two kinds: first, images of momentary peace or fulfillment—glimpses of Nirvana having within them the seeds of
death; and, second, images of conflict at psychic frontiers: between id and ego, for example, and particularly the primordial
human frontier at which the conscious mind grew estranged

from unconscious nature, and across which there is no retreat to the innocence of natural creatures—birds, beasts, and flowers— but only the return, through death, to an inorganic state.

Poem I(f) of *Poems,* 1928, "Consider if you will how lovers stand," warns against reluctance to change and leave the past behind. So do several of its companion pieces which equate individual development with the general theme of weaning from parental influence. They also imply that failure to obey evolutionary law may lead to stagnation, or extinction, in some "sullen valley" of personal fulfillment. And associated with this, there are pervasive images of glimpses of Nirvana: seductive moments of calm, " 'Twixt coffee and the fruit," that are perilous if prolonged.

For such Arcadian moments—when the dancer and the dance seem one—the most common images are gardens or lawns—preferably windless; evening walks; the "homely" gathering of family or friends for an evening meal; or simply the evening hour itself when work is done: ". . . those evenings when / Fear gave his watch no look." (CP, 103) Poem I(a) of *Poems,* 1928, describes a particularly English Arcadian moment: a summer evening with the school cricket match just ended:

> The sprinkler on the lawn
> Weaves a cool vertigo, and stumps are drawn;
> The last boy vanishes,
> A blazer half-on, through rigid trees.
>
> (P, 1928, 3; EA, 437)

A more typical instance of Auden's constant image for peace of mind resembling man's preconscious innocence is the image in Poem XIV, retained in revised form as "Taller To-day," now the second short poem in *Collected Poems,* in which orchard and brook carry overtones of an archetypal Eden while the glacier implies estrangement from nature:

> Taller to-day, we remember similar evenings,
> Walking together in a windless orchard
> Where the brook runs over the gravel, far from the glacier.
>
> (CP, 39)

The phrase "far from the glacier" introduces a contrasting image-cluster—night, winter, and death:

> Nights come bringing the snow, and the dead howl
> Under headlands in their windy dwelling
> Because the Adversary put too easy questions
> On lonely roads.

The closing lines indicate that the conscious personal experience recalled in the poem was a moment of awareness of fellowship or community suspended in time—a moment in which something was "fulfilled . . . loved, or endured"—but which would not itself endure through tomorrow:

> Noises at dawn will bring
> Freedom for some, but not this peace
> No bird can contradict: passing but here, sufficient now
> For something fulfilled this hour, loved or endured.
>
> (CP, 40)

2

Most of the twenty lyrics in the little volume, *Poems*, 1928, are five-finger exercises in this imagery of restless change and the hazardous desire for rest. Technically, they frequently imitate the poetic devices of Wilfred Owen, in particular; but also those of Hopkins, Yeats, and Eliot. Poem I is a cluster of little lyrics, lettered *a* to *g*, which introduce characteristic images: images of journeys, or successive stages of change resulting from conscious choice; and, counterpointing these, images of seasonal return associated with instinctive life. Other poems in this volume develop aspects of these themes and warn, in particular, against the temptation to seek rest in natural harmony—an insistence that may point toward Auden's early preoccupation with the questions raised in his 1929 Berlin Journal entry concerning his specific disagreements with Freud:

The error of Freud and most psychologists is making
pleasure a negative thing, progress towards a state of rest.
This is only one half of pleasure and the least important
half. Creative pleasure is, like pain, an increase in tension. What does the psychologist make of contemplation
and joy?

The essence of creation is doing things for no reason; it
is pointless. Possessive pleasure is always rational. Freud
really believes that pleasure is immoral, i.e., happiness is
displeasing to God.

If you believe this, of course, the death-wish becomes the
most important emotion, and the "reinstatement of the
earlier condition." Entropy is another name for despair.

                                                    (EA, 299)

This journal entry supplies two keys to Auden's art. The first
is revealed in "The essence of creation is doing things for no
reason" and "Creative pleasure is, like pain, an increase in tension." Both axioms might justify the demanding formal patterns
Auden began to impose on his poems about this time: the addition, for example, of patterns of internal rhymes and assonances
to such conventional forms as the sonnet. The second enlighten-
ing point is his disagreement with Freud on the pleasure principle understood as "progress towards a state of rest."
   Auden apparently regarded the theory of creative pleasure
as an important psychological discovery of his own (although it
may owe something to Jung's notions in *Psychology of the Unconscious* on the origins of creativity). Following his comment
on the death wish: "Entropy is another name for despair," Auden has the further note on a compensatory drive: "The real
'life-wish' is the desire for separation, from family, from one's
literary predecessors." (EA, 299) This may echo Jung's view that
archetypal quest myths express a set of fundamental psychological experiences common to all men: "We all have to emancipate
ourselves from parents and other adults and face life and its
challenges independently."[7]
   Even if the theory of creative pleasure was not his own independent discovery, Auden's early images for the creative tension

of leaving "Mother"—for the efforts of the ego, as Freud put it, "to mediate between the world and the id"—have great vitality:

> To throw away the key and walk away,
> Not abrupt exile, the neighbours asking why,
> But following a line with left and right,
> An altered gradient at another rate,
> Learns more than maps upon the whitewashed wall,
> The hand put up to ask; and makes us well
> Without confession of the ill. . . .   (CP, 31)

Poem XX of *Poems,* 1928, "To throw away the key and walk away," re-used as a chorus in *Paid on Both Sides,* provides a good instance of the image of a watershed as the place of mediation and the ground for choice. As distinct from forays into mountains or going to earth in valleys, both manifestations of the death-instinct, this walking away from the past on intermediate ground, neither abrupt nor swooping, is a healing process. Lines of communication are kept open. There is contact with the past and some information about the future—a double process signified by the single word *posts,* which simultaneously suggests letters forwarded from an old address and signposts pointing the way to the new:

> . . . All pasts
> Are single old past now, although some posts
> Are forwarded, held looking on a new view.

But throwing away the key brings no easy walk to freedom. The desire to escape stagnation may meet opposition from the super-ego or the authoritarian father principle, as in the 1929 poem, "No Change of Place":

> For no one goes
>   . . .
> Further through foothills than the rotting stack
> Where gaitered gamekeeper with dog and gun
> Will shout "Turn back."   (CP, 42)

The gamekeeper's gaiters represent a greater psychological imperative than either dog or gun; for gaiters were part of the formal dress of Anglican bishops, and in Auden's case they are associated with his childhood father-image: "My father down the garden in his gaiters." (CP, 108) The voice ordering the trespasser to turn back may speak for super-ego, parent, or puritanical church.

3

The form of wit Auden essayed in these early poems was intellectual in reach and marked by hidden implication and covert cleverness. In them, for example, a spy may personify introspection—our seeking to explore the hidden part of ourselves—and a stranger may personify our human alienation from the wholly natural world. One of his Oxford poems, "The Secret Agent," retained almost unchanged in later collections, is an instance of the type of teasing poem that earned the reputation C. Day Lewis gives him as the fictional detective Nigel Strangeways in the first of his crime novels, *A Question of Proof,* written under the pseudonym Nicholas Blake. Day Lewis's Strangeways, like Auden at Oxford, smokes incessantly, drinks innumerable cups of tea, sleeps under heaped-up blankets, or when these are not provided, under any available window-curtains or carpets, and keeps a revolver under his pillow. (Auden, for a time, openly carried a starter's pistol.) Above all, Strangeways is cryptic enough to deserve the rebuke: "If you'd lived in ancient Greece the Delphic oracle would have had to go out of business. Do cut out the cryptic stuff."[8]

"The Secret Agent," a sonnet about a spy who, having penetrated an alien territory, falls into a trap and expects to be shot, illustrates this cryptic riddling side of Auden quite well:

> Control of the passes was, he saw, the key
> To this new district, but who would get it?
> He, the trained spy, had walked into the trap
> For a bogus guide, seduced by the old tricks.
>
> At Greenhearth was a fine site for a dam
> And easy power, had they pushed the rail

Some stations nearer. They ignored his wires:
The bridges were unbuilt and trouble coming.

(CP, 41)

Because it lacks end-rhyme "The Secret Agent" has commonly been described as an "un-rhymed sonnet," but one of its most attractive features is subtlety of rhyme and a sophisticated musical pattern that compares with the complex texture and highly wrought pattern of assonance in "Missing," which precedes it in *Collected Poems*. These poems show Auden's early inclination to intensify the pattern of sound by such devices as rhyming syllables across lines as in the later "Streams" and "A Permanent Way"—a device employed with comic intention in *Elegy for Young Lovers* where criss-cross rhyming forms an amusing accompaniment to the old lady's knitting in her opening soliloquy. There is vowel play of this sort in "The Secret Agent" where even the end-words are loosely linked by the suggestion of associated sound, usually in the penultimate element: *key, get it; trip, tricks; dam, rail; one, water; had, companion; course, joined.* (*Wires* and *coming* in the second quatrain do not chime as a couplet, but their consonants are picked up by *rail* and *dam* in the companion lines.) Besides this muted suggestion of end-rhyme, there is a firm pattern of internal assonantal rhyme as in *pass, saw; new, who; had, trap; bogus, old:*

Control of the *pa*sses was, he *saw*, the key
To this *new* district, but *who* would get it?
He, the trained spy, *had wa*lked into the *trap*
For a *bog*us guide, seduced by the *old* tricks.

In addition to the rhyme within individual lines, rhymes are carried across lines in both quatrains of the octave: *key* at the end of the first line and *He* at the beginning of the third; and *spy* and *guide* in the third and fourth. There is similar crossing over in the second quatrain; *rail, sta*tions; *ig*nored, *bridges;* but even more significant is the effect of a sustained echo which the ear of a Dylan Thomas, for example, would not miss: *green, easy,* and *nearer; site* and *wires; rail* and *stations; bridges* and *built;* the slant rhyme and alliteration in *near* and *ignored;* and the growling undercurrent in *trouble coming*.

> At Greenhearth was a *fine site* for a dam
> And easy *p*ower, had *they p*ushed the *r*ail
> Some stations *nearer*. They ig*nor*ed his wires:
> The *bri*dges were un*bui*lt and trouble coming.

The sestet has similar harmonies sustained across the lines: *street, weeks; seemed, dreamed, easily;* and *shoot, two;* supplemented by alliteration:

> The *stree*t music *see*med gracious now to one
> For *wee*ks up in the desert. *W*oken by *w*ater
> Running away in the *dar*k, he often *had*
> Re*pr*oached the night for a *c*ompanion
> Dreamed of already. They *w*ould *shoot*, of course,
> Parting easily *two* that were never joined.

At the literal level the sonnet tells the story of an aggressive spy of superior intellect—he has the eye of a skilled engineer, and he can quote Anglo-Saxon verse from memory—who walked into a trap through overconfidence. Like Freud's ego attempting "to mediate between the world and the id," he had penetrated the desert frontier area and marked it for conquest, caring little for emotional or bodily comfort. Captured, he becomes aware of what he had neglected or repressed: the "civitas" of music and the underground running waters of unconscious or emotional nature. This loose paraphrase overlooks two statements in the poem: "he often had / Reproached the night for a companion / Dreamed of already"; and "Parting easily two that were never joined"—this last a line adapted from the Anglo-Saxon poem "Wulf and Eadwacer," spoken by a woman separated from her lover. Since the "companion" and the "easy parting" have no "explicit" literal referents, their significance must be symbolic; and the obvious association in each case is death. These symbolic statements invite an approach to the poem as a psychological allegory; and when the sonnet is so approached, almost any psychological theory will galvanize meanings in it. A remark of Freud's, in particular, suggests the significance of the poem: "It would be possible to picture the id as under the domination of the mute but powerful death instincts which desire to be at peace and (prompted by the pleasure principle) to put Eros, the mischief-maker, to rest . . ."9

The allegorized landscape of "The Secret Agent" suggests that the poem be read as a campaign of conscious intellect to control the instinctive and unconscious. Characteristic imagery distinguishes the two contending territories. The realm of mind, or intellect, is a place of mechanical inventions used to control nature: dams, power-plants, railways, telegraphs, bridges, and so on. The realm of instinct or feeling is a place of running water, "Greenhearth," night, and dreams. The agent of creative consciousness in the "new" territory wants to impose the rational control of a dam on the running water of unconscious feeling. The agent, an intellectual, is "trained"; he recognizes "key" points for "control"; but he is too arrogantly certain of the "fine" site, the "easy" power, and he is almost insolent about the shortcomings of those who had not "pushed" the rail nearer. Not content merely to spy and report, he turns strategist and sends urgent wires. This is both proud and unthinking; and ironically, through thoughtlessness, the agent of the thinking faculty walks into "the trap / For a bogus guide." (Compare, for example, Jung's account of Oedipus and the Sphinx which I cite in Chapter V: "the riddle was . . . the trap which the Sphinx had laid. . . . Overestimating his intellect in a typically masculine way, Oedipus walked right into it"—a view of the Sphinx as Adversary that appears to provide an explicit image in "Taller To-day," the poem that immediately follows "The Secret Agent" in *Poems,* 1930:

> and the dead howl
> Under headlands in their windy dwelling
> Because the Adversary put too easy questions
> On lonely roads.)   (CP, 39)

The sestet of "The Secret Agent" shows the spy, discomfited, in the innocent natural realm of water, night, and dreams. At the end he can regard his own situation ironically. He recognizes that his neglected flesh, instincts, and emotions might welcome divorce from his isolated mind. Here, as Freud said, the antagonistic death instincts "desire to be at peace" and "to put

Eros, the mischief-maker, to rest." There is a corresponding line
in *The Orators* about "perverted lovers" including "haters of
life, afraid to die": "These are they who when the saving thought
came shot it for a spy." (EA, 63)

Other pre-Berlin poems explore variations on the theme of
"The Secret Agent": the Freudian notion of the antagonism set
between aspects of the psyche and the disaster resulting from
the attempt to regress to a simpler state. "The Watershed," the
poem of earliest date retained in Auden's later collections, is a
good instance of this. In it, the agent who attempts to return to
Eden, to restore the "wholeness" of nature before the Fall, is
described as a "stranger" rather than a spy, and the unanxious
realm of nature (mineral, vegetable, animal) that denies him
access comprises the mineral strata (lead mines), the vegetable
"bark of elm / Where sap unbaffled rises," and animals whose
"Ears poise before decision, scenting danger." Nature rejects the
possesser of conscious purposes and "motor-cars and manufac-
tured things":

> Go home, now, stranger, proud of your young stock,
> Stranger, turn back again, frustrate and vexed:
> This land, cut off, will not communicate,
>
> . . .
>
> Beams from your car may cross a bedroom wall,
> They wake no sleeper. . . .

Again, as in "The Secret Agent" the only entry of the "frustrate
and vexed" to preconscious "wholeness" is through death:

> . . . one died
> During a storm, the fells impassable,
> Not at his village, but in wooden shape
> Through long abandoned levels nosed his way
> And in his final valley went to ground.   (CP, 41)

In "The Watershed" the landscape that provides the *"paysage
moralisé"* for the Freudian allegory is derived from an actual
geographical area: the northern Pennine dales in the vicinity of
Alston Moor where lead-mining began before the Romans; but

where nature continues to reject the intruder and reassert herself:

> Who stands, the crux left of the watershed,
> On the wet road between the chafing grass
> Below him sees dismantled washing-floors,
> Snatches of tramline running to a wood,
> An industry already comatose,
> Yet sparsely living. A ramshackle engine
> At Cashwell raises water; for ten years
> It lay in flooded workings until this,
> Its latter office, grudgingly performed. (CP, 41)

The geographical watershed alluded to in this poem is the spine of the Pennines at Cross Fell at the precise center of the ore fields of the Lead Dales: "An industry already comatose." The allegorical watershed is the great psychic divide when man "faulted into consciousness." Geologically, "the crux left of the watershed" is the Cross Fell formation; allegorically, it is the embarrassment and anxiety—"frustrate and vexed"—consequent on consciousness. (The Lead Dales are bisected by the Burtreesford Fault.) What the viewer sees is also an industrial watershed: the retreat of nineteenth-century mining enterprises. The poem itself is a watershed in Auden's art. He discarded all written before it: August 1927. And he kept it with good reason. It is artistically successful in Auden's characteristic mature style which includes a lapidary concern for the music of assonance and internal rhyme, and a masterly handling of syntax and enjambment (two of its sentences run thirteen and eleven lines respectively).

While the theme of this poem, also, owes much to Freud's theories, its artistry bears witness to Auden's dissenting view that Freud and most psychologists erred in identifying the pleasure principle with progress toward a state of rest when, to the contrary, creative pleasure implied an increase in tension. When this poem was in the process of being made, the source of creative tension was the strict pattern of assonance and internal rhyme Auden imposed on it. Some of the consequences are fairly obvious. In the line "Snatches of tramline running to a wood," for example, the word *tramline*—a local word for the narrow-gauge rails used for mine cars—is supplied by the external scene; but the word *snatches* is not. It is a word brought to consciousness in a mind seeking vowel harmony with *tramline* and *dismantled*. Similarly, *Cashwell* is a real place name, but *ramshackle* is a discovery that might have remained unconscious had the place been named *Boston*. The opening lines of "The Watershed" illustrate the intentional complexity of Auden's scheme of assonance or rhyming syllables. Two vowels in the first line rhyme. They also pick up an echo in the second line, in which two vowels also rhyme and echo one in the first line. The crossing of these elements forms a *chiasm* (or cross, or crux): *left,* water*shed,* and *wet; cha*fing *grass* (in Oxonian tones, not Midwestern) and *stands:*

Who *stan*ds, the crux *left* of the water*shed,*

On the *wet* road between the *cha*fing *grass*

Be*low* him sees dismantled *wa*shing-fl*oo*rs,

*Sna*tches of *tram*line running to a *wo*od.

Since there are no end-rhymes this verse is, technically, "blank"; but the ear hears a pattern of rhyme within and across lines: in*dustry,* li*vi*ng; al*ready,* spars*ely;* ram*sha*ckle, *Cash*well; *ten, engi*ne, even though the formal pattern of internal and counterpointed rhymes in a chiastic arrangement is not always as evident as in the final lines:

But *sel*dom this. *Near* you, taller than grass,

*Ear*s poise before *dec*ision, *sce*nting danger.

Apart from their musical qualities, the Oxford poems show a pervasive concern with regression and the death instinct, which are conditions of estrangement from "wholeness." Whatever its origin, Auden brought with him to Oxford a knowledge of *Gestalt* psychology that greatly impressed Stephen Spender. In those undergraduate years, too, he may have come to know the work of Professor R. G. Collingwood of Pembroke College, whose *Metaphysics* he lists among "Modern Sources" of *New Year Letter,* and who later supplied him with a cardinal tenet of his artistic theory, namely, that art is a disenchanting mirror, where, as Prospero puts it in *The Sea and the Mirror,* "all we are not stares back at what we are." (CP, 313) He wrote in 1941: "Art, as the late Professor R. G. Collingwood pointed out, is not Magic, i.e., a means by which the artist communicates or arouses his feelings in others, but a mirror in which they may become conscious of what their own feelings really are: its proper effect . . . is disenchanting." (F&A, 351) What we see in the mirror of Auden's undergraduate art is an ordered pattern, a harmony of elements, and a disciplined technical-aesthetic "whole" at variance with public or private chaos: in the formal arrangement of these poems "all we are not stares back at what we are."

Shortly after he left Oxford the spirit of Auden's work began to change. The conflicts in his allegorical landscapes begin to reflect symptoms of public disorder as well as private inner estrangement; and his psychological imagery shows a shift in emphasis. The theme of the struggle between Eros and the death instinct remains, but becomes fused with an interest in psychosomatic symptoms in the body politic as well as in individuals; and as a consequence of his encounter in Berlin with the psychological ideas of John Layard and Homer Lane, Auden's early poetry begins to show an interest in the healing powers of the unconscious.

IV

Berlin and *Poems,* 1930

1

While Stephen Spender was printing his little volume of Auden's poems in late summer 1928, Auden was himself in Berlin enjoying the freedom of a well-to-do *rentier* through the generosity of his father. There he saw an early performance of Brecht's *Three Penny Opera;* discovered the teachings of Homer Lane, who believed that human nature was innately good and instinctive behavior morally desirable; and wrote or revised most of the poems which together with the charade, *Paid on Both Sides,* supplied the contents of his first conventionally published volume, *Poems,* 1930.

Published in November 1930, this first book of Auden's has been regarded as a landmark in English poetry. Given Auden's youth and the personal tensions he was experiencing at the time—one of his purposes in going to Berlin appears to have included the hope of outgrowing his homosexual condition so that he might marry a Birmingham psychiatric nurse to whom he was engaged[1]—*Poems,* 1930, strikes an oddly authoritative note. The young English poet Charles Madge—adapting T. S. Eliot's metaphor from "Tradition and the Individual Talent" for the effect on the ideal order among existing works of art brought about by the supervention of a really new work—wrote of its impact:

> But there waited for me in the summer morning,
> Auden, fiercely. I read, shuddered and knew,

And all the world's stationary things
In silence moved to take up new positions.[2]

The "fierce," evangelical note in *Poems,* 1930, was often struck
in challenging opening lines as in the following four instances:

Will you turn a deaf ear
To what they said on the shore . . .   (CP, 47)

It's no use raising a shout.   (EA, 42)

Sir, no man's enemy, forgiving all
But will his negative inversion . . .   (EA, 36)

Consider this and in our time
As the hawk sees it or the helmeted airman.   (CP, 61)

In keeping with Auden's dictum equating creative pleasure
with increased tension, *Poems,* 1930, was disposed both to please
and to pain. It was not a book for middle-aged armchair comfort, but rather one that a stern but literate judge might assign
to be read in the stocks. There is touch of the puritanical schoolmaster, or revivalist preacher, in the voice that speaks in it; and
an occasional strident moralizing that could be a mask for inner
uncertainty. Following the Auden family tradition of service to
society, but lacking his parents' qualifications to ease bodily ills
in public health or missionary nursing, the young Auden felt
called to care for man's mind, and to trumpet his witness against
intellectual flabbiness, neurotic evasion, and the decay of mental
powers:

Shut up talking, charming in the best suits to be had in
     town,
Lecturing on navigation while the ship is going down.

Drop those priggish ways for ever, stop behaving like a
     stone:
Throw the bath-chairs right away, and learn to leave
     ourselves alone.

If we really want to live, we'd better start at once to try;
If we don't it doesn't matter, but we'd better start to die.

                                               (EA, 49)

So concludes a poem written in April 1930. But the choice of the meter of Tennyson's "Locksley Hall" rescues it from priggishness and points to one achievement evident in the course of this first volume: a growing mastery of a humorous element that lightens the intensity of the pre-Berlin poems.

Although Auden later wrote admirable light verse, and even though his work in general is memorable for its comic vision, comparatively few lines in his first book have the characteristic quality of his later comic genius—a flash of insight compressed into a daring and unexpected phrase. But he grew quickly in this regard, and, significantly, the later verse in *Poems, 1930,* is more likely to contain such lines than the earlier.

Shortly after arriving in Berlin in 1928—through an introduction arranged by an Oxford friend, David Ayerst—Auden met a man who was to influence his work significantly. This was John Layard, an anthropologist and later a Jungian analyst, now best known for his book, *The Stone Men of Malekula.* Layard had suffered a severe nervous breakdown accompanied by physical paralysis. He became a patient of Homer Lane, an unorthodox American psychologist then practicing in London. Lane, who cured Layard's paralysis, was later accused of malpractice in London and died in France in 1925. Layard thereafter sought psychoanalytical treatment in Vienna and Berlin, where, according to Isherwood who joined Auden there, he continued to study and recommend Lane's ideas: ". . . since the master's death, he was one of the very few people really qualified to spread Lane's teachings and carry on his work." Layard found in Auden "an intelligent listener who became, overnight, an enthusiastic disciple."[3]

Lane's view that human nature was inherently good and that unconscious conflict and suppression of instinctive desire led to both neurosis and physical ills, which had something in common with D. H. Lawrence's views in *Fantasia of the Unconscious,* was reformulated by Layard as a fundamental doctrine: "There is only one sin: disobedience to the inner law of our own nature." Layard equated "God" with the "inner law" of our desires, and held that obedience to this inner law led to spiritual growth and "purity of heart." André Gide whom Auden also met with in Berlin was another who equated "God" with natural desires.

Layard added a further dimension to the "inner law." He was
also a disciple of Georg Groddeck, from whose notion of the
"It" Freud had derived his idea of the *id*. Groddeck, whose work
Auden may have already known, believed that the psychic drives
of the "It" governed not only illness but personal physical characteristics and surface symptoms of various sorts.

Auden soon began to versify the Lane gospel according to
Layard. He apparently saw himself as a diagnostician and healer
in apostolic succession to Lane and Layard, and his Berlin poems
show a new enthusiasm for psychological healers, "Lawrence,
Blake, and Homer Lane once healers in our English land," who
perceived moral disorder beneath surface symptoms. After meeting Layard, he was always ready to offer psychosomatic explanations for illness and even for physical characteristics. He diag-
nosed Isherwood's sore throats as "liar's quinsy" and Spender's
tallness as "heaven reaching"; and he has a rueful self-reflective
couplet of a later date on the comic impact of psychic forces on
the soma in his own case:

> I can't think what my It had on It's mind,
> To give me flat feet and a big behind.   (EA, 189)

Auden compressed the gospel according to Layard into the
Hopkinsian sonnet (discarded from his *Collected Poems*) that
begins:

> Sir, no man's enemy, forgiving all
> But will his negative inversion, be prodigal:
> Send us power and light, a sovereign touch
> Curing the intolerable neural itch,
> The exhaustion of weaning, the liar's quinsy,
> And the distortions of ingrown virginity.   (EA, 36)

Here, the "God" of the inner law of desire is invoked against
the denial of self—"will his negative inversion"—and against the
repression of instinctive urges that results in psychosomatic illness.

Auden's poetry of the thirties owes much to John Layard;
but to repay his obligation for admission to the fellowship of
Homer Lane, Auden had to bear with Layard's neurotic behav-

ior. Auden had introduced Layard to homosexual practices, and Layard became jealous of Auden's bar boys. On one occasion Layard attempted suicide by shooting himself through the mouth. The bullet touched no vital part and he brought the revolver to Auden's rooms requesting to be finished-off out of friendship. Auden said that while willing to perform an act of friendship, he was not willing to be tried for murder; and took Layard to the hospital in a taxi.[4]

2

Auden's Berlin experience brought him new themes and images. It also opened his eyes to the changing character of the times he lived in. He came to realize that his own historical situation was quite other than he had hitherto understood it to be; and he saw that pre-1914 Europe and its generally accepted social order had passed irrevocably. What he learned in Berlin, first hand, was that the social environment he was born into—a comfortable Edwardian, middle-class society where all one's friends had been to elite public school and older university—would never return to its prewar "normality." This circumstance was not yet apparent to Auden's generation of affluent Oxford undergraduates in victorious England in the late 1920s. He said of English society in this period: "Having known neither civil violence, political executions and assassinations, nor inflation, we all thought the world was still as it had been in 1914," and he added:

> . . . my really significant experiences when I went to Berlin in 1928 were not cultural, exciting though the cultural life of the city was at the time. They were two. For the first time I realized that the world was no longer a safe place, that the foundations were shaking. And then as a foreigner stammering in ungrammatical German, I had no class status, and so could make friends with members of the working class in a way I could never have done at home.[5]

The impact of all this becomes apparent in the most ambitious poem in *Poems,* 1930: Poem XX "It was Easter as I walked in the public gardens," which in later collections is titled simply "1929." "1929" is a substantial poem—an annual round in four parts dated April, May, August, and October, 1929. Like other Berlin poems, it draws on stock phrases from Homer Lane's vocabulary of psychosomatic symptoms, and it also brings forward particular people from among Auden's acquaintances to represent Layard's strong and weak types:

> The death by cancer of a once hated master,
> A friend's analysis of his own failure,
> Listened to at intervals throughout the winter . . .
> > . . .
> The happiness, for instance, of my friend Kurt Groote,
> Absence of fear in Gerhart Meyer
> From the sea, the truly strong man.   (CP, 50)

Here, as in the later ballad "Miss Gee," cancer is symptomatic of the denial or repression of one's inner creative urge. The self-analytical friend is John Layard. The first names of Kurt Groote and Gerhart Meyer appear on a list of "Boys had Germany 1928-29" in Auden's journal—the latter here identified as "the truly strong" presumably because he observed in his life-style Homer Lane's maxim: the only sin is disobedience to one's inner law.[6]

The poem "1929" opens with the now familiar image of the garden and unanxious physical nature:

> Hearing the frogs exhaling from the pond,
> It was Easter as I walked in the public gardens,
> Watching the traffic of magnificent cloud
> Moving without anxiety on open sky;

and it moves on to a contrasting image of the human condition:

> But thinking so I came at once
> Where solitary man sat weeping on a bench,
> Hanging his head down, with his mouth distorted
> Helpless and ugly as an embryo chicken.   (CP, 50)

Part Two of "1929" begins with a passage contrasting the
poet's own restless thinking with the placidity of ducks on the
water. The ducks, in harmony with natural necesesity, "find
sun's luxury enough"—a possible echo of André Gide's "to grow
straight you need nothing now but the urge of your own sap and
the sun's call."[7] The poem then meditates on the stages of human development in time, from fetus to infancy and childhood,
and on to anxious adulthood and separation from parents. Part
Three is a further variation on the theme of the process of weaning and of human growth. It begins with a personal recollection
of returning in the summer of 1929 to the Auden family cottage
at Far Wescoe in Cumberland, and meditates on the need for
change in life's process: "As child is weaned from his mother and
leaves home." The lines recall earlier arrivals at Far Wescoe in
more carefree days from school and university and, through such
vigorous images as "slackening of wires and posts' sharp repri-
mand," contrast the spirit of those arrivals with his subsequent
experience of a psychological break from the life the family cottage—and its natural surroundings—represents:

> Being alone, the frightened soul
> Returns to the life of sheep and hay
> No longer his: he every hour
> Moves further from this and must so move,
> As child is weaned from his mother and leaves home. . . .
>
> (CP, 52)

The new notes that emerge in "1929" and that easily lend themselves to apparent Marxist overtones are first, the theme of "a
new country," and second, a new emphasis on "the death of the
grain" in the seasonal imagery that may owe more to Engels's
political parable about the regeneration of society in *Anti-
Dühring* than to Gide, St. Paul, or the myth of Demeter. Perhaps the most attractive feature of "1929" is Auden's apt use of
landscape imagery to represent psychic growth as an entering—
through developing consciousness—into "a new country":

> Moving along the track which is himself,
> He loves what he hopes will last, which gone,

as in the later ballads, "Victor" and "Miss Gee." His apprenticeship in the theater—beginning in 1932 with *The Dance of Death,*
and later his work as writer and assistant director for six months
during 1935 with the Post Office Film Unit that produced the
films *Night Mail* (with his famous verse commentary) and *Cal-
endar of the Year* in which he played Father Christmas—no
doubt helped him to envision a wider audience than his intellectual Oxford friends. But his experiences in Berlin may also
have drawn him to a more public kind of humor. He went there
toward the end of the heyday of the Berlin cabaret; but it still
survived, and he saw one of its best known of its satirical products, Brecht's *Three Penny Opera.*

In 1966 he ascribed the Brechtian use of song in *The Dog
Beneath the Skin* to the "wonderful German cabaret,"[8] and he
ultimately came to approve of carnival as the appropriate mood
for Christian art. "Carnival," he once said, "celebrates the unity
of our human race as mortal creatures, who come into this world
and depart from it without our consent, who must eat, drink,
defecate, belch, and break wind in order to live, and procreate
if our species is to survive." And he added: "We oscillate between wishing we were unreflective animals and wishing we were
disembodied spirits. . . . The Carnival solution of this ambiguity is to laugh, for laughter is simultaneously a protest and an
acceptance." (F&A, 471)

Auden in Berlin was not yet a master of the comic touch, but
some of the pieces in *Poems*, 1930, illustrate the degree of intellectual playfulness with which he was beginning to combine
psychological, evolutionary, and political themes. A good early
instance may be found in Poem XXVIII, a dramatic monologue
given the title "Venus Will Now Say a Few Words" in later collections. The Venus of this poem is an archetypal Mother, like
the Venus of Willendorf. She is spokeswoman for Darwin's natural evolutionary principle; but she speaks also, to some extent,
for a force of history resembling Marx's historical necessity.
Since she presides over the eternal war between life and death,
her monologue is appropriately cast in an adaptation of Wilfred
Owen's technique of slant-rhyme. Moreover, the vowel shift suits
the poem's theme of change; and the demands of the rhyme give
each pair of lines something of the force of an axiom as Venu

Begins the difficult work of mourning,
And as foreign settlers to strange country come,
By mispronunciation of native words
And intermarriage create a new race,
A new language, so may the soul
Be weaned at last to independent delight.   (CP, 52)

These lines, with their sustained *legato* movement, show a distinct advance in poetic power and in mastery of technique.

Some readers of "1929" hear stronger notes than I do of an overture to a call for social or political change in such lines as: "It is time for the destruction of error." But the "error" in this case is more psychological than political. When the poem "1929" recommends "Death of the old gang," it does so less in the voice of revolutionary Marxism than in the voice of D. H. Lawrence preaching liberation from inhibiting custom (or even Wilfred Owen's voice in "Dulce et Decorum Est"). Nevertheless, the beginnings of protest against established social ideas are present in "1929," reflecting aspects of Auden's Berlin experience and his first-hand acquaintance with protest verse recited in the cabarets, for which Bertolt Brecht had shown the way with his "The Legend of the Dead Soldier" in 1922.

While "1929" may be one of the more accomplished of Auden's early poems, it is marred a little by his continued mythologizing of friends and acquaintances. Yeats did this successfully—quite possibly because he brought his friends on stage larger than life. But in Auden's poem Gerhart Meyer and Kurt Groote, who are named, are neither known nor notable; and those friends and acquaintances with more fame, like Layard, remain for the most part anonymous—recognizable only to those in the know who could interpret the psychosomatic symptoms.

3

While Auden never forsook the cryptic obscurities of poems like "The Secret Agent," he grew more capable of casting his favorite psychological themes in openly humorous forms calls on her dependent child—"whose part it is to lean"—to attend to her laws. (In Freud's theory of infant sexuality, the "object-choice" of the mother is *anaclitic* i.e. "leaning up against" for nutrition and preservation; turned in on itself, it is narcissistic):

> Since you are going to begin to-day
> Let us consider what it is you do.
> You are the one whose part it is to lean,
> For whom it is not good to be alone.   (CP, 49)

The "You" addressed by Venus is not, however, simply any child of nature, but is humorously, or ominously, generalized into an upper-class Englishman of the 1920s convinced that he and his society are evolution's masterpiece. This personification is satirically endowed with as many aristocratic virtues as half a dozen lines of slant-rhyme can reasonably accommodate. He is at home in stately halls and excels in climbing, fly-fishing ("that flick of wrist"), and in making love. Relaxed by an evening fire he is even poet enough—in the Wordsworthian sense—to recollect emotion in tranquility:

> Laugh warmly turning shyly in the hall
> Or climb with bare knees the volcanic hill,
> Acquire that flick of wrist and after strain
> Relax in your darling's arms like a stone,
> Remembering everything you can confess,
> Making the most of firelight, of hours of fuss; . . .
> (CP, 49)

The tone of Venus's cautionary monologue accommodates Darwin's emphasis on struggle as an inescapable element in natural selection. Successful species, too well adapted to their environment and impervious to change, may be marked for extinction:

> Lizards my best once who took years to breed,
> Could not control the temperature of blood.

But Venus also seems inclined to dabble in Social Darwinism when she turns commentator and warns against casting out mutants or creative odd ones, who, like exiles, are fitted to adapt to new conditions and so serve her purpose:

> You in the town now call the exile fool
> That writes home once a year as last leaves fall,
> Think—Romans had a language in their day
> And ordered roads with it, but it had to die.   (CP, 49)

The evolutionary theme in these lines easily lends itself to the semblance of a Marxist parable on the fate of conservative societies. Some commentators have read the passage containing these lines not as evolutionary, but as an overt expression of Marxist revolutionary theory. D. E. S. Maxwell, for example, quotes the passage containing them as a specific locus of what he calls the pervasive left-wing social scenario of the thirties. "In both politics and art," says Maxwell, "the stage was seen to be occupied . . . by reactionaries and progressives, fascists and communists. The scenario required revolution and counter-revolution, and the Marxist annotation gave the individual little choice of sides. It was not only virtuous to be left-wing, it was an acceptance of what was historically inevitable."[9] There is certainly an undertone of something like this in Venus's monologue, but it is an ironic undertone far from the stridency of the agitator propagandist.

The authentic voice speaking in the poem derives some of its nuances from the verse form. The imitation of Wilfred Owen's slant-rhyme sometimes tends to end-stop the lines into a series of paired prescriptions, or imperatives with ominous overtones, as in so much of Owen and in many of Auden's imitations. At other times, although a little stagier, the slant-rhyme retains the couplet's playful possibilities for ironic or comic contrast. Auden's Venus combines the ominous and the comic effectively; and what has sometimes been taken for Marxist prescription might equally well be taken as a playful possibility of the form. Apart from *doe(dough)* or *daw*—unlikely in this context—the word *day,* for example, has no other slant-rhyme possibilities in English than *do* or *die.* Auden uses the first of these in the opening lines:

>Since you are going to begin today
>Let us consider what it is you do.

Therefore when he comes to,

>Think—Romans had a language in their day,

the fact that the rhyme form now demands *die* can be looked on, depending on one's attitude to formal elements in verse, as either unfortunate or happy—a sport or chance mutation—and Auden makes the most of it with:

>And ordered roads with it, but it had to die.

In keeping with the generally light tone of the poem's first movement, these lines sound more like the arch punning of a public-school Latin master than the voice of Karl Marx.

But the poem's second movement takes on a more ominous, threatening note, and Venus concludes her monologue with an emphatic declaration that there is no escape from evolutionary change back across the frontier of unconscious innocence:

>Do not imagine you can abdicate;
>Before you reach the frontier you are caught;
>Others have tried it and will try again
>To finish that which they did not begin:
>Their fate must always be the same as yours,
>To suffer the loss they were afraid of, yes,
>Holders of one position, wrong for years.   (CP, 49-50)

In this, her final admonition, Venus may appear to speak not only for evolutionary Eros but in conformity with the Marxist teaching that man's only freedom is the freedom to choose within the restraints of natural necessity. But the poem's pervasive humor does not sit well with any admonitory intent as a Marxist parable.

The poem's primary theme and its imagery are consistent with the concern for "the emergent evolution of mind" so typi-

cal of all the pre-Berlin poems, and indeed it is a kind of re-
writing of the poem "Consider if you will how lovers stand,"
from Spender's little 1928 volume, and it even adapts its final
lines:

> Unanswerable like any other pedant,
> Like Solomon and Sheba, wrong for years.
>
> (P, 1928, 7; EA, 438)

But this poem moves beyond personal concerns and seeks to
satirize the bourgeois class to which Auden belonged. It is a
successful humorous poem, but as satire it falls short of the best
of its kind in *Poems, 1930*: Poem XXX, later titled "Consider."

4

The frequently quoted Poem XXX of *Poems, 1930*,

> Consider this and in our time
> As the hawk sees it or the helmeted airman,

may be the best single instance in this first volume of Auden
finding his mature voice. He once said that what he "most admired in Hardy was his hawk's vision"—his way of looking on
life from a great height (as in *The Dynasts*). Auden adopts a
neutral perspective from above in a number of poems. In "A
Summer Night," for example, the scene is surveyed by the moon:
"the moon looks on us all"; and in *New Year Letter* (1940) by
the sun (on the eve of World War II).

In "Consider," the hawk or helmeted airman—either of whom
can swoop down bringing death—are not quite as neutral as the
moon, the sun, or the mechanical camera's eye in the later poems:
they are symbolically related to one side in the conflict of Eros and
Thanatos. Their presence brings a sense of malign fate offering
a stark contrast to the pervasive sense of providence in Auden's
later poems: "If there when grace dances, I should dance." (CP,
560) The perspective of hawk or helmeted airman, as Auden

employs it in "Consider," permits both the survey of a wide space and a view over the barriers of time. It also permits a double intention: satire on "our time" tempered by comic, or frivolous, undertones that reveal the speaker introducing the scenario to be one of *us* playing a role. Also, in "Consider," the high perspective permits different audiences to be addressed in the poem's three parts. The first part is addressed to the reader from the deadly perspective of hawk and airman; the second is addressed to the "Supreme Antagonist" (the antagonist in the conflict in which Eros is the protagonist, that is, Death); the concluding part is addressed to "seekers after happiness" who turn away neurotically from life's demands: their desire to escape is a form of death wish.

In the first part of this poem the reader is invited to consider, "in our time" those already marked for death:

> . . . look there
> At cigarette-end smouldering on a border
> At the first garden party of the year.   (CP, 61)

This yearly round in the old struggle to recapture the innocent wholeness of nature's first garden is characterized by amusing stage properties from upper-class life in the twenties, when the long cigarette-holder was an obligatory part of every socialite's equipment; when the wealthy enjoyed winter sports and first-class hotels in Switzerland (and the workers spent their annual fortnight in Blackpool) where the new dance bands entertained and were relayed by the new medium, radio:

> Pass on, admire the view of the massif
> Through the plate-glass windows of the Sport Hotel;
> Join there the insufficient units
> Dangerous, easy, in furs, in uniform,
> And constellated at reserved tables,
> Supplied with feelings by an efficient band,
> Relayed elsewhere to farmers and their dogs
> Sitting in kitchens in the stormy fens.   (CP, 61)

As Freud defines the death wish as a desire to regress to an earlier—even inorganic—state, so here the escapist social elite are described in terms of non-living matter: "insufficient units" and "constellated"; and, having none of their own, they are "supplied with feelings" by machines for that purpose: "efficient bands."

The second part of "Consider"—the address to the "Supreme Antagonist"—moves briefly from "our time" to "long ago" when he made the prehistoric highborn mining-captains, in Cornwall, Mendip, or the Pennine moor, "wish to die / —Lie since in barrows out of harm." The poem's perspective then returns to "our time" and catalogues the Supreme Antagonist's "admirers": the "chosen" who seek refuge in bars or in grouse hunting, the psychosomatically ill: "Those handsome and diseased youngsters, those women / Your solitary agents in the country parishes." Part Two of "Consider" concludes with a vision of the epidemic spread of symptoms of anxiety neuroses: "Scattering the people . . . / Seized with immeasurable neurotic dread."

The third part of the poem addresses "seekers after happiness" from the dire perspective of hawk, airman, and Supreme Antagonist. In its first form this final passage began with lines in which the "Financier" is rudely told "the game is up" for him, as it is for the "born nurses"—the Oxbridge intellectuals and higher clergy

> Who, thinking, pace in slippers on the lawns
> Of College Quad or Cathedral close, . . .   (EA, 47)

In revised editions, the passage is addressed to those seekers after happiness who, if they follow "the convolutions of your simple wish," will find no escape:

> Not though you pack to leave within an hour,
> Escaping humming down arterial roads:
> The date was yours; the prey to fugues,
> Irregular breathing and alternate ascendancies
> After some haunted migratory years
> To disintegrate on an instant in the explosion of mania
> Or lapse for ever into a classic fatigue.   (CP, 62)

"Consider" is an early repository of Auden's stock images for the sickness of his own class. The twenties' cult of escape in fast cars (for the idle and rich) appears also in "Missing" and in Isherwood's account of Cape Wrath. The satire on the English preparatory schools, "They gave the prizes to the ruined boys," looks forward to *The Orators;* and "those women, / Your solitary agents in country parishes," looks forward to the ballad "Miss Gee," where repressed Eros turns into a cancer. In "Consider," the judgment on those who seek happiness through escape from life is deprived of some of its harshness by the comic tone. The symptoms of the "immeasurable neurotic dread" they face will appear as "fugue" and "classic fatigue"—terms that embody an elaborate pun. A *fugue* in music employs a counterpointed scheme, and the idea of counterpoint is retained here in the line: "Irregular breathing and alternate ascendancies." A *fugue* in psychiatry is a pathological disturbance of consciousness during which the patient performs apparently conscious acts of which he has no recollection on recovery. The theme of mental disturbance is carried through to the final word *fatigue,* which refers in the context of the war between the Supreme Antagonist and Eros to the fatigue syndrome or combat fatigue: a traumatic psychoneurotic reaction—an anxiety neurosis described as "shell-shock" in World War I and (in American usage) as "combat fatigue" in World War II.

"Consider" is a first try at the theme of *The Orators:* "England, this country of ours where nobody is well." In theme and spirit, including the more public social outlook and the growing mastery of the humorous element, Auden's second long work, *The Orators,* resembles the later poems in his first volume, *Poems,* 1930. His first long work, *Paid on Both Sides: A Charade,* is analogously related in theme and spirit to earlier poems such as "The Secret Agent" and "The Watershed" to which it forms a prologue. *Paid on Both Sides* provided much of the bulk of Auden's first slim volume, *Poems,* 1930. The first version of the Charade, written in 1927, is a dramatization of the eternal unconscious conflict between child and mother. The revised version, written in Berlin, introduces new dramatic machinery to represent the unconscious as a place of healing. Since this is a frequent theme in Auden's later work, notably, for example, in *The Age of Anxiety,* the Charade is a useful introduction to everything that follows it.

V

The Charade
of the Loving and Terrible
Mothers

1

The first of Auden's longer works, *Paid on Both Sides: A Charade*—still placed first in *Collected Poems*, 1976, and in *The English Auden*, 1977—is, ostensibly, an episode in a continuing feud between two families who live some fifteen miles apart in the Lead Dales of the English north country on opposite sides of the Pennine watershed. The conflicting parties are the Shaws of Nattrass House, Garrigill, near Alston, Cumberland, and the Nowers of Lintzgarth House, near Rookhope, in Durham. The central character in this episode, John Nower of Lintzgarth, was born prematurely during his mother's state of shock on hearing that her husband, George, had been ambushed and killed by Red Shaw of Nattrass.

When John Nower grows up he ambushes and kills his father's murderer and several followers, and he has another Shaw executed as a spy; but, eventually, influenced by unconscious forces—and the unconscious is the stage on which the significant action in this drama occurs—he attempts to end the feud and bring about reconciliation by marrying Anne Shaw. During the wedding feast at Nattrass the Shaw matriarch instigates a renewal of the feud. John Nower is killed, and the charade ends as it began, with a wife mourning the death of her husband. A final

chorus recalls the final chorus in *Oedipus Rex* with its warning
to call no man happy:

> Though he believe it, no man is strong.
> He thinks to be called the fortunate,
> To bring home a wife, to live long.

> But he is defeated; let the son
> Sell the farm lest the mountain fall;
> His mother and her mother won.   (CP, 35)

Auden wrote the first version of this Charade in 1927 while
still at Oxford in the hope of having it performed at the Somer-
set country house of the McElwee family, where he was invited
to stay during August—one of the "country houses at the end
of drives" he approved of in the sonnet, "Sir, no man's enemy." The title is taken from the *Beowulf* lines: "That was
no good exchange—that they should pay on both sides with the
lives of friends,"[1] and the imagery of the first version closely
resembles the pervasive imagery of inner psychological conflict,
regression, and the power of the death-instinct characteristic of
Auden's Oxford poems. The Charade was not played at the
McElwees, and Auden expanded it later in Berlin chiefly by introducing new dramatic machinery to represent the unconscious
as a place of healing. Somewhat longer than a one-act play, the
revised Charade is a closet drama that, with a little resourcefulness, can be played out in the mind; but, other than Prospero
who had spirits to command, any producer seeking stageworthy
material might find the Charade as unprepossessing as a half-
plucked chicken.[2] Its machinery is cumbersome. The list of
twenty-six characters in addition to a chorus of three persons
seems extravagant. There are three main groups of characters;
two of these are the hostile parties, the Nowers of Lintzgarth
and the Shaws of Nattrass. To distinguish the opposing sides,
the Oxford version directs, "The Lintzgarth party will wear its
handkerchiefs round their left arms" (EA, 410); the Berlin version significantly directs that the parties be distinguished on
stage by "different coloured arm-bands"—an allusion to the use
of armbands by the militant political parties of the 1920s—Fascist, Communist, Nazi. A third, more heterogeneous group intro-

duced in the course of revision, take part in a surrealist dream scene when the action of the Charade moves into the unconscious. They include, as principals, the conventional mummers' play characters, Father Christmas, the Doctor, and the Doctor's Boy; and, as extras, the White Rabbit from *Alice in Wonderland,* and a jury wearing school caps. (There is an intentional mingling of the atmospheres of the Norse sagas and of English boarding schools in this work.)

Even in its earlier version, Auden seems to have intended the Charade as a vehicle for an ambitious allegory on the life and death instincts—a modern Morality of Eros and Thanatos—that could take its place beside Eliot's *The Waste Land.* Like the equinox poem, "1929," *Paid on Both Sides* is a variation on the Orpheus myth that Auden was to employ again with Marxist overtones in his next dramatic work, *The Dance of Death* (1933) in which the Dancer performs a *"Solo dance as Sun God, creator and destroyer."* (DD, 11) In his Programme Notes for the performances of *The Dance of Death* at Westminister Theatre in October 1935, Auden wrote: "Drama is essentially an art of the body. The basis of acting is acrobatics, dancing, and all forms of physical skill. The music hall, the Christmas pantomime, and the country house charade are the most living drama of today." (EA, 273)

Although it is Freud who supplies the underlying theme of Eros and Thanatos as instinctive energies of the libido, some of the substance of *Paid on Both Sides* appears to be derived from Jung's accounts of the origins of the myths of the Hero and of the Primordial Mother. Jung saw quest Hero myths, particularly those associating the Hero with the sun, as expressions of man's drive toward consciousness; and, recalling Faust's journey to the realm of the Mothers, he noted that "the Kingdom of the Mothers is the kingdom of (unconscious) phantasy."[3] Auden embodies these notions and other aspects of the Oedipal theme in *Paid on Both Sides,* which, like every "country house charade," has its riddle to be solved. For example, the Charade is fairly closely equivalent, in dramatic terms, to Jung's interpretation of the Sphinx as a double being corresponding to "the mother-imago" and representing a force that could not be disposed of by solving a childish riddle: "the riddle was, in fact, the trap which the Sphinx laid for the unwary wanderer," says Jung:

"Overestimating his intellect in a typically masculine way, Oedipus walked right into it, and all unknowingly committed the crime of incest. The riddle of the Sphinx was *herself*—the terrible mother-imago, which Oedipus would not take as a warning."[4] Jung's archetypal Mother, a double being both loving and terrible, who in endowing her children with life also gives death as its end, is a significant figure in a number of Auden's works, including the best of the plays with Christopher Isherwood, *The Ascent of F6*, in which the hero, Michael Ransom, meets both death and mother on the mountain's summit.

Auden was twenty when he composed the first version of *Paid on Both Sides*. He revised it during his subsequent stay in Berlin at which time he introduced his friend John Layard into the opening dialogue on the ambush of George Nower: "To Colefangs had to go, would speak with Layard, Jerry and Hunter with him only." T. S. Eliot liked the Charade, which first appeared in his journal *The Criterion* in January 1930: "I have sent you the new Criterion," he wrote to E. McKnight Kauffer, "to ask you to read a verse play 'Paid on Both Sides' by a young man I know, which seems to me a brilliant piece of work. . . . This fellow is about the best poet I have discovered in several years."[5]

Paid on Both Sides was a late addition to *Poems,* 1930, because having published it in *The Criterion,* Eliot was at first unwilling to include it in the volume. This may account for its placement at the beginning of the book; but Auden continued to place it first in successive collections during his lifetime, and he seems to have tried to draw special attention to this work, particularly in a passage in *New Year Letter,* 1940, where he recalls its geographical setting in the vicinity of Rookhope in the Pennine Lead Dales, and alludes to its allegorical theme of "the Mothers":

> In ROOKHOPE I was first aware
> Of Self and Not-self, Death and Dread:
> Adits were entrances which led
> Down to the Outlawed, to the Others,
> The Terrible, the Merciful, the Mothers . . .
>
> (CP, 182)

2

Although Auden knew Rookhope and the area of the Lead Dales in general (he had gone there on a walking tour with Gabriel Carritt in 1927), it is very likely that he chose the names of the contending houses in *Paid on Both Sides* from ordnance survey maps of the district which confirm, for example, that the following piece of dialogue between George and John Nower contains exact description:

JOHN NOWER: Red Shaw is spending the day at Brandon Walls. We must get him. You know the ground well, don't you, George?

GEORGE: Pretty well. Let me see the map. There's a barn about a hundred yards from the house. Yes, here it is. If we can occupy that without attracting attention it will form a good base for operations, commands both house and road. If I remember rightly, on the other side of the stream is a steep bank. Yes, you can see from the contours.
                                                    (CP, 23)

Maps of the Rookhope area show the farm, Brandon Walls, its nearby barns, and contours indicating a steep drop down Brandon Bank, below the farmhouse, to Rookhope Burn. Across the Burn the contours rise again toward Hanging Wells and Hangingwells Common—called in the play "the hangs."

The map that George and John Nower pore over is the map of an area Auden chose to mythologize as his symbolic landscape, not only in *Paid on Both Sides* but throughout much of his work. "I could draw its map by heart," he says in "Amor Loci," a poem written forty years after *Paid on Both Sides*. He is more specific about its location in *New Year Letter*, where he claims the landscape of the Lead Dales as one of his chief symbolic properties:

I see the nature of my kind
As a locality I love,
Those limestone moors that stretch from BROUGH
To HEXHAM and the ROMAN WALL,
There is my symbol of us all.   (CP, 182)

The moors between Hexham and Brough that are a "symbol of us all" bear traces of continuous human occupation and conscious activity almost since the glaciers retreated: traces ranging from the barrows of Mesolithic man to the trailer parks or caravan villages of this motorized age. But it is not only the stages of man's historical journey that the moors bring to mind. The strata beneath them bear evidence of the stages of his evolutionary heritage, and, behind that again, of geological time stretching back through the earliest epochs: before the Coal Measures, before the Mountain Limestone, and before the Old Red Sandstone. And since lead occurs in the interstices of the most ancient rock strata, lead-mining symbolizes, for Auden, man's interest in his own psychic depths.

It is fairly easy to orient oneself in the symbolic landscape of *Paid on Both Sides.* Anyone driving the fifteen miles from west to east over the spine of the Pennines from Alston in Cumberland (the highest market town in England) to Rookhope in Durham, arrives at the midpoint as well as the highest point on his journey on the summit of Killhope Law near Cross Fell, where Killhope Cross marks the boundary between Cumberland and Durham. This high ground that forms the watershed for Allendale, Weardale, and the upper reaches of Teesdale is at the precise center of Auden's sacred landscape. This high ground is also at the approximate center of the roughly circular limits of the lead-bearing ores of the Lead Dales which occupy an area within a ten-mile radius of Killhope Cross. The road from Alston to Rookhope is the east-west diameter of this lead-mining circle. "There were lead-mines here before the Romans," Auden says in "Not in Baedeker" (CP, 422)—although he does not precisely identify the lead-mining site. The Roman roads and fortifications north of the Lead Dales attest both to the limits of empire here and to the presence, beyond the frontier, of vigorous indigenous tribes of Celts and Picts who resisted imperial

rule. The moors also bear traces of the first successors to the
Romans, from the time of King Arthur who, according to Jessie
Weston in *From Ritual to Romance,* had a seat at Blanchland,
near Rookhope, down to the Norsemen, the memory of whose
isolated farm settlements is still retained in local postal addresses such as those of Auden's two conflicting parties in *Paid
on Both Sides:* the Shaws of Nattrass, Garrigill, Cumberland;
and the Nowers of Lintzgarth, Rookhope, Durham.

Even in the late 1970s, travelers curious about the origins of
Paid on Both Sides could locate on their maps Nattrass House,
Garrigill, about six miles west of Killhope Cross, and, about the
same distance to the east, Lintzgarth House, on Lintzgarth Common, near Rookhope. Above Rookhope, they would also find the
farm Brandon Walls where the Nowers ambushed Red Shaw.
Nattrass House and neighboring East Nattrass were abandoned
in the 1920s and now serve as stables and barns for the nearby
farm Farnbury. The poor agricultural land surrounding Nattrass
is marked by the remains of many old mines on the surrounding slopes, as if generations had attempted to mine it for a very
long time. Lintzgarth, on the other hand is still a handsome
well-kept farmhouse, so set in the slope of a hill with a single
attendant tree that it looks very like the farmhouse that was the
original for *Wuthering Heights.* Auden probably chose it from
the map that he knew by heart simply for its interesting name,
and not because he knew the house or its occupants. Yet, oddly
enough, the name Adamson on the gate to Lintzgarth supplies
a word that also solves the riddle of the Charade as well as any
other. The Adamson family has lived at Lintzgarth for at least
a century; a grandfather was bursar for the old Rookhope smelt
mill that appears in a number of Auden's poems, including the
continuation of the passage already quoted from *New Year
Letter:*

> For lost belief, for all Alas,
> The derelict lead-smelting mill,
> Flued to its chimney up the hill,
> That smokes no answer any more
> But points, a landmark on BOLTS LAW
> The finger of all questions.   (CP, 182)

The tall chimney built to clear away dangerous fumes was for many years a prominent feature on the slopes of Bolts Law—a hill to the northeast of Lintzgarth House. A ground-level flue connected it to the smelting-mill below.

3

The geography of the Lead Dales does not exhaust the allegorical matter in *Paid on Both Sides*. It gives us the symbolism of the place, but not of time. The action is set at approximately Christmastime, for there is talk of Christmas toys and gifts as well as of the killings in old winters that link it allegorically with winter solstice rituals and vegetation myths. After a brief exposition, the play begins with a symbolic tableau introduced by the stage direction: *"Back curtain draws. Joan with child and corpse."* This child is the son prematurely born to Joan Nower under stress of her shock at hearing that her husband was killed in ambush by Red Shaw while on a journey to "speak with Layard." Layard, whom Nower seeks, is appropriately invoked here in a drama of "the Mothers," for he had treated the subject of the manifestation of the "terrible mother" in his accounts of the terrible Goddess of Melanesia. Joan, in the opening tableau with child and corpse, laments her lost husband, welcomes the newborn, and forecasts new killings. An analogous tableau ends the Charade and completes the cycle. In it, this child, John Nower, grown to manhood is killed on his wedding day by another Shaw and is lamented by his bride, Anne. These two lamentation scenes depict recurrences as inevitable as the seasonal cycle they represent; for according to Frazer in *The Golden Bough*, in the earliest vegetation myths associated with Attis and Osiris, "a goddess mourns the loss of a loved one, who personifies the vegetation . . . which dies in winter to revive in spring"; and, further, some of these myths "figured the loved and lost one as a dead lover or a dead husband lamented by his leman or his wife."[6]

The chorus following Joan's lament in the opening tableau speaks of the cycle of birth and death—"Can speak of trouble, pressure on men / Born all the time. . . ." After this chorus, and without any indication of intervening time (Auden apparently omitted a stage direction), we move to the scene in which John Nower, now grown to manhood, ambushes and kills Red Shaw and his companions at Brandon Walls. On returning from Brandon Walls the Nowers discover a Shaw spy, whom John orders to be taken out to be shot. We must assume that John Nower falls asleep during the soliloquy and chorus that conclude this episode; for the next episode begins abruptly with the direction: *"Enter Father Christmas. He speaks to the audience."* This stage direction introduces a surrealist dream scene—an interlude in which unconscious forces within John's mind in sleep seek to mediate the struggle in the outer conscious world. One remnant of his waking day that surfaces in the dream is an encounter with a spy, but this appears to be a manifestation of unconscious forces—the "Other" within himself—in conflict with his conscious ego, not the Shaw spy whom he had ordered shot. (*The Orators* links spying and introspection. In a list of "Perverted lovers" we find: "Others, haters of life, afraid to die, end in hospitals as incurable cases. Those are they who when the saving thought came shot it for a spy." EA, 63) The dream re-enactment of John's inner disharmony has two distinct episodes: a trial scene and a restoration scene, each involving stock characters from mummers' plays. (In his essay "Psychology and Art" Auden finds that both the Elizabethan use of madness—in *Lear*, for example—and the nonsense passages in mummers' plays have correspondences to the techniques of modern surrealism.)

As the trial scene begins John Nower is the Accuser, the spy is the Accused, and Joan (the eternal mother) is "his warder with a gigantic feeding bottle." The court is completed with Father Christmas as President and a jury wearing school caps. At the opening John Nower speaks in the clichés of some jingoistic wartime schoolmaster:

> Yes. I know we have and are making terrific sacrifices, but we cannot give in. We cannot betray the dead. As we pass their graves can we be deaf to the simple eloquence of their inscriptions, those who in the glory of their early

manhood gave up their lives for us? No, we must fight to
the finish.   (CP, 27)

Father Christmas then calls the witnesses, and three manifestations of the unconscious come forward to speak in turn: Bo, Po,
and the Man-Woman. The last represents a primitive life stage
before the distinction of sex and therefore speaks from the remote archetypal depths of the unconscious; but Bo and Po are
closer to the surface. (In the list of characters their names are
linked, as parts to be doubled, with two members of the feuding
houses, George Nower and Aaron Shaw, the latter, in the next
scene, an agent of conciliation prior to the marriage.)
    The first of the unconscious manifestations, Bo, is a spokes-
man for orientation toward the upper world. His cryptic imagery
of migrations, mountains, rebirth, and northern ridges resembles
that of extroverted seekers in Auden's other poems of the period.
He represents in some degree the more positive urge of the
questing hero to emigrate. Bo's concluding lines hint at a
Quixotic, tomb-conscious quest:

                        On northern ridges
            Where flags fly, seen and lost, denying rumour
            We baffle proof, speakers of a strange tongue. (CP, 27)

    Po, on the other hand, echoes Sancho Panza and seems to
favor turning "back to estates / Explored as a child." Po is also
womb-conscious, attracted to the regressive road where sorrow
sits:

                        . . . far from those hills
            Where rifts open unfenced, . . .
            And flakes fall softly softly burying
            Deeper and deeper down her loving son.   (CP, 28)

As each witness concludes, the Spy groans (the groans produced
by jazz instruments) as if some implication had struck home.
Bo and Po are followed by the Man-Woman, who brings associations of war, for this hermaphrodite "appears as a prisoner of
war behind barbed wire in the snow" and speaks in verse with
slant-rhymes reminiscent of Wilfred Owen's war poetry. This

androgynous figure symbolically represents regression to life below consciousness, or at a very early stage of evolution. Darwin,
for example, says in *The Descent of Man:* "In the dim obscurity
of the past we can see that the early progenitor of all the
Vertebrata must have been an aquatic animal . . . with the
two sexes united in the same individual . . ." and Jung points
to the hermaphrodite as an archetypal figure in dreams, who,
like the Atman of the Upanishads, is a "primordial universal
being, a concept which in psychological terms coincides with
that of the libido."[7]

The Man-Woman as a prisoner of war in winter is an aspect
of the libido in need of liberation. Auden's imagery is eloquent
on this point. The Man-Woman begins by declaring that the
occasion does not call for its ordinary role as a life-force or
regenerative power:

> Because I'm come it does not mean to hold
> An anniversary, think illness healed, . . .

Accusations of John Nower's neglect follow:

> Love was not love for you but episodes,
> Traffic in memoirs, views from different sides;

and the bill of particulars goes on to include a series of regressive tendencies toward an infantile narcissistic fixation:

> . . . you made that an excuse
> For playing with yourself, but homesick because
> Your mother told you that's what flowers did.   (CP, 28)

Then the Man-Woman shifts the ground for accusation from
the sexual and instinctive to weakness of will and neglect of the
libido's secondary functions of allurement—or the creative sub-
limation of these: "I tried then to demand / Proud habits"; and
also:

> Lastly I tried
> To teach you acting, but always you had nerves
> To fear performances as some fear knives.   (CP, 28)

The Spy groans at these accusations too, and Nower shoots him. But the new life is at hand. Voices call for a doctor, and the second mummers' episode begins in which the stock figures, the Doctor and the Doctor's Boy, join Father Christmas to revive the Spy. As in conventional mummers' plays, the Doctor boasts of his prowess. Then, to heal the Spy, he "produces a large pair of pliers and extracts an enormous tooth from the body." Georg Groddeck, in the part of *The Book of the It* where he discusses the dual aspects of the mother, the loving and terrible, speaks of how the unconscious draws a symbolic correspondence between a child in the womb and a tooth in the mouth: "For the unconscious, a tooth *is* a child. . . . the mouth is the womb in which it grows, just as the fetus grows within the mother's body. You must know how strongly rooted is this symbol in men's minds."[8] It is appropriate therefore—in the context of unconscious healing—for the Doctor in John Nower's dream to draw from the Spy's body a tooth symbolic of new birth. As the Spy is revived by the Doctor, John Nower also changes—for one moment into the Rabbit in *Alice in Wonderland*—and then joins the Spy in a symbolic ritual, as "the Accuser and the Accused plant a tree." That John Nower and the Spy in this episode are divided parts of the same psyche is implied in their opening line: "Sometime sharers of the same house." (CP, 29)

The joining of a Nower and a Shaw in the tree planting occurs, of course, in the dream and is therefore, like the tooth extraction, a symbol in the unconscious for the revival of the tree spirit, but this mutual undertaking also points toward regeneration, toward reconciliation and marriage between Shaws and Nowers—an event which takes place in the next scene between "John Nower, eldest son of the late Mr. and Mrs. George Nower of Lintzgarth, Rookhope, and Anne Shaw, only daughter of the late Mr. and Mrs. Joseph Shaw of Nattrass, Garrigill." (CP, 32) This reconciliation is short-lived. Anne proposes that they escape the eternal cycle of revenge by emigrating, as John's brother Dick had done, but John elects to stay. At the marriage feast at Nattrass the Shaw matriarch urges the continuation of the feud. John Nower is killed, and the final tableau, of the bride lamenting her dead husband, completes the mythological cycle: "His mother and her mother won."

T. S. Eliot, as we have seen, welcomed *Paid on Both Sides;* but except for Auden's close friend Louis MacNeice, few reviewers greeted its first appearance with enthusiasm. "It can be very profitably contrasted with *The Waste Land*," said MacNeice; "It is tragic where *The Waste Land* is defeatist, and realist where *The Waste Land* is literary. *The Waste Land* cancels out and ends in Nirvana; the Charade (cp. once more the Greeks) leaves you with reality, an agon (see the final chorus)."[9] The Charade courageously attempts to explore the unconscious springs of behavior and in accepting the double significance of the archetypal loving and terrible Mother is a "yea saying" to the whole of life; but in any comparison with Eliot it would take a great deal of generosity to rate it as highly as MacNeice does.

VI

The Orators:
Leaders,
Flying Tricksters, and Mothers' Boys

1

Auden's second book, *The Orators: An English Study*—an attempt to explore the psychology of aspiring leaders and led in the very early thirties—mixes flashes of brilliance with much that is slipshod, silly, and even perverse. He wrote most of it while a schoolmaster at Larchfield Academy, near Helensburgh, Scotland, during the school year of 1930-31. This may account for the substantial presence of schoolboys in the work and for the satire on English schools as tribal places of initiation into a land of the living dead. He also worked on it while holidaying on Reugen Island in the summer of 1931 with Isherwood and Spender and an entourage of the former's homosexual friends and acquaintances from Berlin—a circumstance that may have contributed to the number of rather tiresome in-group jokes and private allusions that spoil much of this work; for *The Orators* is flawed, in particular, by a failure to reconcile in an artistic harmony the private and public themes heralded in the dedication to Stephen Spender:

> Private faces in public places
> Are wiser and nicer
> Than public faces in private places.

At its best *The Orators* sparkles with a surface brilliance—
a sparkle enlivened by clever mimicry of stuffed-shirt oratory
and by playful pilferings from writers Auden admired, or just
happened to be reading, like St.-John Perse, Gertrude Stein,
and Baudelaire; but whereas St.-John Perse's *Anabase,* for
example, may elicit associations with timeless depths, Auden's
gleanings from it are more like surface tinsel. The pilferings
from other writers in *The Orators* may be simply a flashy accompaniment to the psychological theme of kleptomania, which,
in this work, is symbolic of masturbation; for *The Orators* is a
curious work, and some few readers, those willing to give it the
degree of attention that Eliot's *The Waste Land* or Joyce's
Dubliners demands, may be well pleased with it, particularly if
they also find elaborate jokes amusing. Others may regard its
mimicry of many styles as erudite nonsense. While not comparable to either work artistically, *The Orators* resembles
Dubliners and *The Waste Land* to the extent that it represents
the modern world as inhabited, at best, by moral invalids and,
at worst, by paralyzed, moribund, or quite dead souls: "What
do you think about England, this country of ours where nobody
is well?" asks the speaker of the opening oration, "Address for
a Prize Day." The question may contain an ironic allusion to
Ramsay MacDonald's election campaign of September 1931, in
which the Prime Minister called for "a doctor's mandate" to
heal England's economic ills. But on the basis of Auden's diagnosis, the mandate should more appropriately be given to those
who held that traditional society forced repression of the instinctive life: "Lawrence, Blake and Homer Lane, once healers
in our English land." (EA, 49) As Homer Lane had healed the
paralysis that was a psychosomatic expression of John Layard's
neurosis, so Lane and his followers, including Auden, might
diagnose and heal the moral paralysis of English bourgeois society.

Although some of it—particularly in the first edition—is
disguised autobiography, *The Orators: An English Study* is presented as a mock anthropological study, and readers may best
enter its satiric spirit by noting how the title fits into any random list of real or imaginary monographs by anthropologists:
Good Company: A Study of Nyakusa Age-Villages; The Orators:

*An English Study; West African Secret Societies: Their Orga-
nization, Officials, and Teachings; Oral Traditions: The Yo-
ruba.*[1] Amos Tutuola's African novels, *The Palm-Wine Drinkard*
or *My Life in the Bush of Ghosts,* were not available to Auden
when he wrote *The Orators.* Had they been, Auden might have
simply represented England in Tutuola's terms as "Dead's Town"
or "The Bush of Ghosts." But any typical anthropological work
of the 1920s outlining initiation rites in which the initiates are
looked on as having "crossed over" to the land of the dead will
reveal the general basis for the satire in *The Orators.*

In his Foreword to the revised edition of 1966, Auden is
either not quite honest or he is forgetful about his sources when
he says that some of the ideas in the book came from D. H.
Lawrence's *Fantasia of the Unconscious,* and that the stimulus
for writing the section called "Journal of an Airman" came
from Baudelaire's Journals and also General Ludendorff's
memoirs. Although Lawrence, Ludendorff, and Baudelaire contribute something, Auden's more immediate sources were anthropological papers by his friend John Layard: "Degree-Taking
Rites in the South West Bay of Malekula" (1928) and "Malekula: Flying Tricksters, Ghosts, Gods and Epileptics" (1930).
The second of these, in particular, describes an extraordinary
ritual of initiation which, says Layard, "represents in dramatic
form the death of the candidate and his resurrection through
promotion . . . into the ranks of the living dead."[2] Layard's
paper on these flying tricksters had been presented at the meetings of the Royal Anthropological Society in 1929. Both Auden
and Isherwood knew then, or even earlier, of its account of
ghosts, epileptics, and flying tricksters undergoing somewhat
analogous metamorphoses through a real, an apparent, or a
ritual death.

There were obvious possibilities for satire in Layard's paper.
One could transfer the rite of initiation to England and represent the elite public schools, where the sons of the wealthy were
trained for leadership, as places of initiation into the English
ranks of the living dead. And Auden does this. But he also seized
on the matrilineal element, particularly the uncle-nephew relationship, and other recondite aspects of Layard's thesis, and he
handled this material in a way likely to mystify readers less

familiar with his sources than Layard or Isherwood, who knew, for example, that the final section of Layard's paper was subtitled "The Homosexuality of Ghosts and Epileptics." This section caused something of a sensation when it was first presented; for it attempted not only to show correspondences among flying tricksters, ghosts, and epileptics, but to link all of these with homosexual significances in the Egyptian myth of Set and Horus. While the main admonitory theme in *The Orators* is the dangerous element of narcissism or the mother-complex—in the aspiration to leadership as well as in the impulse to sacrifice one's self for a leader—much of its incidental significance derives from variations on the theme of matrilineal inheritances like epilepsy or hemophilia in which the true male ancestor, as in the Malekula rite, is an uncle who may also be homosexual. (Auden himself appears in the first edition as "Uncle Wiz.")

The prologue to *The Orators*—titled "Adolescence" in *Collected Poems*—is a verse parable embodying the book's Oedipal theme. The poem's central figure is an adolescent male both loving toward and loved by his mother:

> By landscape reminded once of his mother's figure
> The mountain heights he remembers get bigger and
>   bigger:
> With the finest of mapping pens he fondly traces
> All the family names on the familiar places.
>
>   (O, 9; O2, 3; CP, 64)

Since much of the satire in *The Orators* concerns schoolboys, "Adolescence," with its theme of mother-fixation, may have seemed a suitable subject for the prologue to a work that also seeks to explore the neurotic desire for self-immolation in the cause of a leader. Auden's Airman in *The Orators* has such a neurotic desire; and he aspires to be a leader of a "new order" like Goering, Ludendorff, and Hitler (who had formed an alliance at the time the work was written). Both cult leaders and their followers are sometimes psychologically associated with a mother-complex. So is homosexuality. The assumption that all this is self-evident is the source of much obscurity in *The Orators.*

In the Foreword to the 1966 edition of *The Orators,* Auden said: "As a rule, when I re-read something I wrote when I was younger, I can think myself back into the frame of mind in which I wrote it. *The Orators,* though, defeats me. My name on the title-page seems a pseudonym for someone else, someone talented but near to the border of sanity, who might well, in a year or two, become a Nazi." Within a year of writing this blunt self-criticism he echoed the phrase "someone talented but near to the border of sanity" in a remark on James Joyce's *Finnegans Wake* during a 1967 interview with the Oxford journal *Isis:* "Joyce was an undoubted genius. But a madman . . . he asked you to stand in the same relation to his writing as you must to your life. It is as if he said 'you must spend your whole life reading me and never give me up or escape.' "[3] He was not alone in so judging *Finnegans Wake.* James Stephens—the friend Joyce asked to finish *Finnegans Wake* if he died before the work was done—said of it: "You need all the rest of your life to read it if you're going to read it, and you will need a life after that again to understand it."[4] And Frank O'Connor, commenting in 1967 on a phrase of his own describing the work as Joyce's putting God's point of view about the universe, said: "Twenty years ago no one would have dismissed *Finnegans Wake* like that without my rising to defend and expound it. Today I can do neither: 'I cannot pay its tribute of wild tears.' "[5] What Auden, Stephens, and O'Connor say of *Finnegans Wake* might equally be said of *The Orators:* that the makers of such labyrinths aspire to the tribute of total devotion the deity demands; and it is because of the implied demand for the humiliation of the reader that Auden can say of himself as the writer of *The Orators:* "someone . . . near to the border of sanity who might well, in a year or two, become a Nazi." Auden was not merely echoing Dryden's line, "Great wits are sure to madness near allied," in diagnosing Joyce, and himself when young, as susceptible to some aspects of madness. In his preface to Dag Hammarskjöld's *Markings* (1964) he identified cynical contempt for others as a minor symptom of the demonic pride of the megalomaniac who, taking on responsibility for God, begins to imagine that he *is*

God. He had associated madness with colossal egoism in "September 1, 1939," where in a reference to "What had occurred at Linz" (the place of Hitler's childhood) he says that accurate scholarship may find "What huge imago made / A psychopathic god." And in the same poem, paraphrasing "What mad Njinsky wrote / About Diaghilev," he implies that even the normal heart is prone to crave "Not universal love / But to be loved alone." His preface to the revised edition of *The Orators* suggests that writers of works demanding total attention are not free from this temptation. And he includes himself.

2

The three books of *The Orators* are variations on a theme derived from John Layard's account of the flying tricksters of Malekula: namely, that the initiation rite of that secret cult represents the death of the candidate and his resurrection into the ranks of the living dead. In Book One, "The Initiates," the speaker, who delivers the "Speech for a Prize Day," is an avuncular "old boy" of the school. He first invites the boys to imagine a Divine Commission of Angels arriving suddenly at Dover to catalogue the rituals and customs of England. He then represents himself as a healer intent on alerting the schoolboys to the moral dangers of the three negative aspects of love enumerated by Dante: excessive love of self or of neighbor, defective love, and perverted love. Beneath the surface moralizing, the Speaker is prone to sly hints at autoeroticism in questionable phrases that, on closer scrutiny, often evoke the more serious psychologizing of Homer Lane or D. H. Lawrence. At the close he turns trickster and encourages the newly initiated boys to assault their masters—to get rid of the old order and its representatives. It seems clear that the Speaker belongs to his own category of "excessive lovers of their neighbours" among whom he includes, in his list of types, "A rich man taking the fastest train for the worst quarters of eastern cities." (EA, 62) He finishes his speech hurriedly: "Time's getting on and I must hurry or I shall miss my train."

The speaker in "Argument," the second piece of rhetoric in Book One, observes the living performing "their annual games under the auspices of the dead." In general the people who inhabit "Argument" have three characteristics: they are bound to a leader, they go abroad to be reborn, and there are among them two kinds of escapist: the introverted who seek escape in detective stories and the extroverted who prefer pubs. The most accessible and most amusing part of "Argument" is the second section comprising a series of mock liturgical invocations, the first eight to fictional detectives—among them Dixon Hawke, Sexton Blake, Poirot, and ·Holmes—and the next twelve to English inns or public houses like the Blue Boar, the White Horse, the Marquis of Granby. (The George in the final invocation could be either an inn or a king.)

The third section in Book One, "Statement," is the most purely musical of the rhetorical forms in "The Initiates." Spoken from the point of view of a detached, almost robot-like observer, it is largely a series of catalogues, although it too moves in three parts through the rhythm of life, death, and resurrection. The first catalogue has homosexual overtones: "One charms by thickness of wrist; one by variety of positions; one has beautiful skin; one a fascinating smell. One has prominent eyes, is bold in accosting. One has water sense. . . ." (O, 30) The rhythms here are reminiscent of Anglo-Saxon cadences and perhaps also of Gertrude Stein's attempts to match language with Cubist techniques, as in her word-portrait "Picasso" (1909): "This one was one who was working. This one was one being one having something come out of him. This one was one going on having something coming out of him. This one was one going on working."[6]

"Statement" goes on to combine a catalogue of deaths with a catalogue of resurrections beginning, "One slips on crag, is buried by guides," and ending "One is famous after his death for his harrowing diary." This last item points forward to "Journal of an Airman."

The rhetorical progression of Book One, "The Initiates," from the public oratory of "Speech for a Prize Day" through the dialectic of "Argument" and the single-minded objectivity of "Statement," leads by a logic of regression to the autistic, self-loving "Letter to a Wound." When Auden reprinted this letter in his *Collected Poetry* (1945), much ink was spilled identifying the wound that prompted the piece. Guesses ranged from the actual wound of surgery, suggested in the "Letter," to the psychological wound of his homosexuality. (This last association would accommodate the homosexual relationship in the initiation rite of the Bwili cult of Malekula.) Isherwood says the "Letter" was inspired by an operation for a rectal fissure in February 1930,[7] which is also recalled in Ode I of Book Three; but identification is unnecessary. The letter-writer, like the speakers in "Address for a Prize Day," "Argument," and "Statement," represents one who leads initiates into some aspect of death or life-avoidance.

3

Book Two of *The Orators*, "Journal of an Airman," is the private diary of a neurotic airman-observer who carries out subversive activities against the authority of the ruling class. The Airman is also a poet. (Two of his poems, "The Decoys" and the interesting sestina "Have a Good Time," are given a permanent place in Auden's *Collected Poems*.) In this respect he represents the artist who, like D. H. Lawrence, takes the side of instinctual liberation against authoritarian constraint. He is also a representative of narcissism in which, according to Freud, the infantile model of the love-object is not the mother but the subject himself.

The many allusions in the Airman's jottings to his own kleptomania and onanism, together with references to his crafty tricks, may owe something to Jung's observation in *Psychology of the Unconscious* that "when onanism confronts the physician it does so frequently under the symbol of frequent pilfering, or crafty imposition, which always signifies the concealed fulfillment of a forbidden wish."[8] The Airman has also a pair of related obsessions: one is with "the enemy" (philistine middle-class society whose homes have names like "The Hollies" or

"The Mimosa" as Auden's first home in Birmingham did: "Apsley House"), and the other obsession is with a leader figure: his Uncle Henry, who was also an airman and, apparently, a suicide.

The Airman reveals himself partly through his attitude toward "the enemy," and partly through his admiration for his uncle. His attitude to his uncle defines him in relation to the Oedipal matrilineal theme which Auden superimposed on the social satire of *The Orators* with undercurrents of a self-portrait. Like Isherwood, Auden also had a homosexual uncle of whom his mother disapproved, and while in Berlin he kept a journal (on which the Airman's is modeled as much as on Baudelaire's) detailing some specifics of his experiences.

It is particularly in relation to the theme of the uncle that the Airman's Journal draws on Layard's anthropological paper describing the initiation rites of the Bwili. Uncle Henry in "Journal of an Airman" is also an initiator; he incurs the mother's disapproval; he has remarkable protruding "eyes going round"; and he is associated with red: "my fascinated fear of his red sealing-ring." And both he and his airman nephew share the power of flight and the pleasure in practical jokes.

4

The various forms of rhetoric in *The Orators* mimic false attitudes. The "Six Odes" of Book Three, with their instances of hero-worship, are no exception: they must be read as mock-heroic and not as an expression of Auden's feelings. Without the extravagant flights of the Odes we might miss Auden's concern for the role of poets, as bards, in the cult of hero-worship; but since the satirical intention of the Odes depends on mimicry, and sometimes on mimicry of mimicry, the reader is confronted with the problem of deciding which voice is the true one. (The fact that Auden reprinted Ode V, "To My Pupils," for many years under the title, "Which Side Am I Supposed To Be On?" shows that this confrontation is part of the game.) The mockery of national bards and the theme of mother-fixation comes out most obviously in Ode IV, "To John Warner, son of Rex and Frances Warner," in which the hero is a newborn infant.

The final Ode moves from the symbolic themes concerned with mother love to those concerned with a father figure. It takes the form of a hymn to an Old Testament God as Father, and its imagery of war and conflict links the zero-hour of World War I trench warfare with the Greek retreat from Persia:

> Not, Father, further do prolong
> Our necessary defeat;
> Spare us the numbing zero-hour,
> The desert-long retreat.

In its metrical form this Ode mimics the Anglican Hymnal much as the discarded Ode II, "To Gabriel Carritt," mimicked Hopkins. Its wrenched syntax parodies those common-measure hymns in which inept metrists contort the normal word order to accommodate stress or rhyme, and, in particular, it parodies Scottish metrical versions of the Psalms which Naomi Mitchison said fascinated Auden. Anyone familiar with these or such popular hymn tunes as "O God our help in ages past" could sing the following stanza from Ode VI; but could he make any more sense of its syntax than of the gabble that choirboys make of hymns, sometimes unintentionally and sometimes intentionally?

> These nissen huts if hiding could
> Your eye inseeing from,
> Firm fenders were, but look! to us
> Your loosened angers come.   (O, 114)

We might assume a logic of syntax something like "If we were hiding from your inseeing eye these nissen huts could be firm fenders." But does all this convolution derive from the need to rhyme *from* with *come?* The parody is far too sophisticated to be merely choirboy mimicry. It draws attention to itself perhaps to remind us that the society into which the schoolboys are to be initiated is not merely one of pubs, press lords, and politicians, but a society of pulpits, too, "Where gaitered gamekeeper with dog and gun / Will shout 'turn back.' "

The enigmatic quality of the odes was the least acceptable element in *The Orators*. Auden was soon made aware of this. Edgell Rickword, for example, writing in the *Auden Double Number* of *New Verse*, 26-27 (1937) drew attention to the lines from Ode IV, "To John Warner"—

> Living in one place with a satisfied face
> All of the women and most of the men
> Shall work with their hands and not think again

(O, 105)

—and remarked: "I don't for a moment suggest that Auden followed out the implications of that last couplet, the essence of Nazi demagoguery with its degradation of women and regimentation of the Strength through Joy variety."[9] Auden seemed to have this criticism in mind in his Foreword to the American revised edition of *The Orators* in 1967 where he says: "In one of the Odes I express all the sentiments with which his followers hailed the advent of Hitler, but these are rendered, I hope, innocuous by the fact that the Führer so hailed is a newborn baby and the son of a friend." (O2, viii)

The Orators had a mixed reception. Douglas Garman's review in *Scrutiny* was noncommittal; and Auden's friend Louis MacNeice who had praised *Paid on Both Sides* highly was less enthusiastic about *The Orators:* "*The Orators* by Auden, an admittedly personal work, is made very obscure by a plethora of private jokes and domestic allusions. . . . these poets make myths of themselves and of each other (a practice which often leads to absurdity, e.g. Day Lewis's mythopoeic hero worship of Auden in *The Magic Mountain*)."[10] But John Hayword, reviewing *The Orators* for Eliot's journal, *The Criterion,* found it to be, without doubt, "the most valuable contribution to English poetry since *The Waste Land*,"[11] and almost forty years later John Fuller concluded his detailed analysis of *The Orators* in *A Reader's Guide to W. H. Auden* by confirming Hawyard's judgment—despite the reservations Auden had meanwhile expressed about the work and his own state of mind when he composed it: "My guess today is that my unconscious motive in writing it was therapeutic, to exorcise certain tendencies in myself by allowing them to run riot in phantasy." (O2, viii)

Auden may have needed to write *The Orators* to exorcise some impish spirit; but the book has some importance now in retrospect, for it points to directions Auden might have taken: the arid introspective road or the arrogant road of the messianic leader of a cult or coterie with faithful entourage, like the poet Mittenhofer in *Elegy for Young Lovers*. Conversely, it points to the degree in which Auden's later experiments in the theater —a public medium impatient of private meanings—were healthy artistically.

By the time *The Orators* appeared, in May 1932, England— and Europe—had crossed the divide between the decade of uphill economic struggle following World War I and the "low, dishonest decade" of political maneuvering leading to World War II. The effects of the Wall Street financial crash of October 1929 did not begin to be felt in Britain until early 1931, when some European banks defaulted on British loans. This gave rise to a crisis in England that brought hunger marches and violent demonstrations by the unemployed in several British cities at a time when the Fascist and Nazi parties were gaining strength in Europe; but the national government, conservative in outlook and troubled by the economic crisis at home, temporized with these threatening foreign movements. After the near-elimination of the Labour Party in the 1931 election, little middle ground remained for critics of the national government. Many middle-class intellectuals and idealists opposed to Nazism and Fascism moved toward the Left and some found the Marxist utopia attractive. Others, equally disturbed by the national government's failure to challenge Hitler's pretensions, made common cause with socialists and Communists in what was termed the Popular Front against Fascism. Between 1932 and 1936 Auden's political sympathies lay with this group although unlike Day Lewis and Spender (for a brief period), he did not join the Communist Party.

VII

Plays for the Group Theatre, 1933-37

1

Robert Medley, the unwitting if providential instrument of Auden's discovery of his poetic vocation while at Gresham's School, was later instrumental in affording him an opportunity to write plays to be staged in London by a group of actors, producers, writers, musicians, and designers seeking alternatives to the conventional drama then available in London's commercial theaters. Rupert Doone, a former Diaghilev dancer and choreographer had conceived the idea, and Medley had helped him in developing the nucleus of a group membership formally organized as the Group Theatre in February 1932. The active membership eventually included artists of such varied talents as Henry Moore, Tyrone Guthrie, Stephen Spender, T. S. Eliot, and Auden (who wrote or edited the Group Theatre's 1934 prospectuses and policy statements). In the autumn of 1932, when Auden was their guest in London at Medley's invitation, Doone, who had worked in Paris with Cocteau (whose *Orphée* he may have had in mind), suggested that Auden write a play for the Group Theatre on the theme of Orpheus and Eurydice with a part for dance or mime. Doone and Medley differ in their recollections; the latter says Doone commissioned two plays: an Orpheus play and a *Danse Macabre*.[1] Auden accepted the idea, and by the following summer, 1933, delivered the script of *The Dance of Death*, which was published by Faber in November that year and received poor critical notices. Apart from the stage direction, *"Solo dance as* Sun God *creator and de-stroyer"* (and a dancer's or choreographer's interpretation of this), there are few discernible survivals in *The Dance of Death* of the original notion of a play on the theme of Orpheus and Eurydice, other than some allusions to vegetation rituals in the chorus that follows the Sun God dance. In some degree the theme of the play is that of Shelley's "Ode to the West Wind" with explicit Marxist references added.

Doone's vague commission had not called for an overt political theme; but the spirit of the play reflects the political climate during the period of its writing: Hitler's rise to power in January 1933 was met with benign neglect by Britain's Conservative-dominated national coalition government, and opposition (after the Reichstag fire incident) from the German Communist Party. *The Dance of Death* is, essentially, a Marxist allegory that owes little to the myth of Orpheus and perhaps a great deal to the well-known Communist parable in *Anti-Dühring* where Engels draws a parallel between the death of the seed-grain before its regeneration and the necessary death of the old order before communism's new order can be brought about.

After trial Sunday performances produced by Tyrone Guthrie in February-March 1934 and well received by professional critics, a modified version of *The Dance of Death,* with Doone in the Dancer's role in a mask designed by Henry Moore, opened the Group Theatre's 1935 season at Westminster Theatre together with T. S. Eliot's *Sweeney Agonistes.* No other London theater could have ensured an audience more sympathetic toward the propagandist theme of *The Dance of Death:* the inevitability of the collapse of bourgeois society and the triumph of Marxism. Many among the Group Theatre's audiences—united at least by anti-Fascist sentiments—could enter into the spirit of some ingenious Brechtian contrivances designed to involve them in the play's action. In this respect the play adhered closely to the prescription for drama laid out in Auden's Programme Note for the Westminster Theatre opening—a brief manifesto beginning with an allusion to vegetation rituals: "Drama began as an act of the whole community. Ideally there would be no spectators. In practice every member of the audience should feel like an understudy." (EA, 273)

In contrast to the puzzling obscurity of earlier works like *Paid on Both Sides* and *The Orators,* the theme of *The Dance of Death* is at once obvious. It is put forward by the Announcer: "We present you this evening a picture of the decline of a class, of how its members dream of a new life, but secretly desire the old, for there is death inside them. We show you that death as a dancer." To this, the middle-class Chorus echoes, "Our death." The opening scene is set in a seaside holiday resort which, like "the Sport Hotel" in "Consider," is a common image in Auden's early works for bourgeois escapism. The Chorus speaks for the idle bourgeoisie:

> Here on the beach
> You're out of reach
> Of sad news, bad news
>
> . . .
> Europe's in a hole
> Millions on the dole
> But come out into the sun.   (DD, 8-9)

The Chorus concludes this scene with a comic-nostalgic "old-time Waltz" bearing Auden's unmistakable signature:

> You were a great Cunarder, I
> Was only a fishing smack
> Once you passed across my bows
> And of course you did not look back
> It was only a single moment yet
> I watch the sea and sigh
> Because my heart can never forget
> The day you passed me by.   (DD, 11)

Leaving their wraps on the beach, members of the Chorus take to the water. The Dancer then performs the dance of the eternal cycle of change—"*Solo dance as* Sun God, *creator and destroyer."* The Announcer's commentary on this dance supplies Marxist overtones for the regeneration theme:

> He dances, and of course the barley and trees grow tall,
> His help is powerful but does not apply to you all.

The bones of the beggared listen from underground:
To them his dancing has long been a familiar sound.

(DD, 12)

Following his dance, the Dancer gathers up and hides the cloth-
ing left on the beach by the Chorus. Returning cold from the
water they are easily persuaded by the Theatre Manager to don
uniforms from an available costume-basket; and the Announcer
persuades them to behave as Fascists and to embrace an Anglo-
Saxon racist form of Fascism: "Our first duty is to keep the
race pure, and not let these dirty foreigners come in and take
our job." (DD, 17) Then, supported by the Chorus, the Fascist
Announcer assaults the German-Jewish Theatre Manager. This
leads to an episode in which the Chorus as English Fascists are
in control of the ship of state—an episode that encourages audience participation; for the audience is here directed to mime,
with appropriate noises, the sea, the storm, and the rocks on
which the Fascist ship of state must founder.

As the ship of the Fascist state founders, the Dancer falls in
an epileptic seizure. Temporarily revived by Sir Edward's injec-
tion, he dances as "The Pilot." When one Chorus member
breaks away and suggests an individualistic creed, "And fly
alone / To the Alone," the Dancer attempts to dance that theme
too, but collapses. At the point of death he makes a will which
the Chorus and the Announcer between them present in a long
ballad, recapitulating the Marxist theory of history, sung to the
tune of "Casey Jones." A typical stanza—this one on the stage of
feudalism—runs:

The feudal barons they did their part
Their virtues were not of the head but the heart.
Their ways were suited to an agricultural land
But lending on interest they did not understand.

(DD, 34)

The ballad's progression through historical stages leads, inevitably, to the appearance in history of Karl Marx. And in the

play itself, when the Dancer dies, Karl Marx comes on stage (flanked by "two young communists") to the strains of Mendelssohn's "Wedding March" in time to declaim the curtain-line: "The instruments of production have been too much for him. He is liquidated."

The Group Theatre's 1935 production of *The Dance of Death* was a theatrical success, well-received by audiences and reviewers, although to the reader of today it may seem merely a period piece with nothing of dramatic value to recommend it beyond the Brechtian cabaret routines and some sparks of wit in the lyrics. But in the climate of the times it did a great deal for Auden's reputation. It brought him early recognition as a dramatist, and it also gave him the status of a senior partner in the Group Theatre with Medley and Doone. Furthermore, the shared billing of *The Dance of Death* with Eliot's *Sweeney Agonistes* gave Auden a place (which his later plays would help to justify) in the flowering of English poetic drama in the second quarter of the twentieth century—a flowering that owed much to Yeats and Eliot.

2

Auden eagerly accepted the role of dramatist offered by his association with the Group Theatre, and casting about for a full-length play to follow *The Dance of Death,* he took up a discarded manuscript of a play he had begun in Germany in the spring of 1929, *The Reformatory,* a version of which he and Isherwood later finished as *Enemies of a Bishop.* He incorporated parts of this and possibly of another unpublished play, *The Fronny,* into *The Chase,* which he sent to Isherwood in Copenhagen in November 1934, requesting suggestions. After Isherwood contributed some new scenes and ideas for scenes, Auden flew to Copenhagen in January 1935 for final work on the play, then called by its present sub-title, *Where Is Francis?*[2] When working with Auden on a substantially cut version for production, Doone proposed the final title, *The Dog Beneath the Skin.* The cutting was essential; for the published text, like so many of Auden's experiments in drama from *Paid on Both Sides* to *For the Time Being: A Christmas Oratorio,* is more readily produced in imagination than in a theater. As in any quest story, the number of episodes is arbitrary. The seekers go out; and they return in a year. Anything can happen in the meantime. The numerous episodes in the published version—some of them surrealist—demand frequent scene changes, and the cast is enormous by present-day standards. There are thirty-three individual parts (although several could be doubled), and a Chorus with fifteen sub-groups: Chorus Girls, Diners, Lunatics, Police, Priests, Procurers, Prostitutes, and so on through the alphabet down to Villagers.

The thread on which the play's many episodes are strung like beads is the folktale theme of the lucky third son whose innocent blunderings succeed where others have failed. In *The Dog Beneath the Skin* we find that Sir Francis Crewe, heir to the Squirearchy of Pressan Ambo, has run away from home and failed to return. Each year a villager is chosen by lot to go in search of him. The first seven seekers—including Sorbo Lamb and Chimp Eagle who reappear briefly in the course of the play—have failed to return. The play opens with the drawing of lots in which an eighth seeker, Alan Norman, is chosen. Accompanied by a large dog that appeared at the selection ceremony, he journeys from Pressan Ambo (a romantic old-world "village of the heart" in Edwardian England) through Ostnia and Westland—the two imaginary European countries that appear in all three plays by Auden and Isherwood. The dog that accompanies Alan Norman is a dog-skin worn as a disguise by the missing heir, Sir Francis. This scenario obviously permits a great deal of comic business with the dog; but its main function is to direct satire against three kinds of political order in which power lies in the hands of right-wing reactionaries. Pressan Ambo is controlled by the feudal clique obligatory in Marxist propaganda literature—the clergy, the military, and the aristocracy—represented by the Vicar of Pressan Ambo, General Hotham, and Miss Iris Crewe, who, in the course of the play, fall for the seductions of Fascism. Ostnia is a decadent autocratic monarchy with a puppet church. In Westland, "Our

Leader," although generalized enough to fit any Fascist dictator, is, essentially, Adolf Hitler. Sir Francis in his dog-skin disguise may represent the revolutionary who heeds Lenin's advice "to hunger, work illegally, and be anonymous."

Beyond and behind the foreground satire on Fascist and reactionary politics, *The Dog Beneath the Skin,* like *The Dance of Death,* also advances the Marxist notion of capitalist society in its death-throes while healthy young socialists stand by ready to come on stage, but it does so with much more comic gusto both in the verse and in the zany theatrics of the episodes. The first section of the opening chorus introduces Pressan Ambo, the imaginary village of nostalgia for England past—"You shall choose its location / Wherever your heart directs you most longingly to look." The second section foresees its moral decay: "Here too corruption spreads its peculiar and emphatic odours." To mimic the sentimental tone and language appropriate to Pressan idealized as the place of English childhood innocence, Auden borrowed shamelessly from the aureate prose of Anthony Collett's *The Changing Face of England.* For example, Collett speaks of the rivers Soar and Trent: ". . . the Trent, or where the Soar comes gliding at leisure out of green Leicestershire to swell the ampler river"; and Auden closes his nostalgic vision with: "As at Trent Junction where the Soar comes gliding; out of green Leicestershire to swell the ampler current."[3] The voice speaking in the opening part of the chorus is not Auden's. To enter the spirit of the play it must be received as a parody, as must other elements including the Vicar's closing sermon which Auden had printed earlier as "Sermon by an Armament Manufacturer," and later in *Collected Poetry* (1945) as "Depravity: A Sermon." (This last gave rise to a great brouhaha by one critic who found this printing out of context deceitful: "intended to be taken in all seriousness as a work of edification.")[4] Some of the comic scenes that parody bad taste and crudeness are among the more memorable in the play: the cabaret scene at the Nineveh Hotel in which Destructive Desmond slashes a Rembrandt, for example. But not all of Auden's choruses between scenes are in keeping with the comic mood or show equal high spirits. Those that deliver the gospel of Homer Lane, like the one following Act II, Scene 3, tend to be preachy:

You who are amorous and active, pause here an instant.
See passion transformed into rheumatism; rebellion into
     paralysis; power into a tumor.

In the final episode Alan Norman and his companion return to England and the play ends with a revolt against the old
order in Pressan Ambo. The Vicar, the General, Miss Iris Crewe,
and their faithful villagers turn into animals, while Sir Francis—
no longer in his dog-skin disguise—and some stalwart volunteers
go off, each "to be a unit in the army of the other side," and the
final chorus concludes: "To each his need: from each his power."
     The first production of *The Dog Beneath the Skin* at the
Westminster Theatre was fairly well received and had a six-week
run from January 30 to March 14, 1936. T. S. Eliot who saw it
about March 1 was pleased by the staging and acting but he
deplored some of the cuts and did not care for the ending. He
found the chorus irritating, not because the players were inept,
but because it kept interrupting the action with Auden's
didactic explanations.[5] As the play's run ended, Doone enquired
of W. B. Yeats, who was visiting London at the time, about the
possibility of moving *The Dog Beneath the Skin* with its London cast to the Abbey Theatre in Dublin. Yeats wrote to Doone
from the Athenaeum on March 18 to say he did not think it
would pay to bring the play to Dublin if he had to bring the
company. He suggested that Doone consult the Dublin producer
of Eliot's *Murder in the Cathedral*.[6] There was a New York
production in July 1947 at the Cherry Lane Theatre for which
Auden provided a revised ending. While in residence as Neilson
Professor at Smith College, 1952-53, Auden "arranged a contest
and offered an award for the best re-writing of the final scene of
The Dog Beneath the Skin . . . open only to students in Freshman English."[7] The unsolved problems with its ending suggest
that the play lacked a coherent, unified action and was for the
most part a pastiche held together by clever cabaret turns.
Thirty years after its first production Auden "ascribed the
'Brechtian' use of song in *The Dog Beneath the Skin* to his admiration for what he called the 'wonderful German cabaret'
rather than to Brecht himself."[8]

3

The theme of a mother's influence on her son comes to the fore again in *The Ascent of F6*, a play about mountain-climbing that takes its name from the world's second highest peak—K2 in the Himalayas—which Auden's mountaineer-geologist brother, John Auden (to whom the play is dedicated), described to him in Berlin in 1929. *The Ascent of F6* combines two interests: the political theme of the urge to power, particularly authoritarian power, and the psychological theme of the Oedipal mother-complex.

For its psychological theme *The Ascent of F6* relies on our recognizing a distinction between two related allegorical figures common in Auden's work: the Dragon and the Demon. The Dragon, an archetypal figure symbolic of the destroying mother, belongs to the realm of the unconscious or instinctive; and the encounter with the Dragon, which is as inevitable as death, is Everyman's maternal inheritance at journey's end. The temptations of the Demon, on the other hand, occur in the course of life and can be consciously dealt with. They differ for different people depending on the form of life-avoidance that may attract each: the longing for ease; or the will to power; or, as in *F6*, the sacrifice of self to others.

The political theme in *The Ascent of F6* turns on rival colonial ambitions: the mountains forming the boundary between two colonial territories, British Sudoland and Ostnian Sudoland, are dominated by an Everest-like peak, F6, locally referred to as the haunted mountain. In response to a rumor that the colonial power whose representatives first climb F6 will rule both Sudolands, the Ostnians have sent out an expedition under the great climber, Blavek. Sir James Ransom of the British Colonial Office offers his twin brother and noted climber, Michael, an opportunity to lead a British expedition to race Blavek to the top of F6. Michael Ransom, who despises the cynical use of political power that his brother James condones, easily rejects James's justification of the expedition. He also rejects the pleas of stock representatives of imperialism who appeal to his patriotism: General Dellaby-Couch, a former military governor of Sudoland, Lady Isabel Welwyn, daughter of a former governor, and Lord Stagmantle, a newspaper peer who is to finance the expedition. But Michael cannot turn aside his mother's accusation that his real reason for refusing the greatest opportunity of his life is simply his hatred for his brother James. Acting on her wish, Michael Ransom leads his companions in the ascent of F6.

In *Christopher and His Kind*, Isherwood says that Michael Ransom was modeled on T. E. Lawrence: "From Christopher's and Wystan's point of view, the Truly Weak Man was represented by Lawrence of Arabia, and hence by their character Michael Ransom in F6."[9] But the play does not bear out Isherwood's assertion. Certainly, as the play begins, Ransom has the destructive quality of the Truly Weak Man within himself. This is revealed, but only very cryptically so, in his opening soliloquy on Pillar Rock in the Lake District where he says: "Under I cannot tell how many of these green slate roofs, the stupid peasants are begetting their stupid children"—a Fascist sentiment of the kind that Auden glosses in a later prose piece: "People who believe that the poor are poor because they are stupid and have stupid children, will not adopt a democratic form of government."[10] But Ransom does not remain Truly Weak, and the development of his character from Truly Weak to Truly Strong is the only significant action of the play. Auden saw Lawrence of Arabia as a rare instance of such a transformation of personality. Reviewing B. H. Liddell Hart's *T. E. Lawrence* in 1934, he said the tendency of the Truly Weak Man is to escape from the demands of consciousness and to enlist "in the great Fascist retreat" from reason and consciousness. He gives Lenin and D. H. Lawrence as well as Lawrence of Arabia as his instances of the Truly Strong. As qualities of the Truly Strong he cites Lenin's characteristics of a revolutionary—"to hunger, work illegally, and be anonymous" that he incorporated also into the lyric, "Our Hunting Fathers" (1934); and in reference to T. E. Lawrence's search for anonymity as Aircraftsman Shaw, he says specifically: "To me Lawrence's life is an allegory of the transformation of the Truly Weak Man into the Truly Strong

Man." (EA, 320) Although Isherwood recalled only the Truly Weak element in Ransom, it appears that *The Ascent of F6* was intended to embody this allegory; but the fact that the authors, by their own admission, "never got that ending right" suggests some confusion in their aims.

Ransom in *F6* is one of the Truly Weak until his recognition of the truth in the Abbot's crystal in the monastery scene. His subsequent colloquy with the Abbot teaches him that only through the abnegation of self can he overcome the temptation of the Demon. Thereafter he climbs not for himself but for the sake of the others, and he becomes absorbed in the climb for its own sake like the anonymous predecessor whose skull they encounter, and like all the other predecessors whose names, as he recalls on seeing the skull, are part of the history mountaineering. (In his review of Liddell Hart's *T. E. Lawrence,* Auden approves of Lawrence's axiom: "Happiness comes from absorption"—not the blind absorption of "the great Fascist retreat," but the absorption required by reasoned choice of action that necessitates further step-by-step rational choice.) It is only when Ransom continues the climb with a sense of dedication to the work of predecessors who prepared the way that we see any glimmer of truth in his mother's earlier insistence that his brother James, the apparent strong man, was Truly Weak and Michael (or M. F. as he is called in the play) Truly Strong: "But you, you were to be the truly strong, / Who must be kept from all that could infect / Or weaken." (F6, I, iii)

The play's most obvious weakness is that its authors do not keep the transformation of Ransom in sufficiently clear focus. This gives the impression that their aim was to compose an anti-Fascist morality play in which all characters were personified types rather than a play about a character's self-discovery. Failure to resolve the ambiguity may account for their difficulties with the play's ending.

Since almost all of the characters are satirical representations of one kind of weakness or another, Ransom stands out by contrast as strong. The stereotyped weaklings include the politically motivated group, James Ransom and his Fascist-minded associates: Lord Stagmantle, General Dellaby-Couch, and Lady Isabel Welwyn. Each of the four mountain climbers who accompany

Ransom fits Isherwood's description of the Truly Weak Man driven by some neurotic form of life avoidance. Gunn, a Don Juan, is also a kleptomaniac, like the Airman in *The Orators;* Shawcross, his narcissistic negative image, also, like the Airman, immolates himself; the botanist, Lamp, is obsessed with his search for the rare five-leaved flower *polus naufrangia;* and the doctor, Williams, is pitifully self-indulgent. Collectively, they constitute two sets of opposing pairs who, as John Fuller has noted, may represent Jung's concept of the disintegrated psyche —the four faculties in isolation: Thought (Lamp), Feeling (Shawcross), Sensation (Gunn), and Intuition (Williams). None of these is granted M.F.'s insight and consequent integration.

All except M.F. die during the ascent. He reaches the summit and dies there in a climactic scene in which his brother James appears in the form of a dragon, and in which a mysterious veiled figure on the summit is revealed to be his mother. Both M.F. and the audience are prepared for this revelation in which the mother and the Demon are the same; for when M.F.'s mother persuades him to undertake the climb, she assures him that she will be with him on the mountain: "Of course you'll get to the top, darling. Mother will help you. . . . Wasn't she with you from the very beginning, when you were a tiny baby? Of course she was! And she'll be with you at the very end." (F6, I.iii) And when he encounters a skull high on the mountain —all that remains of some earlier climber—M.F. addresses it: "Well, Master; the novices are here. Have your dry bones no rustle of advice to give them? . . . Imagination sees the ranges in the Country of the Dead, where those to whom a mountain is a mother find an eternal playground." (F6, II.ii) The psychological theme of the mother-complex, so important to both Auden and Isherwood, did not seem to have too much significance for Group Theatre audiences. In a politically conscious decade, audience interest was drawn to the satire on the stock political figures "whom history has deserted": Lord Stagmantle, General Dellaby-Couch—veteran of colonial wars, and Lady Isabel Welwyn. Auden's anonymous creations, Mr. and Mrs. A, the bourgeois suburbanites who listen to the daily radio reports on the expedition and whose domestic tensions provided a separate little drama on the periphery of the main action of *The Ascent of F6,* drew even greater interest.

One of the present-day ironies associated with *The Ascent of F6* is that time has diminished the two dramatic properties that had great appeal to its first audiences. One was the portrait of the Press Baron, Lord Stagmantle; the other was the device of "listening in" to a radio broadcast to link the average citizen—Mr. and Mrs. A—to the action of the play. The 1930s' forerunners of the mass appeal and the power of network television were the mass-circulation English dailies, *The Daily Express* and *The Daily Mail,* owned by politically ambitious peers, Lord Beaverbrook and Lord Rothermere. Under the motto, "For King and Country," *The Daily Mail* vigorously opposed "Bolshevism and socialism" and derided the League of Nations, whose supporters it dubbed "lovers of every country but their own." *The Daily Express* trumpeted support for the British Empire, trivialized significant foreign events, and played up inconsequential local circumstances through sprightly reporting. Both were deplored by liberals and intellectuals, and Auden had earlier satirized their titled bosses as "Beethameer, Beethameer, bully of Britain" before combining them again in Stagmantle. By 1936 also, radio broadcasting by the BBC had become part of British life, and Auden's use of the radio device for the subplot in *The Ascent of F6* caught the atmosphere of English life in a way new to the theater. (His Narrators in *For the Time Being* (1944) are essentially radio commentators also.) When the play was first performed audiences liked the cabaret songs set to music by Benjamin Britten and sung by Hedli Anderson, particularly the dirge on the death of M.F. (accorded in the printed text to Stagmantle and Isabel) that begins:

> Stop all the clocks, cut off the telephone,
> Prevent the dog from barking with a juicy bone,
> Silence the pianos and with muffled drum
> Bring out the coffin, let the mourners come.   (F6, II.v.)

But the characterization of M.F. also impressed thoughtful observers. Testimony to this may be found in the autobiography of the British-born physicist Freeman Dyson, *Disturbing the Universe* (1979). Robert Oppenheimer ("father" of the American atomic and hydrogen bomb projects) invited Dyson in 1948 to the Institute for Advanced Study in Princeton. By 1953, the year Oppenheimer was put on trial as a security risk they had become close friends. In a chapter of *Disturbing the Universe* titled "The Ascent of F6" that includes illuminating commentary on Auden's play, Dyson analyzes Oppenheimer's character in the light of M.F.'s. Familiar with Eliot's *Murder in the Cathedral* since 1936 and with *The Ascent of F6* since 1937, Dyson first expected Oppenheimer, when on trial, "to behave like the Archbishop in Eliot's play." He later realized he had cast him in the wrong play; and that *The Ascent of F6* was, in some sense, a true allegory of Oppenheimer's life. He enumerates aspects of Oppenheimer's nature illuminated by the play, including: "His combination of philosophical detachment with driving ambition. His dedication to pure science and his skill and self-assurance in the world of politics. His love of metaphysical poetry. His tendency to speak in cryptic poetic images . . ." Dyson draws a specific parallel, for example, between M.F.'s acceptance of Lord Stagmantle's offer to finance the expedition to F6 and Oppenheimer's acceptance of General Grove's offer of the resources of the United States Army for the Los Alamos atomic project: "M.F. refuses at first to be a party to the political game, but afterward accepts the offer. As Oppenheimer said at his trial, 'When you find something that is technically sweet, you go ahead and do it. . . . That is the way it was with the atom bomb.' F6 was technically sweet, too."

Dyson, who had not known Oppenheimer at the time of the Los Alamos project, wondered why his colleagues of that period spoke so admiringly of Oppenheimer's greatness—a quality Dyson also found lacking in M.F.: "Auden and Isherwood succeeded remarkably in painting, or predicting, a good likeness of the character of Robert Oppenheimer as I knew him from 1948 to 1965. But there was one essential feature missing both from the Oppenheimer I knew and from the portrait in the play. The missing element was greatness of spirit to which those who worked with him at Los Alamos bear almost unanimous witness." Dyson at last saw this during 1966-67 when Oppenheimer was dying of throat cancer: "In the twelve months that remained to him, his spirit grew stronger. . . . The mannerisms of M.F. were discarded. He was simple, straightforward, and indomitably courageous."[11]

The Ascent of F6 was the most successful of the Auden-Isherwood collaborations and is occasionally revived; but its successor, *On the Frontier*, had little stage success even though, in retrospect, its diagnosis of the politics of hate may seem acute. Its implied criticism of Communism as well as of Fascism (consequent on Auden's Spanish experience) may not have appealed to supporters of the Popular Front before the Hitler-Stalin pact of 1939, and too few may have been disposed to agree that both Stalin's Russia and Fascist states like Germany were the opposite of "the good place" imagined by the hero, young Eric:

> This is the good place
> Where the air is not filled with screams of hatred
> Nor words of great and good men twisted
> To flatter conceit and justify murder.   (OF, II.i.)

On the Frontier was more tightly constructed and had a more economical cast than the other plays, but it lacked the boisterous cabaret turns that had enlivened them. Primarily in prose, and Auden's prose at that, it was begun at Dover in July 1937 and completed in 1938 during the voyage to China for the travel book *Journey to a War,* in which the prose is Isherwood's and the verse Auden's.

By the time Auden came to write his share of *On the Frontier* he had experienced another moment of revelation. This revelation shook his faith in the cause he had espoused—not the Communist cause, for he had never wholeheartedly espoused that—but the cause of liberal humanism and of liberal democracy for which, at that moment, the focal point of struggle was the war in Spain. The rise and progress of Nazi power in Germany was also much on his mind—the evidence of the plays alone bears that out. He was greatly troubled by the fact that the Nazis made no pretence of believing in justice or liberty. But having lived in Germany and made friends there he was even more deeply troubled that "this utter denial of everything liberalism had ever stood for was arousing wild enthusiasm, not in some remote barbaric land . . . but in one of the most highly educated countries in Europe, a country one knew well and where one had many friends. Confronted by such a phenomenon, it was impossible any longer to believe that the values of liberal humanism were self-evident."

Auden's concern arose from the fact that Hitler did not come to rule Germany through "seizure of power" (as newspapers later tended to say) even though he destroyed German constitutional democracy when in power: "By the summer of 1932 the Nazis controlled 230 seats in a Reichstag of 611, coming closer to an absolute majority than did any other party at any time under the Weimar Republic . . . He had a better right to the chancellorship, and represented, so far as they expressed their feelings through votes, more nearly the wishes of the German people than any of his predecessors."[12] Auden began his reappraisal of his attitude toward the German situation by asking himself if liberalism was really self-supporting, and, if so, what validated its values and invalidated Nazi values. His questioning of Hitler's appeal to intelligent Germans preceded the moment of revelation in February 1937:

> With this and similar questions whispering at the back of my mind, I visited Spain during the Civil War. On arriving in Barcelona, I found as I walked through the city that all the churches were closed and there was not a priest to be seen. To my astonishment this discovery made me profoundly shocked and disturbed. The feeling was far too intense to be the result of a mere liberal dislike of intolerance, the notion that it is wrong to stop people from doing what they like, even if it is something silly like going to church. I could not escape acknowledging that, however I had consciously ignored and rejected the Church for sixteen years, the existence of churches and what went on in them had all the time been very important to me. If that was the case, what then?[13]

This moment of revelation in Barcelona did not result in a dramatic conversion. But the consequences of the self-examination it provoked are evident in the sonnet sequence—later titled "Sonnets from China"—that was Auden's main contribution to his final collaboration with Isherwood, *Journey to a War,* published in March 1939, barely six months after *On the Frontier.* *Journey to a War* is not an attack on Fascism or even on the evils of Japanese aggression; Auden's "Sonnets from China" are first, an exploration of the origins of the writer's own Western values; and then, from the standpoint of those values, a searching look at the suffering of individual Chinese soldiers and reflections on the place of art or of the artistic vocation in a war-torn world. The Auden of "Sonnets from China"—who is not yet the Auden of the later Christian dramatic works like *For the Time Being*—would tend to find some of the shrillness of the Auden of the Group Theatre plays embarrassing.

VIII

Poems of the Thirties:
England, Iceland, and Spain

1

The decade of the 1930s coincided in the West with the Great Depression and the rise of Fascism, and in the USSR with the consolidation of Stalin's power. (Trotsky was exiled in 1929 and murdered in 1940.) That "low dishonest decade," as Auden called it in "September 1, 1939," saw Hitler's accession to power in Germany in 1933, the Japanese occupation of Manchuria, civil war in Spain and China, and Mussolini's war in Ethiopia; and it drew toward a close with Japan's expansion of the war in China on July 7, 1937, and the outbreak of "total war" in Europe on September 1, 1939. It also witnessed gross inhumanities perpetrated in the name of political ideology. By its end Stalin had "liquidated" millions of independent peasant farmers; Hitler had sought to exterminate the Jewish people and, with them, any Germans who had the courage to voice protest; Mussolini had brought weapons of modern warfare to Ethiopia in search of a colonial empire; and all three dictators had intervened in the Spanish Civil War, thereby transforming what had been a struggle for liberal democracy into a Communist-Fascist confrontation and testing-ground.

At such a time it was no surprise to find poets being concerned with politics, particularly a poet like Auden who knew Germany, had German friends, and whose parents sheltered a succession of Jewish refugees more fortunate than the speaker in his "Refugee Blues" written in New York in 1939:

114

Thought I heard the thunder rumbling in the sky;
It was Hitler over Europe, saying: "They must die";
We were in his mind, my dear, we were in his mind.

Saw a poodle in a jacket fastened with a pin,
Saw a door opened and a cat let in:
But they weren't German Jews, my dear, but they weren't
   German Jews.   (CP, 210)

Such verse reflected ugly realities, not the doctrinaire and abstract theory of history embodied in *The Dance of Death*. When
one looks for manifestations of Marxist ideology in Auden's
work of the thirties, the span narrows down to the period
1932-34, when, besides *The Dance of Death,* there are three or
four poems of quasi-Marxist orientation reflecting a belief that
"history had deserted" bourgeois society and that only a socialist
revolution could cure England's ills. Among these were two
poems he wrote in August and September of 1932: "Brothers,
who when the sirens roar," and "I have a handsome pro-
file. . . ." The first of these had appeared in March 1933 in
New Country, an anthology of left-wing poems and prose edited
by Michael Roberts, whose preface advanced the notion that
England's future hope lay in the triumph of a socialist revolution. In Roberts's anthology the poem in question appeared to
cherish the same hope, for it was titled "A Communist to
Others" and its opening line read "Comrades, who when the
sirens roar." Another poem of Auden's in *New Country,* "A
Happy New Year: To Gerald Heard," was similar in spirit
to the longer work, later abandoned, that convinced Harold
Nicolson of Auden's dedication to revolution although not
necessarily to Communism. Nicolson's diary entry of August 4,
1933, supplies a valuable account of the effect of Auden's work
on a sensitive mind at the time:

> Wystan Auden reads us some of his new poem in the
> evening. It is in alliterative prose and divided into Can-
> tos. The idea is Gerald Heard as Virgil guiding him
> through modern life. It is not so much a defence of com-
> munism as an attack upon all the ideas of comfort and
> complacency which will make communism difficult to

achieve in this country. . . . I go to bed feeling terribly
Edwardian and back-number, and yet, thank God, delighted that people like Wystan Auden should actually
exist.[1]

Auden retained none of these poems in *Collected Poems,*
Part IV, 1933-38; but he begins that section with a revised version of "A Summer Night," a poem he wrote in June 1933 in
which the view of history foresees the inevitable overthrow of
the bourgeois ruling class by the proletariat. Originally a poem
of sixteen six-line stanzas, but reduced in its revised form to
twelve, "A Summer Night" moves swiftly and easily in allegro
rhythms through two contrasting phases: the first evoking a
moment of felt peace and harmony in one's private and personal world and the second giving a simultaneous sense of
ominous events in the outer public world. At first, in a beatific
mood, the thinker in the poem basks in his own enviable situation: he is comfortably reclining on the lawn of a walled garden, in congenial company, looking up at the moon. In the
second phase, he contemplates, with mixed feelings, the world
the moon looks down on beyond the garden wall. The tone
of the original version of "A Summer Night" fits comfortably with
the outlook of someone who could say "I thought I had done
with Christianity for good." The smug bourgeois thinker experiences a moment of Nirvana—ironically, a death-wish; and
his vision of a force working in the world beyond the garden
wall is the Marxist vision of the historical inevitability of purga-
tive revolution. The revised version in *Collected Poems* exor-
cises this vision. The process of revision is of some interest
because the first and second versions of "A Summer Night" are
essentially two different poems; each, in its historic setting, reflecting Auden's outlook on history at the time of its composition.

"A Summer Night" was probably occasioned by an unusual
personal experience of a sense of peace and of concord with
others—a lived experience corresponding to the Nirvana image
of his early poems. Auden told of this "vision" thirty years later
in a section titled "The Vision of Agape," in his long Introduction to Anne Fremantle's collection, *The Protestant Mystics*

(1964). He begins this subsection by defining "the vision of Agape" as a mystical experience of which "the classic Christian example . . . is, of course, the vision of Pentecost." And he adds, "but there are modes of it which are not overtly Christian." Lacking instances of these in the collection he was introducing, he provides an account of one, "for the authenticity of which I can vouch." The vision Auden recounts has for its setting a calm evening scene in June 1933 on the grounds of the private boarding school where he was then teaching. He begins the account as follows:

> One fine summer night in June 1933 I was sitting on a lawn after dinner with three colleagues, two women and one man. We liked each other well enough but we were certainly not intimate friends, nor had any one of us a sexual interest in another. Incidentally, we had not drunk any alcohol. We were talking casually about everyday matters when, quite suddenly and unexpectedly, something happened. I felt myself invaded by a power which, though I consented to it, was irresistible and certainly not mine. For the first time in my life I knew exactly—because, thanks to the power, I was doing it—what it means to love one's neighbor as oneself. (F&A, 69)

He then says that after the power had faded, the memory of the experience did not prevent him "from making use of others grossly and often." But he claims that the recollection of the experience made it much more difficult for him to deceive himself about his intentions, and he adds: "among the various factors which several years later brought me back to the Christian faith . . . the memory of this experience and asking myself what it could mean was one of the most crucial, though, at the time it occurred, I thought I had done with Christianity for good." (F&A, 70)

It seems likely that Auden recorded his recollection of "The Vision of Agape" in 1963 to supply the want of a ready instance in the book he was introducing. If so he was in some degree describing the experience of a different person—his younger self thirty years before; and his recollection is filtered through a mind committed in the interim to Christianity and to the theological concept of "the vision of Pentecost" which presupposes that the course of history is providential. This view of history was brought home to him by Charles Williams's *The Descent of the Dove: A History of the Holy Spirit in the Church*, first published in 1939, and later edited by Auden (who said he had been "reading and rereading" it "for some sixteen years") in a new American edition in 1956.

"A Summer Night" begins with a series of images for the ideal moment of peace and harmony already familiar in Auden's earliest poems: the evening hour, a windless night, and congenial company. The third stanza contains a remarkably skillful image comparing the force that confers beatitude on the thinker with the "dove-like pleading," logic, and power of light which enchants the flowers into bloom:

> Equal with colleagues in a ring
> I sit on each calm evening
>   Enchanted as the flowers
> The opening light draws out of hiding
> With all its gradual dove-like pleading,
>   Its logic and its powers: . . .

The thinker in the poem pauses momentarily in a transitional stanza to remember friends not present in the garden:

> Now north and south and east and west
> Those I love lie down to rest;
>   The moon looks on them all . . .   (CP, 103)

The tone and rhythms of this stanza are reminiscent of the children's nursery prayer known as the "White Paternoster"—in effect a celebration of the day—that associates the four Evangelists with the four bed-posts. And as Paul Fussell has pointed out, this stanza is, significantly, the stanza of Christopher Smart's "A Song of David": "a poem which visits Auden's in other ways as well, not least in its canvass of the particulars of the Creation (moon, flowers, lion, bird, sun, gardens, creepers, tree, sea, wheat, tigress) as components of the joy it celebrates. And once we are alerted to Auden's awareness of Smart, we see their kinship elsewhere, in 'The Creatures,' say, or in Auden's rhetorical instinct for prayer and praise."[2]

In the 1933 version of "A Summer Night" the childhood prayer echoed in this transitional stanza appears to be but a passing reflection of the outmoded order surveyed more fully in the second part of the poem from the perspective of the moon which observes with equal indifference our English "picnics in the sun" and Hitler's claims on Danzig, "where Poland draws her eastern bow." Auden's revisions make no change of real consequence in the first section of "A Summer Night" other than the deletion of the rather arch and technically weak fifth stanza that hints—with a trace of homosexual overtone—at a loved one waiting. (There are also minor changes in two lines that improve them artistically.) But the second part of the poem dealing with the public world beyond the wall undergoes radical revision. In the 1933 version this second portion of the poem developed the theme of the class struggle in the manner of *The Dance of Death* and foresaw the destruction of Britain's upper classes. The revision emasculates this theme by excising three stanzas, of which the first opens with lines on the spectre of proletarian forces gathering outside the garden wall in the hungry thirties:

> The creepered wall stands up to hide
> The gathering multitudes outside
> Whose glances hunger worsens;

and the third opens with lines on the death-wish of the grouse-hunting, Oxford-educated, ruling class:

> For what by nature and by training
> We loved, has little strength remaining. . . .
>
> (EA, 137-38)

Without the ironic contrast provided by these three stanzas, the new life looked forward to in the revised poem's concluding stanzas is, simply, new life—not post-revolutionary new life:

> But when the waters make retreat
> And through the black mud first the wheat
> In shy green stalks appears,

> When stranded monsters gasping lie,
> And sounds of riveting terrify
> Their whorled unsubtle ears.   (CP, 104)

In the unexpurgated version, the "stranded monsters," like the
nursery prayers, seemed to stand for something outmoded by the
new "Power Stations" and so forth that the revolution would
bring. In the revised poem, these images fit with a generalized
theme of renewed life linked to distant hope for social "wholeness."

Auden revised "A Summer Night" to fit his changed outlook
on history for his 1945 *Collected Poetry*. In *Modern Canterbury
Pilgrims,* having outlined some of the events and occasions that
cumulatively contributed to his return to Christian belief toward the end of the thirties including his shock at finding
churches closed and priests proscribed in Barcelona, he adds,
"Shortly afterwards, in a publisher's office, I met an Anglican
layman, and for the first time in my life felt myself in the presence of personal sanctity. . . . So, presently, I started to read
some theological works, Kierkegaard in particular, and began
going, in a tentative and experimental way, to church."[3] Auden
enlarges on the effects of his meetings with Charles Williams in
his Introduction to Williams's *The Descent of the Dove:* "I
count them among my most unforgettable and precious experiences . . . in his company one felt twice as intelligent and in-
finitely nicer than, out of it, one knew oneself to be."[4] As *New
Year Letter* (1940) shows, Williams's books, particularly *The
Descent of the Dove,* profoundly influenced Auden's later work
and may have largely contributed to the pervasive presence in it
of the vision of Pentecost. But in 1933 all that was in the future.

2

Auden's *Collected Poems,* Part IV, 1933-38, includes all
the poems he wished preserved from the period when he was
looked on in England as politically committed. The omission of
poems once widely admired brings the quality of those retained

into sharper focus; and what these surviving poems from the mid-1930s convey without doubt is that Auden was then a superb lyric poet. Rhythmic certainty, verbal dexterity, and a *con brio* movement of the verse characterize poem after poem such as "On This Island," "What Is that Sound," "Paysage Moralisé," and "Musée des Beaux Arts." Auden's lyric genius was then prodigal. To take a single striking example: the table of contents contains the entry "Twelve Songs"—an umbrella title that denies individual recognition to any particular song. Yet this throwaway title is the reader's only lead to a little anthology of songs perhaps without equal in modern poetry. To compare this unheralded dozen with, for example, James Joyce's baker's dozen in *Pomes Penyeach,* is to be convinced that Joyce wisely chose not to continue writing verse. Even when compared with earlier and later groupings of Auden's own lyrics in *Collected Poems,* the "Twelve Songs" of Part IV stand out as particularly accomplished.

Although some poems written during 1937-38 initially appeared in Auden's first American volume, *Another Time,* most of the lyrics and songs retained in Part IV, were originally included in a volume of Auden's with variant English and American titles: *Look, Stranger* (London, 1936) and *On This Island* (New York, 1937). (While Auden was visiting Iceland in the summer of 1936, Faber, in London, chose the title *Look, Stranger* from the opening line of the lyric "Look, stranger, on this island now." Auden thought this choice of title sounded "like the work of a vegetarian lady novelist" and insisted that Random House in New York not use it. They therefore chose the next three words from the same opening lines.)

The line that supplies both titles introduces an accomplished lyric of great technical as well as thematic interest. As a metrical performance, "On This Island" transforms a series of risky moves into a smooth flow of sustained rhythmic activity with the daring of a skilled gymnast. There is, for example, the unexpected turn from the stiff formality of the invitation in the opening line to the eager rhythms and internal rhyme of the second line—a liveliness countered, in turn, by a hushed admonition in the two short lines:

> Look, stranger, on this island now
> The leaping light for your delight discovers,
> Stand stable here
> And silent be,
> That through the channels of the ear
> May wander like a river
> The swaying sound of the sea.   (CP, 112)

This soft "ebb music" is followed shortly by a long line of six stresses in the Hopkins manner, introducing a passage in which Auden risks dividing a word for the sake of effective rhyme:

> When the chalk wall falls to the foam and its tall ledges
> Oppose the pluck
> And knock of the tide,
> And the shingle scrambles after the suck-
> ing surf,
> And the gull lodges
> A moment on its sheer side.   (CP, 112)

Besides effectively combining varying line-lengths, this passage employs a variety of rhyme forms. These include both end-rhyme and internal rhyme, either of which may be either full or partial, or—as in the case of *ledges* and *lodges* above—may be precise instances of Wilfred Owen's slant rhyme.

The metrical virtuosity of "On This Island" attracts attention to itself to some purpose; for the poem quite intentionally invites comparison with Matthew Arnold's "Dover Beach." The poems share the same setting: the chalk cliffs at Dover overlooking the English Channel; Arnold's at night, Auden's in the morning. In each a speaker invites someone to contemplate the view while listening to the rhythmic movement of pebbles on the strand as the waves ebb and flow. Arnold's poem finds in these sounds an echo of the rhythms of tragedy, and foresees, fatalistically, the decline of civilization into the clash of "ignorant armies" on a "darkling plain." Arnold seeks solace in personal trust: "Ah, love, let us be true to one another . . ."

Auden's poem, by contrast, is optimistic. Addressed to a stranger—that is to a representative of humankind (including the speaker) estranged from simpler creatures by consciousness and volition—it affirms the resourcefulness and civilizing capacity of human consciousness. The contrast with Arnold's outlook is intentional. Early in Arnold's poem the light on the French coast "gleams and is gone," and the poem thereafter moves in darkness. Early in Auden's the "leaping light" discovers ships "like floating seeds" moving on "voluntary errands"—an imagery of life, potentiality, and conscious choice—of "Eros, builder of cities"—that gainsays Arnold's vision of a darkling plain where ignorant armies are fated to clash. The conclusion of Auden's poem is calm, confident, and affirming; and it culminates in a low-keyed but effective image linking a vision of civilization to such capacities of the mind as memory and imagination:

> Far off like floating seeds the ships
> Diverge on urgent voluntary errands,
> And the full view
> Indeed may enter
> And move in memory as now these clouds do,
> That pass the harbour mirror
> And all the summer through the water saunter.
>
> (CP, 113)

The final image implies that "the full view" of England's cliffs, the harbor, and the ships at sea can be seen again, at will, in the waters of memory, as clearly as the passing clouds are mirrored at that moment in the harbor.

In its meticulous shaping, rhythmic certainty, and quiet affirmation, "On This Island" confirms that in the late thirties Auden saw conscious choice as the hope and nurture of civilization. The obvious correspondences with "Dover Beach" also imply that, at thirty, he had the confidence to challenge an acknowledged master on his chosen ground. Companion lyrics in *On This Island*—several of them set to music by Benjamin Britten—show that this confidence was well-founded.

3

However good his songs and individual lyrics, Auden seems to have preferred, when possible, to undertake more sus-

tained works. He had spent time on the long work that Harold
Nicolson heard him read from but abandoned it after writing
about a thousand lines of alliterative verse. He had better success with another, less political, venture: a satirical epistle to
Lord Byron in rhyme-royal stanzas. "I want a form that's large
enough to swim in, / And talk of any subject that I choose," he
said at the beginning of this work, *Letter to Lord Byron*—an
eclectic verse commentary modeled on Byron's *Don Juan*. This
epistle was Auden's main contribution to *Letters from Iceland,*
a volume on which he and Louis MacNeice collaborated during
a visit to Iceland in the summer of 1936 at a time when travel
literature was in vogue. Some of this poem is autobiographical;
but it is, in the main, light, witty traveler's verse that is still en-
tertaining. The work has no superb passages comparable for
instance to the Waterloo stanzas in *Childe Harold* where Bryon
fades into the background, or even to those parts of *Don Juan*—
the tales of Donna Inez or Haidée, for example—where the characters in the tale so absorb our interest that we forget the writer.
We are almost always aware of Auden in *Letter to Lord Byron,*
but he narrowly escapes censure for being unduly self-centered
because he sustains the lightness and dexterity necessary for
the possibilities of comic rhyme in the seven-line rhyme-royal
stanza:

> Ottava Rima would, I know, be proper,
>   The proper instrument on which to pay
> My compliments, but I should come a cropper;
>   Rhyme-royal's difficult enough to play.
>   But if no classics as in Chaucer's day,
> At least my modern pieces shall be cheery
> Like English bishops on the Quantum Theory. (CP, 80)

If not quite up to Byron's *Don Juan,* Auden's *Letter to Lord
Byron* is still readable, the more so in its later, and shorter, revised form.

Some of the other verse in the travel-book *Letters from Iceland* also keeps well, particularly the poem "Journey to Iceland"
originally beginning:

And the traveller hopes: "Let me be far from any
Physician"; and the ports have names for the sea.

(EA, 203)

This poem, subtitled, "A Letter to Christopher Isherwood," was
followed in *Letters from Iceland* by a prose letter to Isherwood
beginning: "Thank you for your letter. No. You were wrong. I
did not write 'the ports have names for the sea' but 'the poets
have names for the sea.' However, as so often before, the mistake
seems better than the original idea, so I'll leave it." (LI, 27) Almost thirty years later in his *Elegy for Young Lovers* Auden
shows us the self-centered poet Mittenhofer in a towering rage
because his secretary has transcribed *ports* for *poets* in a similar
line. Since the line is Auden's and the rage Mittenhofer's, it is
difficult, as we shall see in a later chapter, to assess how much of
his earlier self Auden intends to satirize—along with Yeats—in
the character Mittenhofer.

Auden wrote much of *Letters from Iceland* after returning to
England in September 1936. On completing this book with Mac-
Neice, he decided to join the International Brigade then fighting against General Franco in Spain, and he went there in January 1937 intending to drive an ambulance, but when he got to
Valencia "the government refused him permission and put him
to work broadcasting propaganda." (EA, xviii) He did this only
briefly, and there is no record of what else he may have done
during his seven weeks in Spain besides visiting Barcelona. But
he did compose a substantial work in verse: the poem *Spain,*
which he later repudiated.

Auden's *Spain* is a solemn Pindaric ode in which allegorical
voices speak on behalf of History (understood in the Marxist
sense of a dialectical process moving inevitably toward a Communist society) or on behalf of Spain (representing a crucial
stage in that process). The scheme turns on a central stanza:

What's your proposal? To build the just city? I will.
I agree. Or is it the suicide pact, the romantic
    Death? Very well, I accept, for
I am your choice, your decision. Yes, I am Spain.   (S, 9)

Stephen Spender has described *Spain,* with its Yesterdays, To-days, and To-morrows, as built on a framework suggested by the Marxist dialectic of history. There are certainly overtones of the Marxist dialectic in it; but the poem departs from conventional expressions of that dialectic in at least one respect: it seems less certain—less assertive—about the future than the Marxist rubric ordinarily demands.

The poem *Spain* has some fine lines and stanzas, particularly in the second half where it describes the response of those who have flocked to the aid of Republican Spain migrating "like gulls or the seeds of a flower":

They clung like birds [*sic*] to the long expresses that lurch
Through the unjust lands, through the night, through the
          alpine tunnel;
     They floated over the oceans;
They walked the passes. All presented their lives.   (S, 10)

Behind the choral cadences of the Yesterdays, To-days, and To-morrows, and the voices of History and of Spain, one senses the voice of the public Bard proclaiming what is expected of him—like Tennyson in his "Ode on the Death of the Duke of Wellington"; and the poem is what many, schooled on Tennyson or Yeats, or other "foudroyant masters," might expect poetry to be—eloquent, Delphic, prophetic. But the obligatory rhetoric had its dangers, and it tripped Auden up in such lines as:

To-day the deliberate increase in the chances of death,
The conscious acceptance of guilt in the necessary murder;
     To-day the expending of powers
On the flat ephemeral pamphlet and the boring meeting.
                                                  (S, 11)

George Orwell balked at the phrase "necessary murder" in an article in the December 1938 issue of *The Adelphi* where he attacked "this utterly irresponsible intelligentsia" and the alliance of "the gangster and the pansy": "Mr. Auden can write about 'the acceptance of guilt for the necessary murder' because he has never committed a murder . . . possibly never even seen a murdered man's corpse."[5] When Auden revised the poem late in 1939 for publication in *Another Time* (1940) he omitted three stanzas and altered some words and phrases. The line with the phrase "necessary murder" became "The conscious acceptance of guilt in the fact of murder," not so much, in Edward Mendelson's view, because of Orwell's criticism, but because Auden "could no longer see the movement of History as a simple struggle between rising and dying forces"; and Mendelson interprets the line about "the conscious acceptance of guilt" as a reference to Auden's involvement in broadcasting propaganda: "By speaking for the Republic, he accepted a degree of complicity for the actions done in its name, actions that included political and judicial murders."[6]

Apart from the publication of *Spain*, 1937—Auden's thirtieth year—was a year that brought him a great deal of public adulation beginning with the publicity attendant on his visit to Spain. In February, during his absence, the Group Theatre produced *The Ascent of F6* at the Mercury Theatre; and the spotlight continued on him with the summer publication of *Spain* and *Letters from Iceland*. He also completed *The Oxford Book of Light Verse* during 1937. *New Verse* paid him the extraordinary honor that same year, of a special issue, the *Auden Double Number,* 26-27 (November 1937) devoted to his work; and he was awarded, and—to the surprise of some—accepted, the King's Gold Medal for Poetry, conferred on him by King George VI. By year's end also, he and Isherwood had accepted a commission from the publishers of their plays to write a travel book on Asia, and toward the end of the year the Group Theatre was advertising *On the Frontier* among its plays for 1937-38, with "special terms for trade union members and students."

IX

China and America: Journey to a War and Another Time

1

Auden and Isherwood were both newsworthy in England by the end of 1937; and newspapers carried photographs of their departure when they set out for China on January 19, 1938, via Suez, the Red Sea, and Hong Kong to report on the Sino-Japanese war. (In China, the combination of civil war and foreign intervention that characterized the struggle in Spain was magnified. While Mao Tse-tung's communists and Chiang Kai-shek's nationalists struggled internally, the Japanese who already occupied Manchuria in 1931 used a minor confrontation at the Marco Polo Bridge on July 7, 1937, as a pretext for launching a full-scale invasion.) This new war came before the advent of television when war correspondents often gained quick fame. Writing of his Spanish Civil War experience in "Impressions of Valencia," Auden said: "The foreign correspondents come in for dinner conspicuous as actresses." (EA, 361) Isherwood certainly implied that such reputations were enviable when he described how he and Auden were in awe of an American war correspondent they met, by chance, on the Pearl River ferry from Hong Kong to Canton: "Thrilled and goggling, we were prepared to hang upon his words; but he was bored and tired. . . . We retired, not wishing to bother him further, and viewed him from a respectful distance, with awe. A disillusioned journalist is the

Byron, the romantic Hamlet, of our modern world." (JW, 30) Their own setting out to report on a war had a touch of the Byronic.

That both were then figures in the public eye—celebrities in the American sense—was evident alike from their send-off in London and their reception on arrival in Asia. Before leaving London they were given an elaborate party, stage-managed by their Group Theatre associate, Rupert Doone. Auden and Benjamin Britten prepared songs for the occasion that were performed by cabaret singer Hedli Anderson. (These appeared in Auden's first American collection, *Another Time,* as "Four Cabaret Songs for Miss Hedli Anderson"; but Britten's music was not published.) Most of the guests at this send-off were writers, artists, or theater people—among them, E. M. Forster, to whom Auden and Isherwood eventually dedicated their book on China: *Journey to a War.*

Their arrival in the Far East was also marked by publicity attendant on social occasions and receptions—so much so that Isherwood recalled their stay in Hong Kong as a kind of dream: "all about dinner-parties at very long tables, and meetings with grotesquely famous newspaper-characters—the British Ambassador, the Governor, Sir Victor Sassoon." (JW, 28) On their arrival in mainland China on February 27, 1938, they were driven to interview the mayor of Canton in the British consul's beflagged and chauffeured limousine; in Hankow—then the Chinese capital, containing both the headquarters of Chiang Kai-shek and of the Communist Eighth Route Army—they had similar consular support; and in Shanghai, the last city they visited, and from which they sailed for America on June 12, 1938, they were guests of the British Ambassador, Sir Archibald Clark-Kerr. Such connections facilitated entry to high levels of Chinese officialdom. They were even entertained at tea—as her sole guests—by Madame Chiang Kai-shek, and joined later by the Generalissimo, whose official chop on their travel documents helped to smooth the way. Their left-wing reputations and contacts were helpful also, particularly their friendship with Agnes Smedley, who had the goodwill of the leaders of the Communist Eighth Route Army, and at whose house Auden had met and photographed Chou En-lai.

In their well-publicized journeys to the battlefronts—reported, for example, in the *New York Times* as well as in British papers—they went north from Hankow to combat areas in the Yellow River zone near Soochow, and south over difficult terrain to the shifting Japanese front that fanned out from Shanghai past the beautiful city of Hangchow. They traveled mostly by train, but sometimes on foot or on horseback; and they did see something of war at first hand: the railroads they traveled were bombed; and they experienced, or observed, air raids on cities like Canton, Hankow, and Shanghai. Background information of this kind is conveyed not so much in Auden's verse in *Journey to a War* as in Isherwood's prose narrative compiled from his and Auden's diaries, which also reveals that they did not suffer discomfort all the time. Besides enjoying formal diplomatic occasions, they indulged themselves in the fleshpots of Shanghai, where they found homosexual bath-houses, or massage-parlors, to their liking.

On one occasion they escaped the war for a few days of relaxation at Journey's End, a resort hotel in the Kuling Hills—a nostalgically British and colonialist retreat as inauthentic as a dude ranch, but with idyllic charm that reminded them of the Demon's temptation of Michael Ransom in *The Ascent of F6*: to abandon the climb and remain forever in the quiet of the monastery. A section of the diary gives an amusing account of this episode which nevertheless carries an undertone of Auden's concern for the temptation to escape from the quest into a Nirvana or false Eden—an almost obsessive theme in his poetry early and late.

Their sensitivity to this particular manifestation of the Demon—the forbidden garden, or false Eden that tempts the voyager to rest—may point to a profound sensing of the need for change in their own lives; for between their setting out for China on January 19, 1938, and their emigration to America exactly one year later, January 19, 1939, they made decisions that altered the courses of their lives, and, in Auden's case, changed his view of the poet's role in society. His earlier travel-book, *Letters from Iceland*, had directly invoked the spirit of Byron in the cantos of *Letter to Lord Byron*. But however Byronic their setting out from London as war correspondents, their book on China is remarkably un-Byronic; and in the course of Auden's verse contribution, the sonnet sequence "In Time of War," there emerges the new notion of a hero with everyday virtues, like the characters in E. M. Forster's novels—or as Auden's "Verse Commentary" puts it: "the Invisible College of the Humble, / Who through the ages have accomplished everything essential." (JW, 298) The artists whose spirit the sonnet sequence invokes are the quiet-voiced Forster and Rilke, not the posturing Byron.

2

Journey to a War has four parts. The first, "London to Hong-Kong," is a series of poems by Auden on the outward journey via the Mediterranean, Suez, and the Red Sea. (It includes "The Voyage," "The Sphinx," and "The Ship," written on the journey, and "Macao" and "Hong-Kong" added later.) The second part, "Travel-Diary," is Isherwood's prose account of their experiences in China—derived from their separate diaries—which comprises most of the book. The third part, "Picture Commentary" has forty-five photographs, mostly by Auden, and two stills from the Chinese film *Fight to the Last*. The fourth part is Auden's main verse contribution: "In Time of War: A Sonnet Sequence with a Verse Commentary." Of the twenty-seven sonnets in this sequence, twenty are retained, slightly revised and rearranged, as "Sonnets from China" in *Collected Poems*.

Both in form and theme the sonnets in this sequence signal a change in Auden's outlook. Technically they follow Rilke, a poet who endured war but had no wish to glorify it, and who greatly respected individual human worth and creativity. Many of these sonnets are not directly about the war in China. They are wartime reflections on the human condition and on the role of the artist in time of war. In the revised and rearranged form "Sonnets from China," the first three sonnets constitute a prologue on the evolution of human consciousness. They imply, as much of Auden's later poetry frequently does, that only plants and animals are innocent or good by nature, and that man may use his freedom for either good or evil as he chooses. The next seven, a retrospect of human history markedly anti-Romantic and far from Marxist in outlook, combine the evocation of a series of historical epochs with portraits of personified types who supplied successive ages with models of heroic personality: the Agriculturalist, the Soldier, the Prophet, the Poet, and so on. The Poet depicted in Sonnet VII, for example, is the Rousseauean Romantic, god-like in his self-esteem:

> And honoured him, a person set apart,
> Till he grew vain, mistook for personal song
> The petty tremors of his mind or heart
> At each domestic wrong.

He is also the self-righteous satirist:

> He stalked like an assassin through the town,
> And glared at men because he did not like them,
> And trembled if one passed him with a frown. (CP, 152)

The tenth sonnet, closing the first half of the sequence, is an interesting sonnet on the Enlightenment (for which Auden sometimes uses the German *Aufklärung*). Its theme is that the Enlightenment, by banishing the mythical, the mysterious, and the illogical, prepared the way for their reappearance in the unconcious:

> . . . The vanquished powers were glad
> To be invisible and free; without remorse
> Struck down the silly sons who strayed into their course,
> And ravished the daughters, and drove the fathers mad.
>
> (CP, 153)

Auden made Sonnet X the culmination of the retrospective survey of his own Western intellectual heritage—a placement that gives weight to its questioning of wholly rational values (expressed elsewhere in his view that Hitler's rise in a center of humane learning cast doubt on the proposition that liberalism was self-supporting). Since this sonnet was composed in 1936, prior to his visits to Spain and China, it confirms that the stages of his return to Anglicanism enumerated in *Modern Canterbury Pilgrims* are stated in exact sequence: first the puzzle of the election of Hitler in an advanced liberal society; second Auden's recognition of religious persecution in Barcelona; third, his meetings with Charles Williams and his reading of Kierkegaard.

The second half of the sequence "Sonnets from China" moves on to the immediate situation in China by way of a transitional sonnet affirming the value of song: "Certainly praise: let the song mount again and again"; but insisting that even song must take account of human doubleness—of the capacity for evil as well as good:

> The quick new West is false, and prodigious but wrong
> The flower-like Hundred Families who for so long
> In the Eighteen Provinces have modified the earth. (CP, 153)

There follows a group of sonnets dealing directly with scenes from the war, with individual sonnets devoted to the dead, the wounded, air-raids, diplomats exchanging views, and so on. There are fewer of these vignettes in the revised sequence than in the original, but all share the detached viewpoint of an observer from outside the struggle. They are, in a sense, photographic, and a number are directly related to photographs in Auden's "Picture Commentary." One of them in particular, a Petrarchan sonnet on a dead soldier, has an interesting history. Auden had finished writing it on April 20, 1938, the day he and Isherwood returned to Hankow after a visit to the front near Soochow during March, and a subsequent visit to the ancient capital, Sian. On the following day they attended a party with a number of Hankow intellectuals including the poet Mou Mou-tien who presented them with some verses written in their honor. Not to be outdone Auden replied with the sonnet he had written the day before. There was also a journalist present, Ma Tong-na (anglicized to Macdonald), who interviewed them for the newspaper *Ta Kung Pao*. His interview, printed on April 22, included a Chinese rendering of Auden's sonnet together with a manuscript facsimile. The second line, "Abandoned by his general and his lice," was too brutal for the Chinese translators; or, as Isherwood puts it, "maybe, even, a dangerous thought (for generals never abandon their troops under any circumstances)." The Chinese translators emended the line to read: "The rich and poor are combining to fight." (JW, 161) This modification marks, perhaps, the first of many expressions of embarrassment at Auden's new determination to view events not with the single-mindedness of a propagandist but in the double focus of the struggle between good and evil.

The revised arrangement of "Sonnets from China" gives the sequence a tighter structure and a much more pointed conclusion. The anti-Romantic theme, for example, becomes more pronounced. The three final sonnets, which now include the sonnet to E. M. Forster used as a dedication to *Journey to a War,* justify the work of artists and also of ordinary people who live simple, creative lives even in the face of apparent defeat by an all-powerful tyranny:

> When all our apparatus of report
> Confirms the triumph of our enemies.   (CP, 156)

As a representative of artists who cultivated the inner life rather than public attitudes, Sonnet XIX calls on Rilke, "Who for ten years of drought and silence waited, / Until in Muzot all his being spoke." Sonnet XX develops this theme of voluntary personal commitment to justify the sacrifice of the nameless soldiers killed in China, and to set them above narcissistic tyrants "Who want to persist in stone forever." Sonnet XXI moves to the particular case of E. M. Forster, an artist who, in contrast to the god-like poet of Sonnet VII, neither domineers nor lectures us on what to do, but quietly sets before us parables in which we may see ourselves:

> As we dash down the slope of hate with gladness,
> You trip us up like an unnoticed stone,
> And, just when we are closeted with madness,
> You interrupt us like the telephone.   (CP, 157)

This sonnet on E. M. Forster not only justifies the artist as observer, but insists that art and the inner-life have a place in our affairs. It is the first of an extraordinary series of poems, mostly

elegaic, on art and artists that Auden wrote within a year of his journey to China.

The sequence "Sonnets from China" shows that Auden had reached a critical point in his intellectual development between early 1937, when he went to Spain, and late 1939, when he assembled the collection *Another Time*. Several of the poems in *Another Time* are on existentialist themes and show that within a year after his arrival in America his beliefs had unquestionably changed. By the end of the thirties he had become, philosophically, not a Communist, but a would-be Christian—at first existentialist, or Kierkegaardian, in outlook. "Sonnets from China" and its successor, "The Quest: A Sonnet Sequence," show that at the time of their writing Auden had adopted an anti-Utopian vision that accepts doubt and ambiguities in place of doctrinaire certainties.

In essays and reviews of the same period Auden frequently returns to the themes that the Renaissance is at an end and that the liberalism it nurtured is not self-supporting. Reviewing Reinhold Niebuhr's *The Nature and Destiny of Man* in June 1941, he said: "For the past hundred years Occidental liberalism has lain snug in the belief that the relation of its arts and sciences, its ethical and political values, to the Christian faith was simply historical. It has taken Hitler to show us that liberalism is not self-supporting."[1] And some ten years later while discussing Romanticism in *The Enchafèd Flood* he said: "We live in a new age in which the artist neither can have a unique heroic importance nor believes in the Art-God enough to desire it, an age, for instance, when the necessity of dogma is once more recognized, not as the contradiction of reason and feeling but as their ground and foundation." (EF, 153) In retrospect, "Sonnets from China" may be seen as an overture to Auden's major American themes.

3

On leaving China on June 12, 1938, Auden and Isherwood continued eastward round the world—across the Pacific from

Shanghai, via Japan, to Canada and the United States. There they gave a number of reports on their experiences in press interviews and lectures, and in a magazine article that they prepared for *Harper's Bazaar*. It was during this visit, apparently, that Auden decided to leave England and to return to live in New York. Years later, in a BBC interview, he said that he felt his situation in England was becoming impossible for him. He compared himself to a child who needs to break away from family ties in order to mature: "I couldn't grow up. That English life . . . is for me a family life, and I love my family but I don't want to live with them."[2] By *family* he meant the English literary and intellectual establishment. This is clear from his brother John's account of their conversations in Brussels in December 1938. "His reasons for going to America," says John Auden, "were not then so much disgust with Chamberlain as dislike of the narrow intellectualism of the English establishment, and the desire not to become a 'court' poet."[3]

In August 1938, on the final leg of their round the world trip, he and Isherwood sailed from New York to England where they were occupied for a time with preparing *Journey to a War* for publication, and with the opening of their play *On the Frontier* at the Arts Theatre, Cambridge. (During October and November Auden also found time to review nine books for the Birmingham *Town Crier*.) In December they left England for Brussels where Auden not only finished his sonnet sequence for *Journey to a War*, but wrote "Musée des Beaux Arts," "The Novelist," and other poems in the remarkable series on art and the artistic vocation in *Another Time* that occupied him also during 1939, his first year in America. (Brussels itself is commemorated in "Brussels in Winter" and "Gare du Midi"—and besides the Royal Museum with its Breugel collection in "Musée des Beaux Arts," the Bourse visits his elegy on Yeats, and the fountain sculpture, Manneken Pis, was evoked in the first version of "In Praise of Limestone.")

Auden and Isherwood sailed from Southampton to New York on the French liner *Champlain* on January 19, 1939, the anniversary of their setting out for China. The ostensible purpose of their voyage was to gather material for a book on America in the travel-book format of *Letters from Iceland* and *Journey to a*

War on the basis of a commission given them by John Lehmann at the Hogarth Press. But both had reasons to prolong their stay. They arrived in New York harbor on January 26, 1939, delayed by storms in the Atlantic during a week of record low temperatures, snowstorms, and northeast gales. Isherwood recalled that as they sailed past the Statue of Liberty it was blurred by swirling snow—a memory caught in the line, "And snow disfigured the public statues," in Auden's elegy on Yeats, who died January 28, 1939, two days after their arrival in New York.

In the first week of April 1939, Auden, Isherwood, and Louis MacNeice had collaborated in a forum on "Modern Trends in English Poetry and Prose" for the League of American Writers. An eighteen-year-old freshman student of English literature at Brooklyn College named Chester Kallman was in the audience and asked if he might interview Auden for a college literary magazine he edited. Isherwood gave him the address of the Yorkville apartment where the two writers and Isherwood's New York friend were living. When Kallman came there two days later for the interview, their friendship began. Besides approaching Auden's ideal of physical beauty—he had the appearance of youthful innocence, golden-blond hair, and blue eyes—Kallman had a sensitive appreciation of music and literature and a quick wit that rivaled Auden's in intellectual dexterity. Ultimately it was through their shared interest in music and literature that their friendship survived the tribulations of a life-long, unequal association in a shared ménage; for, at least on Kallman's side, the sexual attraction soon palled, and within two years he turned his attention elsewhere.

Auden, who had associated (as in Berlin) with uneducated or delinquent youths, was disposed to romanticize his meeting with Kallman. He wrote shortly afterwards to Mrs. Dodds: "Of course I know that Love as a fever does not last, but for some years now I've known that what I really needed was marriage, and I think I have enough experience and judgment to know that this relationship is going to be a marriage with all its boredoms and rewards."[4] Auden took to wearing a wedding ring, and by July he was writing to John Lehmann: "My heart is so full and I am so mad with happiness that I don't know what to do."[5]

His meeting with Kallman was to have profound influences

on Auden's life and work. From adolescence on, he had always
been, in some sense, "homeless." He had lived in his parents'
home or summer cottage from time to time since leaving school
and university, but he grew increasingly estranged from them; his
teaching posts at schools where he lived-in were mostly short
term; and he traveled abroad alone a great deal. Kallman made
him feel at home in New York in various ways. He had a great
aptitude for mimicry, and for the droll ways of New York Jewish
humor that intrigued Auden. Kallman also gave Auden entrance
to the warmly humane culture of his "extended" family, and beyond it, to a local ethnic atmosphere in New York. Some months
after their first meeting they began to share an apartment. Kallman was a gourmet cook and his influence brought a semblance
of civilization to Auden's always barbaric eating habits. (He
usually "wolfed" his food and once amazed the fastidious Igor
Stravinsky by swilling down a fine vintage Château Margaux the
composer had selected for an occasion.)[6]

Auden's relationship with Kallman had two kinds of immediate influence on his work: Kallman had been from childhood an aficionado of Italian opera, and it was he who introduced Auden to the world of Italian opera in New York with
lasting consequences. (Auden had visited Bayreuth in 1925.) A
more immediate influence was the eliciting of love poems addressed in an indulgent tone of genuine affection and with a
saving touch of humor to a specific person. The tone of these
lyrics offers a contrast to Auden's earlier generalized and guilt-
laden lyrics—even the very successful "Lay your sleeping head
my love"—and also to the skittish and bum-slapping innuendo
that marked passages in *The Orators,* for example. The Kall-
man-inspired love poems in Auden's first American volume, *Another Time,* include "The Prophets," in which Auden implies
that his childhood infatuation with mining machinery was but a
forecast of his mature absorption in a loved person. (The "all
you prefiguring" note may equally well allude to Shakespeare's
Sonnet 106, since one of their shared interests was Shakespeare.)
Other poems in *Another Time* apparently inspired by his relationship with Kallman include "Like a Vocation," "The Riddle," and "Law Like Love," to which may be added the dedica-

tory poem to Kallman, "Every Eye Must Weep Alone," and, in lighter vein, the poem now titled "Heavy Date."

In time, his relationship with Kallman was to bring the experience of tribulation to Auden's life and poetry. About two years after their first meeting, Kallman found another lover and told Auden that although their friendship might continue their relationship could no longer be physical. Thereafter Kallman sometimes behaved like a wayward son rebelling against a parent. He would go off on his own affairs, neglecting to contact Auden or to respond to his letters; meanwhile depending on him for money. Kallman's first infidelity, in July 1941, dismayed Auden. And he refers to his distracted emotional state on that occasion in listing the sequence of experiences that contributed to his return to his Anglican faith. Following his account of religious persecution in Barcelona and the impression made on him by Charles Williams, he speaks of his own irrational response to Kallman's infidelity, when he seriously thought of murdering his rival:

> So, presently, I started to read some theological works, Kierkegaard in particular, and began going, in a tentative and experimental sort of way, to church. And then, providentially—for the occupational disease of poets is frivolity —I was forced to know in person what it is like to feel oneself the prey of demonic powers, in both the Greek and Christian sense, stripped of self-control and self-respect, behaving like a ham actor in a Strindberg play.[7]

Their friendship endured, nevertheless, in its own way, and produced their collaboration on several opera libretti.

4

Auden's first American volume, *Another Time,* containing poems from the three years that had passed since the publication of *Look, Stranger* in 1937, appeared in October 1939. This collection reveals the direction of the shift in poetic sensibility that distinguishes his American work from the politically engaged verse acclaimed in *New Signatures, New Country,* and *New Verse* in England in the 1930s. While it is noticeable that much of the more boisterous lighter verse in *Another Time* dates from 1937—the three psychological ballads, "Miss Gee," "James Honeyman," and "Victor," for example—the volume has a more varied range of tone, mood, and technique than any previous collection of Auden's lyrics. The poems in *Another Time* written after his arrival in America are nevertheless remarkable for two departures. Some are the light-hearted love poems, already noted, expressing a measure of contentment not previously noticeable in Auden. Others wrestle with existentialist themes: anxiety in time, the present moment and its choices, and the journey toward death. These include "Our Bias," one of Auden's most accomplished sonnets on his perennial theme of how the natural world of the creatures is separated from man's time-conscious world, beginning (with an echo of Shakespeare's Sonnet 19):

> The hour-glass whispers to the lion's roar,
> The clock-towers tell the gardens day and night
> How many errors Time has patience for,
> How wrong they are in being always right.
>
> Yet Time, however loud its chimes or deep,
> However fast its falling torrent flows,
> Has never put one lion off his leap
> Nor shaken the assurance of a rose.   (CP, 218)

Other poems on man's anxiety in this 1940 collection include the enigmatic "Hell" and the obviously existentialist poem "Another Time" that supplied the volume's title—a poem that opens by dwelling on consciousness in time and the moment of choice:

> For us like any other fugitive,
> Like the numberless flowers that cannot number
> And all the beasts that need not remember,
> It is to-day in which we live;

and that ends:

Another time has other lives to live.   (CP, 218)

Closely related to these existentialist poems on time and on existence understood as "being-towards-death" (Heidegger) were the several elegies and poems in elegaic mood included in *Another Time*. Part Two, for example, contained seven elegiac poems on artists and thinkers: "A. E. Housman," "Edward Lear," "Rembrandt," "Herman Melville," "Pascal," "Voltaire at Ferney," and "Matthew Arnold." Part Three, "Occasional Poems," had an even more noteworthy concentration of these. Besides "September 1, 1939," the famous poem on the outbreak of war in Europe, Part Three contained the elegies, "In Memory of W. B. Yeats (d. Jan. 1939)," "In Memory of Ernst Toller (d. May 1939)," and "In Memory of Sigmund Freud (d. Sept. 1939)." Part Three also contained a rather abstract "Epithalamion (for Guiseppe Antonio Borgese and Elizabeth Mann, Nov. 23, 1939)," which Humphrey Carpenter identifies as a disguised celebration of Auden's "marriage" to Kallman.[8] Grouped with these as a companion occasional piece—its title made to conform with theirs by including the date—was "Spain, 1937."

The fact that Auden later discarded two of the more celebrated of these poems—"Spain" and "September 1, 1939"—and significantly revised a third, "In Memory of W. B. Yeats," displeased a number of critics who trumpeted their displeasure loudly enough to draw a following suspicious of Auden's motives, with some among them apparently dedicated to the task of preserving the originals from his unwarranted interference. A. Alvarez, reviewing *Collected Shorter Poems* (1957) in *The Observer,* rebuked Auden from an Olympian perspective: "Some of the axed poems have already become part of the language and literature, whether Auden accepts them or not."[9] In the 1967 *Shenandoah* special issue, "A Tribute to Wystan Hugh Auden on His Sixtieth Birthday," his old friend Naomi Mitchison departed from the spirit of the occasion to deprecate his "cutting out the most essential verse" of "September 1, 1939" and to complain: "I can't find myself reading him these days."[10] While Auden did not ordinarily reply to critics, he drafted a reply (which he did not send) to this old friend whose early review had prepared the way for the favorable reception of his *Poems,*

1930: "I expect personal friends like you, my dear, to respect my judgment on poetry, which is a professional judgment, rather than yours. . . . If, by memorability, you mean a poem like 'Sept 1st 1939,' I pray to God I shall never be memorable again."[11] Given the insensitivity, even of friends, to his diagnosis of the dangers of Romanticism in himself, Auden's vehemence was pardonable.

X

Disenchantment with Yeats: From Singing-Master to Ogre

1

Did those of Auden's friends who arranged for his memorial in the Poets' Corner of Westminster Abbey think of him as the poet of only one poem, "In Memory of W. B. Yeats," as one might think, for example, of Henley as the poet of "Invictus," or of Gray as the poet of "Elegy in a Country Churchyard"? At the Abbey ceremony in October 1974, John Gielgud read the third movement of "In Memory of W. B. Yeats" (chosen for the occasion by Chester Kallman), beginning with lines that seemed a little inappropriate for the unveiling of Auden's stone:

> Earth, receive an honoured guest:
> William Yeats is laid to rest;

and ending with the lines permanently inscribed on the memorial:

> In the prison of his days
> Teach the free man how to praise.   (CP, 198)

Set in isolation these lines refer to poets in general, including Auden. But would he want lines that brought Yeats to mind inscribed on his monument? I believe he would not. In fact I feel certain that should his ghost visit the Poets' Corner the inscription would vex it.

Of course Yeats had been one of Auden's first singing-masters (although perhaps not always quite so fervently invoked as Yeats invoked his sages in "Sailing to Byzantium": "O sages standing in God's holy fire / . . . / Come from the holy fire, perne in a gyre, / And be the singing-masters of my soul"). Auden's earlier masters were Thomas Hardy and Robert Frost, for whom he says he developed a passion while still at school. Then T. S. Eliot, particularly as the poet of *The Waste Land,* attracted him during his Oxford years. So did Wilfred Owen, whose technique of slant-rhyme as we have seen helped to shape the best of his undergraduate poems. But W. B. Yeats, once Auden had discovered his later work, exerted a much more powerful fascination than any of these. This fascination grew in time into a kind of obsession. And when Auden's own changed attitudes caused him to turn so strongly against Romanticism, and to deplore the notion of the inspired "national Bard," the Irish singing-master became an Ogre.

Auden had edited *Oxford Poetry* in 1927 with Cecil Day Lewis. Forty years later in a Preface to *C. Day Lewis, the Poet Laureate,* he recalled that it was he who introduced Day Lewis to the poetry of Frost and Hardy, and that Day Lewis had introduced him to the later poems of Yeats. He remarked on Hardy's subsequent good influence on Day Lewis, and added: "I wish I could say the same about Yeats' influence on me. Alas, I think it was a bad influence, for which, most unjustly, I find it difficult to forgive him."[1]

A number of Auden's undergraduate poems are quite evidently influenced by Yeats, in tone, rhythm, or rhetoric; but his early debt to Yeats goes much deeper. It was Yeats who invented a viable modern form for a particular kind of poem—the occasional poem in conversational style—at which Auden was eventually to become a master among poets writing in English. In 1918 Yeats wrote "In Memory of Major Robert Gregory," beginning with the lines:

> Now that we're almost settled in our house
> I'll name the friends that cannot sup with us
> Beside a fire of turf in th' ancient tower,

> And having talked to some late hour
> Climb up the narrow winding stairs to bed.[2]

The opening lines of Poem XIII of the hand-printed volume, *Poems,* 1928 show that Auden as an undergraduate had tried to emulate this elegy:

> Tonight when a full storm surrounds the house
> And the fire creaks, the many come to mind,
> Sent forward in the thaw with anxious marrow;
> For such might now return with a bleak face,
> An image pause, half-lighted at the door . . . ;

> (P 1928, 28)

And when, in "Yeats as an Example," Auden sought to identify Yeats's chief poetic legacy, he credited the Irish poet with transforming the occasional poem in English from an official performance of impersonal virtuosity, like Tennyson's "Ode on the Death of the Duke of Wellington," into a serious reflective poem having at once personal and public interest; and he identified Yeats's elegy for Robert Gregory as the first successful instance of this transformation: "A poem such as 'In Memory of Major Robert Gregory' is something new and important in the history of English poetry. It never loses the personal note of a man speaking about his personal friends in a particular setting—in *Adonais,* for example, both Shelley and Keats disappear as people—and at the same time the occasion and characters acquire a symbolic public significance."[3]

As the thirties wore on, Auden's admiration for Yeats as an occasional poet was tempered by his dislike for Yeats's fondness for the trappings of aristocracy and his flirtation with General O'Duffy's Irish fascist organization, the Blueshirts. But this was mere distaste for Yeats's foibles. In the second half of his life Auden developed an almost obsessive fear of the danger of Yeats's kind of outlook, and much of the story of Auden's development as a poet after 1940 is also the story of his struggle to exorcise the persistent spirit of Yeats. The stages of his growing disenchantment with Yeats mark the hardening of his conviction that the greatest threats to individual freedom in the

modern world—the Utopias of both left and right—were a direct
legacy of the Romantic outlook on which Yeats prided himself.

In a number of works—beginning with "Sonnets from China"
(1938)—Auden distinguishes two effects of Romanticism on the
modern mind. The first is the persistence into the twentieth century of the nineteenth-century notion of a national Bard: a poet
who regarded himself or who was regarded by others as the embodiment of the soul of his nation. Wagner, Whitman, and
Tennyson represent this nineteenth-century notion in varying
degrees. Kipling is an obvious instance of the notion persisting
into the twentieth century. So also, with individual differences,
are D. H. Lawrence, W. B. Yeats, and of course Auden himself
broadcasting on Spanish radio for the Republican government
in February 1937, for in an age of ideologies the notion of the
Bard persists in the official propagandist; and some of those who
welcomed Auden's revolutionary zeal in the thirties (not all of
them lovers of poetry) may have been merely on the lookout for
an effective Bard—a Kipling for the Popular Front. In time he
became acutely conscious of a kinship between the cult of the
poet as national Bard and the cult of the "inspired" national
leader—Hitler, Mussolini, Stalin—that threatened the survival
of European democracy in the thirties. In the fifth volume of
Poets of the English Language (1950) he warned that to the
would-be poet in whom the notion of the Bard persists—since
the Bard must be an apostle of something—"the thought of a
tyrant who will provide him with a myth of terror, of the prospect of total war as a cult, are not unwelcome. . . ." (PEL,
5, xx) It is in the light of this view of the Bard as Bellman or
court poet for the national leader who expects all to follow his
dark intuitions that Auden eventually came to see Yeats as one
of the Ogre's party.

Three things in particular mark the successive stages of Auden's disenchantment with Yeats: first, his revisions of "In
Memory of W. B. Yeats," and second, his discarding of the
highly popular poem, "September 1, 1939." The third and most
direct repudiation of what Yeats stood for is the opera *Elegy for
Young Lovers* (1961) in which the "great poet" Mittenhofer not
only browbeats his devoted admirers but sacrifices the lives of
the young lovers on the twin altars of his ego and his art.

2

Auden arrived in New York harbor in a near-blizzard on Thursday January 26, 1939. Yeats died in the south of France two days later, on Saturday, January 28. Auden, who probably read the obituary notice in New York newspapers on Monday, immediately commemorated Yeats's death in two ways. One, "The Public *vs.* the Late Mr. William Butler Yeats," was a prose exercise in the two voices of rhetorical dialectic in which "The Public Prosecutor" and "The Counsel for the Defence" present cases for denying or according to Yeats the title of "great" poet. The other was one of the most justly famous of his own occasional poems, "In Memory of W. B. Yeats." The law-court antagonists rely on formal argument, civilized and witty in the tradition of London's Old Bailey, to sway the jury, but the elegy emphasizes the healing power of the unconscious and the need for psychic wholeness attendant on the reconciliation of human intellect and feeling in a world on the brink of war:

> Intellectual disgrace
> Stares from every human face,
> And the seas of pity lie
> Locked and frozen in each eye.

Although its opening has the plangent quality of the poetry of Yeats's old age, this memorial to Yeats is not an overflow of powerful feeling. Speaking about his elegies on Freud and Yeats, Auden said: "These elegies of mine are not poems of grief. Freud I never met, and Yeats I only met casually and didn't particularly like him. Sometimes a man stands for certain things, which is quite different from what one feels in personal grief."[4]

The first of the elegy's three movements draws on Auden's first experience of a New York winter to set Yeats's death in an allegorical landscape freezing into inactivity—

> He disappeared in the dead of winter:
> The brooks were frozen, the airports almost deserted,

And snow disfigured the public statues;
The mercury sank in the mouth of the dying day.

(CP, 197)

The word *disappeared* in the opening line is not an evasive substitute for *he died;* it is a measure of Auden's close reading of Yeats who uses this word in *A Vision* as a technical term for death.[5] The initial imagery of airport and public statues—typical products of consciousness which in this winter landscape seem almost returned to natural tracts and shapes—gives way to a scene of natural permanence alien to—and even threatening to—the civility of the urbane "fashionable quays":

Far from his illness
The wolves ran on through the evergreen forests,
The peasant river was untempted by the fashionable quays.

(CP, 197)

The wolves and forests evoke the instinctive natural world, beneath consciousness, of timeless Mother Earth; and the fashionable quays, like the airports and statues that are also man-made, suggest the distinctively human world of consciousness. The initial imagery of natural vitality and conscious fabrication is followed by an image of the city of the mind in dissolution. This image depicts the Irish poet's creative consciousness as ebbing, and its energy transferred to the living who read his poems:

The provinces of his body revolted,
The squares of his mind were empty,
Silence invaded the suburbs,
The current of his feeling failed; he became his admirers.

(CP, 197)

The imagery therefore emphasizes the role of the poet's consciousness rather than his unconscious (as the Bardic notion would have it) in the making of a poem.

The second movement of the elegy (added after first publication) addresses Yeats on shared human frailty:

> You were silly like us; your gift survived it all:
> The parish of rich women, physical decay,
> Yourself. . . .   (CP, 197)

These lines pass over Yeats's personal shortcomings with just a
flicker of recollection. The phrase "physical decay" may possibly
glance at Yeats's decision to undergo the Steinach surgical procedure thought at that period to confer a measure of glandular
rejuvenation and some stay against geriatric ills.[6] More specifically, the phrase "the parish of rich women" casts Yeats in the
role of the pastor of an admiring flock, and therefore in the role
of Bardic apostle or priest of the imagination.

In the prose companion piece the Prosecutor also dwells on
aspects of the parish of rich women. He points, for example, to
the inconsistency of Yeats's extolling the life of the peasantry
while preferring to live in "noble houses, of large drawing rooms
inhabited by the rich and the decorative, most of them of the
female sex." The Prosecutor also chides Yeats for his obsession
with the occult and mocks his failure to outgrow his folly: "In
1900 he believed in fairies; that was bad enough; but in 1930
we are confronted with the pitiful, deplorable spectacle of a
grown man occupied with the mumbo-jumbo of magic and the
nonsense of India."[7] Elsewhere, speaking in his own voice, and
possibly with a malicious eye on Isherwood's Southern California
mysticism, Auden again deplores Yeats's interest in the occult:
"How on earth, we wonder, could a man of Yeats's gifts take
such nonsense seriously? I have a further bewilderment, which
may be due to my English upbringing, one of snobbery. How
could Yeats, with his great aesthetic appreciation of aristocracy,
ancestral houses, ceremonious tradition, take up something so
essentially lower-middle class—or should I say Southern Califor-
nian . . . ?"[8] Yet neither in his own voice nor the voice of the
Prosecutor does Auden name the several women close to Yeats,
all of whom were in some degree devoted to occult practices or
psychic studies. These included, for example, Yeats's wife, from
whose mediumship he profited in *A Vision;* Lady Gregory, who
shared his interest in psychical research; Annie Horniman, who
helped finance the Abbey Theatre when her Tarot cards re-

vealed the time was right;[9] and both Maude Gonne and Florence Farr, who were fellow members of the Order of the Golden Dawn. But Auden was less reticent twenty years later in his comments on the origins of the opera *Elegy for Young Lovers* which satirizes Yeats and his entourage.

The second movement of the elegy also addresses Yeats on the limitations of art which, it implies, can no more moderate the madness of civil or international strife than it can change Irish weather:

> Mad Ireland hurt you into poetry.
> Now Ireland has her madness and her weather still,
> For poetry makes nothing happen: it survives
> In the valley of its making where executives
> Would never want to tamper, flows on south
> From ranches of isolation and the busy griefs, . . .
>
> (CP, 197)

The phrase "poetry makes nothing happen" retains a faint echo of Wilfred Owen's "Preface": "All a poet can do today is warn" —an echo heard more distinctly in Auden's poem on the outbreak of war later that year, "September 1, 1939": "All I have is a voice. . . ." Such disclaiming of poetry's power to influence events may pain those who wish to cling to the notion of the Bard; yet Auden has bluntly said that no poem of his, or of another, saved even one Jewish victim of the death camps. The context invites the understanding that poetry is not a proper medium for Apostles, and is misused by Bards who think themselves called to an apostolate. In his unpublished 1939 Journal Auden said, referring to the Nazi propaganda minister: "If the criterion for art were its power to excite to action, Goebbels would be one of the greatest artists of all time." (EA, 406) Significantly, in his final revision of this poem Auden changed the wording of his statement on poetry from "it survives / In the valley of its saying" to "it survives / In the valley of its making." The substitution of *making* diminishes the expectation of inspired Bardic utterance that *saying* may hint at. (Despite his fussiness on this point, his revision overlooks his unexamined assumptions in the phrases about "mad Ireland" and Ireland's "madness still." Books rather than life often supplied him with his impressions, and he assumes here wide recognition of G. K. Chesterton's rather condescending

> For the great Gaels of Ireland
> Are the men that God made mad,
> For all their wars are merry
> And all their songs are sad.)

To speak of the phrase "For poetry makes nothing happen" in isolation from the highly figurative elaboration that follows it may lead to misinterpretation. The "valleys," "ranches of isolation," and "busy griefs" speak of inner creativity in the language of Auden's allegorical landscapes; and the word "executives" has associations with the movers and shakers who get things done, including the scaling of mountains. (See the sonnets "Who's Who": "though giddy, climbed new mountains"; and "Two Climbs": "Fleeing the short-haired mad executives.") The key symbolic phrase in this elaboration is "flows on south," because in the general tradition of English poetry, and particularly in the Nordic myths that Auden knew from childhood, the north is represented as the abode of evil forces. In Jung's orientation of the psyche of the "thinking type" (personified by Malin in Auden's *The Age of Anxiety*), the north is associated with isolated, even malign, intellect, and the south with feeling submerged in unconsciousness. The achievement of a "whole" or "healed" personality requires that these opposing faculties move toward reconciliation. Therefore to say poetry "flows on south" is to represent it as an agent of emotional healing, capable of restoring harmony between intellect and feeling. This notion—central to theme of the final movement of the poem—is stated explicitly in the final stanza:

> In the deserts of the heart
> Let the healing fountain start, . . .   (CP, 198)

In this final movement the elegy for Yeats contrasts the ideal order the artist has power to command with the disordered

European body politic—a disorder reflecting the dissociation of feeling and intellect in the consciousness of individual citizens. The artist, whose skill is limited to imposing order on his materials, cannot manipulate the political order; neither can he heal the disordered personality. Yet his "farming of a verse" can, by analogy, provide a glimpse of ideal, even paradisal, order; and so "make a vineyard of the curse." Also, his successful creativity within the bounds of formal necessity provides a model for the conscious exercise of human freedom within the constraints of natural necessity: "In the prison of his days / Teach the free man how to praise." Furthermore, although "the farming of a verse" cannot directly produce a wholesome psychic balance between intellect and feeling and thereby bring emotional warmth to thaw "the seas of pity" frozen by national pride, the poetic process, and the constraints of poetic form may bring hidden emotions to consciousness—a process transcending the dialectic which, when re-created in the mind of the reader, can "In the deserts of the heart / Let the healing fountain start." Auden—who admired E. M. Forster's thought—may have in mind in these lines Forster's outlook on the colonial mentality summed up in a remark about Ronnie, the complacent young Anglo-Indian in *A Passage to India:* "One touch of regret—not the canny substitute but true regret from the heart—would have made him a different man, and the British Empire a different institution."

At least one image for poetry's intermediary role in establishing a dialogue between mind and heart—between isolated intellect and unconscious feelings—appropriately brings together William Blake's poem on the creation of opposites, "The Tyger," and the thought of psychologists who explore the "night side" of life. The appeal to poets:

> Follow, poet, follow right
> To the bottom of the night,

adapts a phrase of Blake's—"at the bottom of the graves"—to which Auden draws attention in his "Notes" to *New Year Letter* as "quoted by Yeats in *A Vision*" (NYL, 111); and in the context of similar rhythm and syllable count, the reference to "the bottom of the night" may recall Blake's vision of the tension between good and evil:

> Tyger! Tyger! burning bright
> In the forests of the night,
> What immortal hand or eye
> Could frame thy fearful symmetry?

The third movement of the elegy originally contained three quatrains—with Kipling and Paul Claudel as cautionary instances of Imperialist and Fascist leanings—on how the passage of time erases the memory of an artist's personal shortcomings. Revised versions omit these quatrains on time for good reasons. One reason for the change was his recognition of the injustice done Claudel by equating his Catholicism with Fascism—a facile equation commonly made by English writers like George Orwell, for example, during the Spanish Civil War. Reviewing *Voltaire* by Alfred Noyes in March 1939, Auden accepts and elaborates on this equation in a passage beginning: "For if I know the good, then it is my moral duty to persecute all who disagree with me. That is why the Catholic church can never compromise with liberalism or democracy, and why it must prefer even fascism to socialism."[10] There is a mild modification of this absolute stand in an unpublished passage he wrote three or four months later: "Artists even when they hold religious or political dogmas, do not mean the same things by them as the organizers of their church or party. There is more in common between my view of life and that of Claudel than there is between Claudel's and that of the Bishop of Boston." (EA, 404) Some months later, while reading Charles Williams's *The Descent of the Dove,* he would have encountered a passage on Claudel's regard for Pastor Niemoller—imprisoned by the Nazis for his opposition to their regime—likely to cause him to rethink his superficial judgment on Claudel: "The separations . . . in Christendom remain . . . ," Williams wrote. "But the vocal disputes are a little suspended, and courtesies between the clamant bodies are easier; as when the Roman Catholic Paul Claudel wrote in honour of the Lutheran Niemoller—'*ce courageux confesseur de*

Christ.' It might be possible now to praise the confessors of
other obediences without supposing that we compromised our
own."[11] An even weightier reason for eliminating these stanzas
might be that their theme: "Time . . . / Worships language and
forgives / Everyone by whom it lives," comes too close to echoing Shelley's Romantic claim in his *Defense of Poetry* where, in
a parody of Scripture, he says that the faults of such illustrious
poets of the past as Homer, Virgil, and Spenser "have been
weighed and found to have been dust in the balance; if their
sins were as scarlet they are now white as snow; they have been
washed in the blood of the mediator and redeemer Time."

Finally, in 1967, Auden changed the first of the repeated resonant lines:

> O all the instruments agree
> The day of his death was a dark cold day,   (EA, 242)

to the more matter of fact understatement, "What instruments
we have agree," and it is this change that best indicates the
arena in which Auden wrestled with the spirit of Yeats. The
change may seem slight, but anyone familiar with his poetry will
recognize the voice of Yeats in the line "O all the instruments
agree" (compare the line "O sages standing in God's holy fire"
quoted above), while those familiar with Auden's work will recognize the more matter of fact "What instruments we have
agree" as authentically his own. (There is more to poetry than
."O Altitudo," Nevill Coghill had said in 1927.) The original
line written in the voice of Yeats demands declamation. It gen-
erates an impulse to mount on a stage, or on a box, or on a
boiler—and to intone like Bard or patriotic orator. One can
imagine it spoken by the Delphic oracle, or by the god Apollo
himself. The revised line, by contrast, shorn of its apostrophe
and of its certainty, is spoken by a man banished from Eden:
"What instruments we have agree." Earlier changes in "In
Memory of W. B. Yeats" came from dissatisfaction with the
poem; but this one, by muting the Yeatsian resonance and typical staginess that Auden referred to among friends as "walking
in high heels," indicates disenchantment with the spirit of Yeats.
The main battleground for this struggle was not the elegy for

Yeats, but the even more popular poem of the same period "September 1, 1939."

3

In October 1939 *The New Republic* printed a poem of Auden's that took its title from the date on which Hitler's armies attacked Poland at the start of World War II. This poem, "September 1, 1939," was modeled quite closely on Yeats's "Easter 1916." It soon became a favorite anthology piece, at least in America where it was much in demand at poetry readings during the 1950s. At such times Auden would feel compelled to explain his revisions and deletions.[12] His initial dissatisfaction was with the final line of stanza eight: "We must love one another or die," which accommodates both Christ's injunction and echoes of the love duet in *Tristan and Isolde,* which (taking Isolde's part) he used to sing as a child with his mother. He first altered this line to: "We must love one another and die." Still dissatisfied, he excised the stanza before including the poem in *Collected Poetry,* 1945; but, eventually, he discarded the entire poem. He told the whole story of his revisions and his rejection of the poem in his Foreword to B. C. Bloomfield's bibliography: "Re-reading a poem of mine, '1st September, 1939,' after it had been published, I came to the line 'We must love one another or die,' and said to myself: 'That's a damned lie! We must die anyway.' So, in the next edition, I altered it to, 'We must love one another and die.' This didn't seem to do either, so I cut the stanza. Still no good. The whole poem, I realized, was infected with an incurable dishonesty and must be scrapped."[13] He eventually found an appropriate place for the line "We must love one another and die" in his final work, *An Entertainment of the Senses,* where with the *and* italicized it caps the final chorus of the Senses in the presence of Death:

> When you get a little older
> You'll discover like Isolde:
> "We must love one another *and* die."   (TYF, 58)

The simple explanation for Auden's dissatisfaction with "September 1, 1939" was his conviction that if his poems were to be *authentic,* the tone of voice must be unmistakably his own. He defined an authentic poem as one that convinces the reader that the poet has seen its vision of truth with his own eyes, and not through someone else's spectacles.[14] Expanding on this idea, he said that every poet in reading other poets, "has to distinguish between their merits, which may be very great, and their influence upon himself which may be very pernicious. It was not the fault of Yeats or Rilke that I allowed myself to be seduced by them into writing poems which were false to my personal and poetic nature."[15] Auden also says that he finds in much "serious" poetry an element of theater, "of exaggerated gesture and fuss, of indifference to the naked truth," that revolts him. Yeats was one of those whose too theatrical gestures he found himself imitating in "September 1, 1939."

But Auden's disenchantment with Yeats ultimately went deeper than his dislike for exaggerated fuss and staginess. It went deeper also than the political differences that divided them in the thirties. Auden's distrust of the imaginative Romantic genius who makes an infallible dogma of his own intuitions—a quality akin to the self-deification of intuitive Führers like Hitler—extended to what he called Yeats's "determinist and 'musical' view of history." For some of the same reasons he also came to distrust the theories of D. H. Lawrence who, like Yeats, had influenced his early works, particularly *The Orators.* At least in Auden's view, poets like Yeats and Lawrence, imbued with the notion of the Bard, made infallible dogma of their own intuitions quite as readily as Marx or Hitler. He says, "works like *A Fantasia of the Unconscious* or Yeats's *A Vision* are not humble attempts at private myths, but are designed as the new and only science."[16] And reviewing Yeats's posthumous volume *Last Poems and Plays* in June 1940, he faulted Yeats most of all for "his utter lack of effort to relate his esthetic Weltanschauung with that of science, a hostile neglect which was due, in part at least, to the age in which he was born when science was avidly mechanistic."[17] Both statements confirm that by 1940 Auden found Yeats's Gnostic outlook—his regard for truth self-derived from the God-within—more deplorable than his politics in the 1930s.

4

In his later career Auden's preoccupation with Yeats tended to increase rather than diminish. In *Elegy for Young Lovers* (1961) he created the character Gregor Mittenhofer to embody, in caricature, the nineteenth-century notion of the Bard. It was Yeats who provided the chief model for Mittenhofer, as Lady Gregory provided the model for Mittenhofer's devoted admirer and unpaid secretary, the aristocratic Carolina, Gräfin von Kirchstetten. Other characters in the opera were given qualities in common with Mrs. Yeats and with Yeats's friend and physician, Dr. Oliver Gogarty.

Cyril Connolly reviewing *Dublin Portraits* by W. R. Rogers quotes a remark of Austin Clarke's (which he mistakenly attributes to Frank O'Connor): "As far as the younger generation of poets are concerned here in Ireland, Yeats was rather like an enormous oak-tree which, of course, kept us in the shade. We always hoped we would reach the sun, but the shadow of the great oak-tree is still there." Connolly suggests that this remark of Clarke's gave Auden the idea of creating Mittenhofer: "this, and some anecdotes of Yeats's life at Coole," says Connolly, "formed, I believe, the genesis of Auden's opera *Elegy for Young Lovers*."[18]

Auden himself gives two accounts of the genesis of *Elegy for Young Lovers*. The first, "Genesis of a Libretto," which is signed by both Auden and his collaborator Kallman, tells us that the composer Henze wanted a chamber opera for a small cast and no chorus. To the librettists this seemed to call for "five or six persons, each of whom suffered from a different obsession." They first thought of a character obsessed with the past like Miss Havisham in Dickens's *Great Expectations*—an idea which survived in Hilda Mack, the old lady whose visions supply Mittenhofer with matter for his poems, as Mrs. Yeats's automatic writing supposedly supplied Yeats with matter for *A Vision*. For a variety of attitudes and operatic voices, they decided also on a boy, a girl, and a doctor. Their first idea for a central character with a suitably Romantic obsession was an actor whose supreme ambition was to play the lead in Byron's *Manfred*. But on asking themselves "What kind of person can dominate an opera both dramatically and vocally?" and "What kind of mature man can be intimately and simultaneously involved with a young girl and a mad old lady?" they decided the answer was "the artist-genius of the nineteenth and early twentieth century"—which is to say the poet as Bard. They go on to claim that this idea of the artist-genius is a genuine myth "because the lack of identity between Goodness and Beauty, between the character of a man and the character of his creations, is a permanent aspect of the human condition." And they add:

> The theme of *Elegy for Young Lovers* is summed up in two lines by Yeats:
>
> > The intellect of man is forced to choose
> > Perfection of the life or of the work.
>
> Aesthetically speaking, the personal existence of the artist is accidental; the essential thing is his production. The artist-genius as the nineteenth century conceived him, made this aesthetic presupposition an ethical absolute, that is to say he claimed to represent the highest, most authentic mode of existence. (EYL, 64)

The librettists say they chose Vienna as the setting because the myth of the artist-genius was a European myth at the time when Paris and Vienna were the centers of European culture; and having coyly warned us not to think of Mittenhofer's outrageous behavior an Austrian characteristic, they say "As a matter of fact, the only things about him which were suggested by historical incidents were drawn from the life of a poet—no matter whom—who wrote in English." (EYL, 63)

Yeats's life supplied most of this, but some identifiable material from Auden's own experience as a poet is also used to flesh out Mittenhofer. For example, Mittenhofer berates his aristocratic patron and devoted secretary, Carolina, Gräfin von Kirchstetten, for mistyping the word *poets* in his draft of verses as *ports*. Such a transposition had actually occurred in the case of Auden's "Journey to Iceland," and Auden, unlike Mittenhofer, accepted the change as unconscious wisdom. To some extent, at least, Auden in his earlier Byronic phase is the butt of his own satire in *Elegy for Young Lovers,* as to some degree Wagner and Ibsen are also; but Yeats seems to be the primary target.

"Genesis of a Libretto" does not directly name Yeats as the model of Mittenhofer, but Auden's T. S. Eliot Memorial Lecture, "The World of Opera," in *Secondary Worlds,* comes very close to doing so. Speaking of the Miss Havisham character, Frau Hilda Mack, Auden says: "Remembering that Yeats had a wife from whose mediumistic gifts he profited, it seemed plausible that Mittenhofer should have discovered Frau Mack and made it his habit to visit her from time to time, bringing his entourage with him." (SW, 104)

From so direct a revelation of "historical incidents drawn from the life of a poet—no matter whom," it seems safe to conclude with Cyril Connolly that anecdotes about Yeats's life at Coole Park supplied the character Carolina, Gräfin von Kirchstetten, who corresponds to Lady Gregory (and in Auden's own life to his American patroness, Carolyn Newton); and also to conclude that a second character, Mittenhofer's personal physician, Dr. Wilhelm Reischmann, who keeps Mittenhofer "in good health and youthful vigour with medicines and hormone injections," corresponds to Dr. Oliver Gogarty, Yeats's physician, who first suggested to him the Steinach procedure for rejuvenation.

To return briefly to the claim made by Auden in the quotation above, that *Elegy for Young Lovers* embodies a universal myth of the artist-genius, it is evident that the language in the quotation assumes wide acceptance of Kierkegaard's categories, the Aesthetic, Ethical, and Religious, as themselves universal. (This claim, fundamental to Auden's outlook, marks him as author-in-chief of "Genesis of a Libretto" and not Kallman, who found Kierkegaard's ideas uncongenial.) The immediate points

made in the quotation are two. The first is that there is a dialectical tension between the Aesthetic and the Ethical modes as
Yeats had recognized in his lines:

> The intellect of man is forced to choose
> Perfection of the life or of the work.

The second point—aptly illustrated above by the quotation on
"the blood of the . . . redeemer" from Shelley's *Defence*—is
that when the Aesthetic mode takes itself too seriously and refuses to be content to play, it mistakenly presumes not that its
sphere is the Ethical, but that it is, in fact, the Religious in Kierkegaard's scheme; which is to say that where the notion of the
Bard persists, the public, like the "list'ning crowd" in Dryden's
"Alexander's Feast," shout "A present deity," and the artist
preening himself like a deified Alexander, or Mussolini, as Dryden puts it:

> Assumes the god,
> Affects to nod,
> And seems to shake the spheres.

The relative proneness of Auden and Yeats to this temptation may possibly be gauged by their attitudes toward biogra-
phies of poets. Auden felt that, ideally, poets should be as
anonymous as the builders of the pyramids. Yeats, on the other
hand, declared: "A poet is by the very nature of things a man
who lives with entire sincerity . . . his life is an experiment in
living and those who come after him have the right to know it."[19]
    To Auden, the most dangerous legacy of Romanticism was
the tendency to confuse the artist, the custodian of beauty, with
the Apostle, the witness to truth. And it is no doubt his anxiety
to proclaim this danger, not personal animosity toward Yeats,
that led to the invention of Mittenhofer who so confuses the
Aesthetic and Ethical—the spheres of beauty and truth—that he
contrives the actual death of two young lovers to provide matter
for his elegy.
    Auden's quarrel with Yeats's aestheticism reflects his more

fundamental quarrel with the Platonism that lay at the heart of the Romantic sensibility. One of his more ambitious undertakings—that has perhaps gone unrecognized among those he had hoped would find his views congenial—was an effort to formulate a Christian theory of art that would replace Greek aesthetics. His first podium for this was the weekly column he wrote for *Commonweal* during November and December of 1942. He called this column "Lecture Notes"—an allusion, no doubt, to that other famous reply to Plato: Aristotle's *Poetics*— and he signed it "Didymus," possibly to represent the tension between faith and reason in the Apostle Thomas who was called Didymus; and also to represent a Kierkegaardian double focus, or dialectic, running counter to the single-minded Romantics whom he had dubbed "the either-ors, the mongrel halves / Who find truth in a mirror" in "New Year Letter" the year before. (The first title of that work, *The Double Man,* was intended to convey some of the same significance as "Didymus.")

Auden began his second column in *Commonweal* (November 13, 1942): "As a writer, who is also a would-be Christian, I cannot help feeling that a satisfactory theory of Art from the standpoint of the Christian faith has yet to be worked out. With the exception of Kierkegaard, most theologians . . . have accepted Greek aesthetics too uncritically." Then, having distinguished three religious standpoints, "Natural, Revealed, and Christian," he sought to color the second of these Gnostic: "The second believes that the Unconditional is, objectively, perpetually *absconditus,* but occasionally subjectively manifest to exceptional groups or individuals. . . ." By contrast, the third "believes that the Unconditional was objectively manifested upon one unique occasion (The Word was made Flesh and dwelt among us). . . ." Auden first developed these ideas in *New Year Letter* (1940) and later in the long dramatic works, *The Sea and the Mirror* and *For the Time Being: A Christmas Oratorio.* Simeon, in the latter, puts the case for a Christian aesthetic: "Because in Him the Flesh is united to the Word without magical transformation, Imagination is redeemed from promiscuous fornication with her own images." In so refuting the Gnostic way of the *illuminati* in all ages, Auden may have had in mind the

imaginary world of Yeats's *A Vision*—privately revealed through
the instrumentality of his wife's mediumship and his own fictional creations, Aherne and Robartes.

One of the last poems Auden composed before he died, "No,
Plato, No," shows him still, in some degree, preoccupied with
Yeats; for this poem is not merely a general rejection of Plato
as is "On Installing an American Kitchen in Lower Austria,"
later retitled, "Grub First, Then Ethics." "No, Plato, No," is
also a satirical response to "Sailing to Byzantium," in which
Yeats, philosophically following Plato and Plotinus, longs for
his soul to be free from the prison of the flesh:

> Once out of nature I shall never take
> My bodily form from any natural thing,
> But such a form as Grecian goldsmiths make . . .

Auden's "No, Plato, No" rejects such Platonic yearning to be
"out of nature." It offers instead a novel personification of
bodily organs yearning to be free from servitude to consciousness, to return to a quiescent mineral state, and to become, once
more, irresponsible matter. (This is the "desire to be at peace"—
the death-instinct of the early poems.) Ironically, because of the
lines inscribed on his memorial in the Poets' Corner of Westminister Abbey—that national mausoleum for English Bards—
Auden does not escape the shadow of the great Celtic oak-tree
even in death. Furthermore, English reviewers of Auden's *Collected Poems* (1976) continued to deplore his revision of the line
"O all the instruments agree." David Bromwich, in the *Times
Literary Supplement,* found the change "painful" and wrote:
"the poem has stopped singing."

Auden may have succeeded in exorcising the Bardic spirit—
including the spirit of Yeats—in himself; but that spirit was still
to bedevil him, unexorcised, in sundry friends and admirers—
nostalgic for the thirties—who were reluctant to accept his revisions of his own poems. Among those contemporaries who survived him, few shared, or even approved of, his anti-Romanticism.
One negative consequence has been the comparative neglect of
his American achievement, particularly in the longer philosophical works, *The Sea and the Mirror, For the Time Being,* and
The Age of Anxiety.

XI

America 1939-41:
The Gift of Double Focus

1

In November 1939 Auden attended a cinema in Yorkville (then a German-American district of New York where the Nazi Bund was active) to see the wartime Nazi propaganda film *Sieg in Polen* (Victory in Poland). He was horrified to hear some members of the audience scream, "Kill them!" when Poles appeared on the screen. This experience reawakened his interest in the light theology might shed on the human capacity for evil as well as good. More than thirty years later he told Alan Levy in an interview at Kirchstetten: "There was no hypocrisy [in the audience]. I wondered why I reacted against this denial of every humanistic value. The answer brought me back to the church."[1] His experience in the Yorkville cinema was not so immediate a cause of his conversion as this statement may imply; but it was a stage on the way, for he felt that it called into question some assumptions of the scientific-humanist perspective of his own intellectual *apologia,* "The Prolific and the Devourer," written just four months previously. The experience in the Yorkville cinema strengthened his growing conviction that the world crisis of the times was a consequence of the exhaustion of Europe's intellectual reservoirs; that the humanist hopes of the Enlightenment for the advent of the Rational City had foundered on its unconcern for the irrational; and that the Romantic political doctrines nourished by belief in man's natural innocence overlooked the human capacity for evil.

A concern for these aspects of the West's intellectual inheritance from the Renaissance informs the first of his longer philosophical works in America, "New Year Letter (1940)"—a work that may owe some of the fervor of its anti-Romantic polemic to his experience at *Sieg in Polen,* but which may also owe much of its wide-ranging philosophical concern to the intellectual ferment in New York (and in America at large) during the period of its composition in 1940 before the United States, too, was involved in the war. At that time, with its established research institutes, art galleries, universities, theological centers, and publishing houses offering a form of sanctuary to exiles from European terror, New York was the intellectual capital of the West. There were artists, philosophers, and theologians among the European immigrants as well as leading scientists like Einstein. Among artists, Bertolt Brecht and Kurt Weill were there from Germany, as was the architect Mies van der Rohe. Igor Stravinsky, with whom Auden was later to collaborate, had already come from Paris to settle in America; and at the fall of France in June 1940, all the leading Surrealists, led by André Breton, left Paris for New York. Among these were Salvador Dali, André Masson, and Max Ernst, whose wife Peggy Guggenheim founded the Art of This Century Gallery. Klaus and Erika Mann (and their father Thomas Mann) were among the German exiles closest to Auden.

When Auden began to teach at the New School for Social Research, he met Wolfgang Köhler, the German pioneer of *Gestalt* psychology, who was a member of the faculty there, as was Eduard Heimann, a German-Jewish philosopher who had been associated with Paul Tillich in the "Kairos Group" in Berlin in the 1920s; and Tillich himself, who had come to the United States after Hitler's advent to power in 1933, was a professor at the Union Theological Seminary. Some of these, and Tillich in particular as well as Reinhold and Richard Niebuhr who had invited Tillich to the United States, were to influence Auden's thought within a year or two; but he appears, first, to have endeavored to familiarize himself with the American background.

In the summer of 1939, accompanied by Chester Kallman, he had traveled south by bus to Washington, D.C.; on through

Georgia to New Orleans; and west to Taos in New Mexico where D. H. Lawrence had died. Auden rented a house from Lawrence's widow Frieda who lived nearby, and there he wrote portions of a book, "The Prolific and the Devourer"—a title drawn from Blake to signify the tension between the creative artist (the prolific) and the politician (the devourer). This work was an ambitious and intellectually self-assertive *apologia pro vita sua* modeled both in its aphoristic style and philosophical aspiration on Pascal's *Pensées*. It criticized those poets of "the last eight years" who, like himself, sought a political role; and it expanded on the general theme already evident in "In Memory of W. B. Yeats": that poetry was helpless to intervene directly in the political realm. In its three parts "The Prolific and the Devourer" (which was not published in Auden's lifetime) examined three topics from a humanist standpoint: Art and Politics, Religion, and the Christian Church.[2]

The altitude at Taos had an adverse affect on Chester Kallman, who had had rheumatic fever as a child. They moved on to California for a time, and returned to New York during the last week in August 1939, arriving there on the eve of the outbreak of war in Europe. Auden wept at the news, but his writing at that period shows no nostalgia for England. He reviewed books by British authors which came to him routinely, but there is hardly ever a backward glance; and the topics he chose to write on reveal his eagerness to acclimatize to things American. There are sustained passages in the third part of "New Year Letter (1940)," for example, particularly the section of about 130 lines on America past and present, that provide evidence of this and of Auden's new conviction that

> More even than in Europe, here
> The choice of patterns is made clear
> Which the machine imposes, what
> Is possible and what is not,
> To what conditions we must bow
> In building the Just City now. (CP, 190)

His interest in acquiring an American background may also account for his frequent reviews of books by American authors: James Thurber, Edmund Wilson, Jacques Barzun, and Reinhold Niebuhr, for example; and, in particular, for his review of Carl Sandburg's *Lincoln: The War Years;* and it finds expression in his verse in such poems as "At the Grave of Henry James."

He also plunged—some thought brazenly—into American folk-myth when he wrote the libretto for *Paul Bunyan*—a "choral operetta" with music by Benjamin Britten—on the doings of the legendary giant of the lumber camps of the American frontier. *Paul Bunyan,* delayed for a time by Britten's illness, was produced at Brander Matthews Theater, Columbia University, May 4-10, 1941, but not well received. Reviewers faulted Auden's libretto for being tiresomely "literary"; and some apparently thought it impertinent of two Englishmen to annex an American legend. Auden's libretto was not published nor was the opera revived in his lifetime. But it was revived in slightly modified form in 1976 by both the BBC and the English Music Theatre Company, and again the following year in New York by students of the Manhattan School. (It was written to be technically feasible for high school students.) This school production elicited an interesting reappraisal of the opera from Andrew Porter in *The New Yorker.* While admitting the obvious faults in Auden's libretto, from which two of the most "literary" numbers had been removed, Porter found Britten's score, in particular, to be "one of those early works of genius—like Mozart's *Idomeneo,* Verdi's *Nabucco*—whose youthful freshness and abundance of invention set the audience's spirits soaring."[3]

It was through Benjamin Britten that Auden met the woman who was to become a kind of mother-figure for him in America, Elizabeth Mayer, to whom the first of his longer philosophical works, "New Year Letter (1940)," is addressed; with whom he translated Goethe's *Italian Journey* (1962); and who is the subject of his poignant and compassionate 1970 poem, "Old People's Home." Britten and Peter Pears had met Elizabeth Mayer on board ship in 1936 when she was coming from Hitler's Germany with her children to join her husband, William Mayer, a psychiatrist, who had left Munich to escape the Nazi persecution of Jews. Elizabeth Mayer, who had studied to be a concert pianist before her marriage, invited Britten and Pears to stay at her Long Island home when they again came to New York in

1939, and Auden, visiting them there, became friendly with the Mayers. These visits to the Mayer home at Amityville, Long Island, would later provide Auden with symbolic moments of "wholeness" (resembling the "Vision of Agape" in "A Summer Night") that he could transfer to significant historical dates like September 1, 1939—a day on which the sun "whose neutral eye" had watched events in Europe:

> The very morning that the war
> Took action on the Polish floor,
> Lit up America and on
> A cottage in Long Island shone
> Where Buxtehude as we played
> One of his *passacaglias* made
> Our minds a *civitas* of sound
> Where nothing but assent was found,
> For art had set in order sense
> And feeling and intelligence,
> And from its ideal order grew
> Our local understanding too.   (CP, 161-62)

Auden was certainly at the Mayer home for such a musical occasion on November 22, 1939, when he brought Kallman for the first time. This was a day of double significance, since it was both Britten's birthday and St. Cecilia's Day. Auden was apparently at the Mayers' again for Christmas—an occasion recalled in the third part of "New Year Letter." On January 1, 1940, he wrote to Elizabeth Mayer: "1939 was a very decisive year for me and one of its most important events was meeting you." And he concluded: "I want to start my poem to you."[4] The poem was the first of his longer works in America: "New Year Letter (1940): To Elizabeth Mayer." He completed it in April 1940 and published it first in a book called *The Double Man* (1941).

2

Before Auden and Isherwood sailed for America in January 1939 they had accepted a commission from their friend John

Lehmann at the Hogarth Press for a book on America to be
called *Address Unknown,* and probably to be modeled on the
loose travel-book format of *Letters from Iceland* and *Journey to
a War.* Their separation at mid-year ended prospects of collaboration; but Auden, having submitted *The Double Man* to his
New York publisher, submitted it also to Lehmann to repay the
advance. *The Double Man* had some of the bravura of the earlier travel volumes, but was more "bookish" than its predecessors. It reflected Auden's new interest in historians, theologians,
and existentialist philosophers; and as part of its polemic against
the one-sided certainty of the *Aufklärung* it advocated the tension of double focus. It conspicuously employed images of ambiguous reality drawn from contemporary science and, besides
being more cerebral than anything he and Isherwood might
have done together, was probably wittier and possibly more
careless. *The Double Man* reached print without much benefit
of proofreading and had some inexplicable lines like: "Art in
intention is nemesis." (Auden had written: "Art in intention is
mimesis." CP, 162)

Like the earlier travel books, it was a collection of loosely related pieces. It opened with a verse "Prologue" on Auden's now
familiar theme of man's regressive longing for the pre-conscious
innocence of "lives without language"—a state, ironically, all too
easily attained in wartime "on battlefields where the dying /
. . . / Repair the antique silence the insects broke / In an architectural passion." The "Prologue," which Auden did not retain
in *Collected Poems,* was written in the same Alcaic stanza as his
Horatian ode "In Memory of Sigmund Freud." It concluded
with lines on the vital urge toward wholeness or harmony within
the human mind arising from the struggle between creative Eros
and the death-wish:

> Our bones cannot help reassembling themselves
> Into the philosophic city where dwells
>   The knowledge they cannot get out of;
>   And neither a Spring nor a war can ever
>
> So condition his ears as to keep the song
> That is not a sorrow from the Double Man.   (DM, 12)

This "Prologue" was followed by the three-part letter: "New Year Letter (1940): To Elizabeth Mayer," comprising 1707 lines in octosyllabic couplets—a discursive, philosophical, and humorous epistle ranging outwards in space from New York on New Year's Eve ("our parish of immediacy") to "the situation of our time" in war-torn Europe and Asia, and backward in time seeking the etiology of the present world malaise in the history of Western thought—from Plato, the Renaissance, and the Enlightenment to Darwin, Marx, and other "monists" whose rational theories neglect the claims of the irrational:

> Twelve months ago in Brussels, I
> Heard the same wishful-thinking sigh
> As round me, trembling on their beds,
> Or taut with apprehensive dreads,
> The sleepless guests of Europe lay
> Wishing the centuries away,
> And the low mutter of their vows
> Went echoing through her haunted house,
> As on the verge of happening
> There crouched the presence of The Thing.
>
> (DM, 15; CP, 161)

The poem touched on topics as various as the uses of poetry, disillusionment with Marxism at the end of the thirties, and the American Dust-Bowl *Völkerwanderung* of that decade; and the whole was set against an American background shadowed by the war in Europe.

The verse letter was followed by some eighty pages of "Notes to Letter" comprising the bulk of the book. These "Notes," which resemble a shorter version of Auden's commonplace book *A Certain World* (1970), consisted of commentaries or quotations in prose and verse offering amplification or explanation of the lines they were appended to. The "Notes" concluded with a list of twenty-eight books headed "Modern Sources" containing some hints of Auden's background reading on America. It named works by Henry James, Henry Adams, and Vachel Lindsey as well as *Middletown in Transition* by the Lynds. Among more general works it listed Jung, *The Integration of Personality;*

Groddeck, *The Book of the It;* Whitehead, *Appearance and Reality;* Hyman Levy, *Modern Science;* Kierkegaard's *Journals* translated by Alexander Dru; Hans Spemann, *Embryonic Development and Induction;* Paul Tillich, *The Interpretation of History;* and Wolfgang Köhler, *The Place of Value in a World of Facts.*[5] But it did not list *The Descent of the Dove* by Charles Williams or Goethe's *Faust,* the two works upon which—together with Kierkegaard—the poem most obviously depends. While these works by Williams, Goethe, and Kierkegaard are not the sole sources of the ideas versified in Auden's letter to Elizabeth Mayer, they constitute a literary trinity informing its spirit.

The list of "Modern Sources" in *The Double Man* was followed by "The Quest," a sequence of twenty Rilkean sonnets employing one technique of double focus. When first published in *The New Republic* (November 25, 1940) this sequence was preceded by the note:

> The theme of the Quest occurs in fairly tales, legends like the Golden Fleece and the Holy Grail, boys' adventure stories and detective novels. These poems are reflections upon certain features common to them all. The "He" and "They" referred to should be regarded as both objective and subjective.

The sonnets are highly symbolic and allusive. Their general theme "is, roughly, that most of our troubles, political and personal, stem from the unconscious."[6] The sonnet sequence was followed by an "Epilogue" (titled "The Dark Years" in *Collected Poetry*) in the same Alcaic stanza as the "Prologue." Its theme, like that of "In Memory of Sigmund Freud," is the mutual exchange between conscious and unconscious elements in the mind.

Auden drew on *The Descent of the Dove* for his first title, *The Double Man,* which he found in Williams's quotation from the *Life of Antony* by Athanasius of Alexandria:

> A certain brother said: "It is right for a man to take up the burden for them who are near to him . . . and, so to speak, to put his own soul in the place of that of his neighbour, and to become, if it were possible, a double man, and

he must suffer, and weep, and mourn with him . . . as if
he had put on the actual body of his neighbour . . . and
he must suffer for him as he would for himself . . .[7]

What Auden had hoped to convey by the title *The Double Man*
is more clearly revealed in his "Introduction" to the American
edition of *The Descent of the Dove* (1956) where he says of Williams's works: "the basic theme which runs through all of them
is a doctrine of exchange and substitution . . . the first law of
the spiritual universe, the Real City, is that nobody can carry
his own burden; he only can, and therefore must, carry someone else's."[8] (The general notion of exchange, interdependence,
and double focus or symmetry of opposites provides a link
between the ideas of Freud, Blake, and Rilke in this poem
and the spiritual theme drawn from Williams.) *The Descent of
the Dove* also furnished the epigraph from Montaigne (unfor-
tunately omitted from *Collected Poems*): "We are, I know not
how, double in ourselves, so that what we believe we disbelieve,
and cannot rid ourselves of what we condemn."

The Double Man appeared only as the title of the first New
York printing of 2000 copies of this work published on March
21, 1941. Subsequent editions have the title *New Year Letter*.
When John Lehmann in London received the typescript of *The
Double Man* from Auden in 1940 he announced the title as
forthcoming from the Hogarth Press; but received a letter from
T. S. Eliot informing him that Faber had the English rights to
Auden's books. Auden left the matter to be settled between
them.[9] Eliot compensated Lehmann for the advance he had
given Auden, but was unwilling to use a title announced by another publisher, and without consulting Auden he changed the
title to *New Year Letter* and substituted the phrase "the invisible twin" for the phrase "the Double Man" in the "Prologue."
Eliot's decision to change the title from *The Double Man* to
New Year Letter did both the work and its readers some disser-
vice. It removed a valuable signpost to the letter's deeper philosophical and religious themes. Later New York editions adopted
the London title with its better edited text on which the definitive versions of "New Year Letter" in *Collected Longer Poems*
(1969) and *Collected Poetry* (1976) are based.

3

"New Year Letter"—to give the poem its permanent title from *Collected Poems*—is a fluent, witty, aphoristic work in rhymed octosyllabic couplets. The coinherence in it of humor and seriousness is a reflection of its theme of "doubleness" or double focus. One of Auden's terms for this in the poem is "a reverent frivolity" which, in a verse note to line 1649 (". . . the powers / That we create with are not ours"), he associates with both physical and spiritual expressions of love: "The reverent fury of couples on the wedding night, / Jacob wrestling with a river demon at the ford, / St. Francis bleeding from the five stigmata of Christ. . . ." (NYL, 157) The octosyllabic couplets offer a suitable vehicle for the tension of this double mood. They incline, on the one hand, toward the comic mode of Samuel Butler's "Hudibrastics," and on the other, toward the lucid use of the heroic couplet for reasoned argument by Dryden and Pope.

In its serious purpose this verse letter espouses coinherence and dialectical tension as approaches to truth, and attacks all one-sided claims to the whole truth, whether these be Darwinian, Freudian, or Marxist, without denying each some truth, or even a good measure of it. The work is harshest toward the claims of "the lost Romantics"—a phrase Charles Williams had used to characterize Romantics of all ages including the early Gnostics who esteemed *illuminati* as possessing truth. "The lost or pseudo-Romantic in all times and places has the same marks, and he had them in the early centuries of the Faith. He was then called a Gnostic."[10] In "New Year Letter" Auden uses the term *impatient* rather than *lost* for the one-sided Romantic. In his note to line 821: "The either-ors, the mongrel halves, / Who find truth in a mirror," he writes: "i.e., the impatient romantics. (Definition of Romanticism: unawareness of the Dialectic.)" And he goes on to characterize "the impatient romantics" by quoting A. E. Housman's description of a certain textual editor: "He is like a donkey between two bundles of hay who fondly imagines that if one bundle of hay be removed he will cease to be a donkey." (NYL, 119)

Auden drew on Williams for much of his diagnosis of the Western historical malaise, and he also raided *The Descent of the Dove*—like a magpie in search of glitter—for specific words and phrases including the key line on coinherence related to the title *The Double Man* which is adapted from the motto of Williams's Real City: "Your life and death are with your neighbour." (Auden simply changed each adjective to *our.*) Some of the items drawn directly from Williams include the repeated Latin phrase (slightly transformed), "*Quando non fuerit, non est,*" and the climactic line, "*Da quod jubes, Domine,*" and also the Greek term for "thinking," *dialegesthai,* incorporated into the couplets:

> The *dialegesthai* of the rich
> At cocktail parties as to which
> Technique is most effective in
> Enforcing labour discipline,
> What Persian Apparatus will
> Protect their privileges still
> And safely keep the living dead
> Entombed, hilarious, and fed . . .   (CP, 186)

The expression "Persian Apparatus," signifying elaborateness, is from Horace, *Odes,* I,38; but the last-quoted line had its origin in a passage of Williams's on the Roman government at the beginning of the Christian era: "The Government's own business was to keep their world fed, to keep their world quiet, and to keep their world 'hilarious.' (It was *Hilaritas Populi Romani* on which, at a later period, the coins of Hadrian, as it were, congratulated the Emperor.)"[11]

The three parts of "New Year Letter" deal with three modes of responding to experience: through imagination, reason, and doubt; and the literary manner of each part reflects its theme. The stages of the poem's development have therefore correspondences to Kierkegaard's triad. Part One, which treats of art, the lives of artists, and the perfection of their works, employs a series of figurative devices; Part Two, by contrast, employs—or ironically mocks—such dialectical devices of rhetoric as argument and syllogistic logic; and Part Three, appropriate to its theme of the process of becoming, in doubt and uncertainty, employs the literary device of a quest: a searching for "the Way." And since Kierke-gaard's thought has a significant place in this work, these three parts may be seen to correspond to his three categories of experi-ence: the Aesthetic, the Ethical, and the Religious (for which the threshold is doubt, or anxiety, spurring the "leap of faith").

Part One of "New Year Letter" is highly successful both in its definitions of art and in its series of miniature portraits of great artists. These are introduced, in part, to illustrate the courage —despite the conflicting demands of their art and their lives (which may be disorderly)—necessary to create lasting examples of artistic order:

> All the more honour to you then
> If, weaker than some other men,
> You had the courage that survives
> Soiled, shabby, egotistic lives, . . .   (CP, 163)

Among those whom Auden chooses as keepers of his own artistic conscience are Dante and Rimbaud, and also "choleric" William Blake who

> Broke off relations in a curse
> With the Newtonian Universe,
> But even as a child would pet
> The tigers VOLTAIRE never met,
> Took walks with them through Lambeth, and
> Spoke to Isaiah in the Strand,
> And heard inside each mortal thing
> Its holy emanation sing.   (CP, 164)

Part One concludes with an examination of the baffling "situation of our time." It laments the inability of art to erase the guilt of social disorder—a theme developed here through an analogy to the detective story in which the interest, as Auden has said elsewhere, is the "dialectic of innocence and guilt." (DH, 147) So, here, ". . . all are suspects and involved / Until the mystery is solved." (CP, 165) A brief and witty comparison between police methods in democracies and in dictatorships extends the scene of the crime from "Our parish of immediacy" to those global conflicts in which the guilt for national and international crimes involves all mankind. The concluding paragraph laments the helplessness of poetry to rescue the social order, but finds some hope in the ambivalent *form* of the aesthetic pronouncements of the delphic Oracle: "For through the Janus of a joke / The candid psychopompos spoke." (CP, 166)

Auden turns in Part Two of "New Year Letter" to the limitations of those one-sided systems, ideologies, and Utopias which human reason has, from time to time, proposed as ultimate order. In this section the chief apologist for reason as a guide is Mephistopheles who has stepped out of Goethe's *Faust* still bound by his wager with God in the "Prologue in Heaven"—that he can satisfy man's restlessness which is the reflected image of God's own nature: "the changing Essence that ever works and lives." In "New Year Letter" Mephistopheles is an expert in the devious devices of logic. He is familiar with the rhyme beginning *"Barbara, Celarent . . . ,"* a mnemonic for a complex system of syllogistic logic:[12] and he asks, "Could one not almost say":

> That Eve and Adam till the Fall
> Were totally illogical,
> But as they tasted of the fruit
> The syllogistic sin took root?
> Abstracted, bitter refugees,
> They fought over their premises,
> Shut out from Eden by the bar
> And Chinese Wall of *Barbara*.   (CP, 170)

The Devil's task is to entice the troubled intellectual to rest in some Utopia, and this is given an ironic twist when he enters a debate with disillusioned Utopians who were eager Marxists in the thirties: "We hoped, we waited for the day / The state would wither clean away / Expecting the Millennium. . . ." The Devil's duplicity points both to the weakness inherent in monist absolutes—"the either-ors"—and to the positive value of dialectic, "the gift of double focus":

> So, hidden in his hocus-pocus,
> There lies the gift of double focus,
> That magic lamp which looks so dull
> And utterly impractical
> Yet, if Aladdin use it right,
> Can be a sesame to light.   (CP, 176)

Reviewing Carl Sandburg's *Lincoln: The War Years* while working on "New Year Letter," Auden said: "The one infallible symptom of greatness is the capacity for double focus. Great men
know that all absolutes are heretical but that one can only act
in a given circumstance by assuming one. . . . They are skepti-
cal about human nature but not despairing, they know that they
are weak but not helpless. Perfection is impossible but one can
be or do better or worse."[13] (Auden's most significant examination of literature from the viewpoint of double focus is the
extended essay: "Baalam and His Ass: The Master-Servant Relationship in Literature."[14])

The influence of Goethe's *Faust* on "New Year Letter" is only
a little less pervasive than that of Williams's *The Descent of
the Dove,* and approximately equivalent to that of Kierkegaard,
whose presence is manifest in several ways. He is ostensibly
quoted at times:

> Ironic KIERKEGAARD stared long
> And muttered "All are in the wrong";   (CP, 185)

and he is also characterized:

> As out of Europe comes a Voice,
> Compelling all to make their choice,
>
>   . . .
>
> What none before dared say aloud,
> The metaphysics of the Crowd . . .   (CP, 180)

His thought is represented more indirectly by the emphasis in
this work on the value of the dialectical approach, "both-and,"
and the rejection of "either-or"—the one-sided commitment,
and his thought is pervasive in Part Three which might be
regarded as a Pindaric hymn in praise of doubt:

O once again let us set out,
Our faith well balanced by our doubt,

. . .

And keep in order that we may
Ascend the penitential way
That forces our wills to be free,
A reverent frivolity
That suffers each unpleasant test
With scientific interest. . . .

(NYL, 50; CP, 179)

Part Three traces the sickness of war-torn Europe to the exhaustion of the rationalist quest begun at the Renaissance; and it sustains the anti-Romantic theme chiefly by associating the notion of *illuminati*—shared by party leaders, cadres, and national Bards—with Plato's "lie of intellect" and Rousseau's "falsehood of the flesh"—both deriving from "one common cloud / Up in the Ego's atmosphere." He says of the Ego:

And our political distress
Descends from her self-consciousness,
Her cold *concupiscence d'esprit*
That looks upon her liberty
Not as a gift from life . . .

. . .

But as the right to lead alone
An attic life all on her own . . .   (CP, 187-88)

Part Three also contains the fine survey in memorable verse well worth preserving on America as the prime example of the conditions the machine age imposes:

To what conditions we must bow
In building the Just City now.

From America the focus moves to awakening Asia: "Clocks shoo the childhood from its face." Looking forward in time to Asia's future, lines 1580 to 1602 envision "what ought to be / The nature of society":

> How readily would we become
> The seamless live continuum
> Of supple and coherent stuff,
> Whose form is truth, whose content love . . .
>
> (CP, 191)

The penultimate verse paragraph of Part Three (lines 1685 to 1707) takes the form of an invocation to the deity under a series of symbolic names: Unicorn, Dove, Ichthus, and so on. Here, through masterly use of assonance and internal rhyme, Auden succeeds in imposing a devotional tone on the octosyllables of "New Year Letter." The invocation opens with the lines:

> O Unicorn among the cedars,
> To whom no magic charm can lead us,
> White childhood moving like a sigh
> Through the green woods unharmed in thy
> Sophisticated innocence,
> To call thy true love to the dance . . .   (CP, 192)

These lines show how Auden draws consistently on Kierkegaard's categories for details of the imagery of the concluding hymn. For example, since magic is encompassed by the Aesthetic sphere, the line "To whom no magic charm can lead us" re-affirms Kierkegaard's view that art cannot directly represent the Religious sphere. But it can nevertheless provide analogies for its perfect order. One common analogy for both the perfect order of art and the ultimate order of paradise is the dance; and to express this, Auden borrows (with altered pronoun) the line, "To call my true love to the dance," from a medieval lyric in which the speaker is Christ.

Even though it depends for so much of its matter on the works of Christian thinkers like Kierkegaard and Charles Williams, "New Year Letter" is not a poem of Christian commitment; for Auden had completed it before the final stage of his conversion; that is, before he suffered his equivalent of what Kierkegaard called "the great earthquake" in his own life: his discovery in July 1941 that Kallman no longer shared his commitment to a "marriage." His second long work of the 1940s, *For the Time Being: A Christmas Oratorio* (dedicated to the memory of his mother who died in August 1941) is the work of a man who has known anguish and acquired a personal revelation through it.

XII

Kairos and Logos:
For the Time Being

1

Having earlier found metaphors for poetry in the writings of Freud, Groddeck, and Homer Lane, Auden in the 1940s drew new metaphors from the works of Kierkegaard and other existentialist theologians. He made imaginative use of Kierkegaard's three categories of existence—the Aesthetic, Ethical, and Religious—in several ways, one of them a logic of arrangement. The three parts of *New Year Letter*, devoted to art, to reasoned argument, and to the purgatorical Way, show a measure of correspondence to the triad; as does the later arrangement of *The Dyer's Hand:* from the aphoristic *pensées* on the arts of reading and writing partly derived from his own unpublished aesthetic work, "The Prolific and the Devourer"; through the analysis of Christian art (with its ethical component) in "The Shakespearean City"; to the final essays on the art of music, which, because it needs no material shape of words or clay to embody its harmonies, comes closest to the perfected state of Being associated with the religious sphere. (This is the theme of the second part of Auden's "Anthem for St. Cecilia's Day.")

Kierkegaard had embodied the categories in psychological types: the aesthetic personality, for example the Poet in *Either-Or*, responds subjectively to experience; judges things on the basis of beauty or ugliness, fortune or misfortune; and is a prey to boredom. Ibsen's Hedda Gabler who says, "Let it be beautiful," as she encourages Lövborg to shoot himself may be

the fullest intentional representation in literature of Kierkegaard's aesthetic personality. But Kierkegaard himself, who
evolved the notion of the first two categories in his studies of
literature, points for his instances of aesthetic behavior to
classical literature—to those tragic and epic characters who are
always what they were fated to be, and who do not *become*
what they ought to through choice. Hence the ironic question
in the first semi-chorus of Auden's *For the Time Being:* "Can
great Hercules . . . reinvigorate the Empire?" Kierkegaard's
ethical personality—Judge William in *Either-Or*—respects law,
evaluates on the basis of reason, and, like Aristotle's megalopsych, may be dedicated to "the Good"; but, like Auden's
Herod in *For the Time Being*, he is apt to be unnerved by the
irrational: by the "absurd" claim of the Wise Men, for example,
that "God has been born." Kierkegaard's third category of existence, the religious, is an inward relation to God and cannot be
recognized by external signs; neither, in Auden's view, can art (the
aesthetic mode) reflect it, except as a distorted or ironic parody:
"the voice of Agape, of holy love, speaks comically" he says in
"Baalam and His Ass," where, typically, he alludes to all three
categories—represented by Hector, the megalopsych, and "the
Way"—within a sentence: "For Christ is not a model to be
imitated, like Hector, or Aristotle's megalopsych, but the Way
to be followed." (DH, 135) Condensed reference of this kind,
reducing the categories to a symbolic alphabet, is common in
the poems. The extent to which Auden felt that Kierkegaard's
three categories and his concepts of anxiety, boredom, and "the
Crowd" offered insights into the contemporary human situation
is made clearly evident in his prefaces to *The Portable Greek
Reader* (1948) and *The Living Thoughts of Kierkegaard* (1952).

Auden read theological works other than Kierkegaard's during 1939-40. Ursula Niebuhr recalled that she and her husband,
Reinhold, first met Auden "some time in 1940," and that "he
was then reading Kierkegaard of whom translations had been
coming out on both sides of the Atlantic." The Niebuhrs lent
to Auden a copy of Tillich's *The Interpretation of History*
(from which he quotes in his Notes to *The Double Man* completed in April 1940). They also lent him "the mimeographed
propositions for his Systematic Theology which were handed

out in Tillich's classes. These in distilled and stripped form appealed to Wystan, and he found Tillich 'exciting.' "[1] This excitement soon carried over into his work. Some of Tillich's special terms began to appear in his writing, among them: the Abyss, the Void, the Demonic, and *Kairos*. In *The Dyer's Hand* he defined "the Greek notion of Kairos" as "the propitious moment for doing something." (DH, 140)

Tillich's influence first appeared in "Kairos and Logos," the suite of four sestinas, that Auden composed in 1940. The imagery of the opening stanza of the first sestina seeks to convey the notion of the despair and exhaustion of the Classical world on the eve of the Christian era:

> Around them boomed the rhetoric of time,
> The smells and furniture of the known world
> Where conscience worshipped an aesthetic order
> And what was unsuccessful was condemned;
> While, at the centre of its vast self-love,
> Sat Caesar with his pleasures, dreading death.   (CP, 238)

Auden's image in this sestina for Christ's nativity—in Tillich's terms "the One Great Kairos" and "the Center of History"—is: ". . . when predestined love / Fell like a meteor into time": a poetic phrasing much inferior to T. S. Eliot's lines in "Gerontion": "In the juvescence of the year / Came Christ the tiger."

While they are not uniformly successful, the four sestinas of "Kairos and Logos" are of some technical interest. Auden had written sestinas before: the well-known "Paysage Moralisé," for example, in 1934 and the Airman's sestina in *The Orators* (1932); but he had not undertaken a set of four bound by an exacting sequence of variations on the end-words. Each sestina of "Kairos and Logos" has a different set of end-words. But in all four the order of repetition is constant: each stanza varies the order of words in the preceding stanza in a sequence that groups the odd and even numbers and encloses the two extremes (1 and 6) between their companions: 3, 1, 5, 2, 6, 4. While demonstrating unusual technical resourcefulness, the mechanical rigidity of the form makes for some dull lines like "The fountain sinks into a level silence," or "Defined by an indefinite confusion," and similar abstractions. What "Kairos and Logos" lacks to be truly Kierkegaardian is a quality of painful irony in the moment of revelation, the existential anxiety of which Kierkegaard often speaks figuratively as sailing alone over seventy thousand fathoms: ". . . the martyrdom of believing against the understanding, the peril of lying upon the deep, the seventy thousand fathoms, in order to find God."[2] This quality was not lacking in Auden's next attempt to find an artistic embodiment of *kairos:* the opening movement, "Advent," in the Christmas Oratorio, *For the Time Being.* Meanwhile he experienced some anguish.

In July 1941 Kallman had asserted his independence from their "marriage." This occasioned the frightening loss of rational control that Auden listed as the final step in his return to religious practice. He had been reading theological works and going, "in an experimental and tentative sort of way," to church. Then he says, "I was forced to know in person what it is like to feel oneself the prey of demonic powers, in both the Greek and Christian sense, stripped of self-control and self-respect, behaving like a ham actor in a Strindberg play."[3] Isherwood came from California to help smooth things out between them while they were staying near Jamestown, Rhode Island, during August at the summer home of Carolyn Newton, then Auden's patron. It was there that Auden received the news of his mother's death: "I was surprised at the violence of my feeling," he wrote, "though I had known it was likely. When mother dies, one is, for the first time, really alone in the world, and that is hard."[4] A month later, having started his year of teaching at the University of Michigan, he began work on *For the Time Being: A Christmas Oratorio* and dedicated it: "In memoriam Constance Rosalie Auden, 1870-1941."[5] While he worked on it at Ann Arbor, the Japanese attack on Pearl Harbor on December 7, 1941, brought America into World War II.

3

For the Time Being is an ambitious major work intended for musical setting as an oratorio; but it was written, for the most part, without much consultation with Benjamin Britten, the composer Auden had in mind. He began work on it in the autumn of 1941 while teaching at the University of Michigan and may have had it near completion in December 1942 when the fifth movement, "At the Manger," appeared in *Commonweal* with directions for vocal assignments: soprano solo, tenors, sextet (three Wise Men and three shepherds), and so on. Auden sent the finished script to Benjamin Britten who was reluctant to undertake a setting of such magnitude; but Auden did not reply to his request for cuts. Apart from a separate score for the short "Chorale" in "The Summons" (and a "Shepherd's Carol" not in the final text) for a BBC radio program in 1944, Britten did not set the Oratorio.[6] An abridgement set by Marvin David Levy had its premiere at Carnegie Hall, December 7, 1969.

Auden's Christmas Oratorio is unparalleled in the tradition of Nativity literature principally because he chose to make it a vehicle for the theories of existentialist theologians. Kierkegaard identifies certain anxious or despairing states of soul which indicate that a person has plumbed one of the inferior stages to its depths, and may be prepared for "the leap of faith." That such moments of darkness were signs that the time was ripe for renewal, and that such critical moments could obtain in history as well as in the life of an individual, was a common element in the thought of Tillich and Kierkegaard—and this is essentially the theory dramatized in Auden's Christmas Oratorio.

"The Meditation of Simeon," is the key to the philosophical attitude of the poem. It puts forward the pertinent theological view in such phrases as: "Before the Unconditional could manifest itself under the conditions of existence it was necessary that man should first have reached the ultimate frontiers of consciousness" (CP, 298), and "The Word could not be made Flesh until men had reached a state of absolute contradiction between clarity and despair in which they would have no choice but either to accept absolutely or reject absolutely . . ." (CP, 299). These are declarative phrases, but the other episodes in the Oratorio seek to dramatize this concept in various ways.

The choruses in the opening movement, "Advent," employ both of Tillich's terms for the experience of meaninglessness and despair that can lead to renewal: the Void and the Abyss.

They also employ an imagery resembling that of the first sestina of "Kairos and Logos" for the mood of boredom and exhaustion in the Greco-Roman world in "the fullness of time":

> Darkness and snow descend;
> The clock on the mantlepiece
> Has nothing to recommend,
> Nor does the face in the glass
> Appear nobler than our own
> As darkness and snow descend
> On all personality.
> Huge crowds mumble—"Alas, . . ."
>
>   . . .
>
> Portly Caesar yawns—"I know";
> He falls asleep on his throne,
> They shuffle off through the snow . . .   (CP, 271)

Two semi-choruses in "Advent" declare that neither the aesthetic hero, Hercules, nor the ethical ideal, the civil garden of philosophy, could comprehend the irrational event of the Incarnation.

The theme of the limits of rationality is also developed in the speech of the Narrator in "Advent," which begins with a reassuring commentary on the political situation in the idiom of the complacent official spokesman or bland radio announcer. But the Narrator soon adverts to "a Horror" invading his comfortably urbane world (there may be a veiled allusion to the "Revelation came to Luther in a privy" of a later poem):

> But then we were children: That was a moment ago,
> Before an outrageous novelty had been introduced
> Into our lives. Why were we never warned? Perhaps we were.
> Perhaps that mysterious noise at the back of the brain
> We noticed on certain occasions—sitting alone
> In the waiting room of the country junction, looking
> Up at the toilet window—was not indigestion
> But this Horror starting already to scratch Its way in?
>   (CP, 273)

The Narrator finds that the advent of this Horror makes his world as unreal as Alice's: "as if suddenly the living room had

changed places / With the room behind the mirror over the fire-
place"; and he concludes with expressions of despair in the face
of what he calls—in Tillich's term—the Void: ". . . for no nightmare / Of hostile objects could be as terrible as this Void." The
development of this Narrator speech, from the trite common-
places of the opening to the troubled observations of the close
indicates the potential for *kairos* in the mood of "Advent." The
Narrator has arrived at an extremity—a "limit situation"—which
may be a prelude to renewal.

But the rational mind may also reject the invitation to renewal. This is dramatized in Herod's speech in "The Massacre
of the Innocents." Unlike Simeon, whose inner communion takes
the form of meditation, Herod reveals himself as a rhetorician
whose style is that of the public orator. His oratorical flourishes
are by the book—his speech develops step by step in line with the
seven rhetorical elements in a Classical oration. He is the orator,
par excellence, in Auden's long line of orators. His speech begins with a burlesque presentation of the qualifications of the
orator—a clever parody of Marcus Aurelius who began his *Golden
Book* with references to the various tutors, relatives, and ances-
tors to whom he owed the virtues of a worthy Roman emperor.

Herod argues three points: if, as the Wise Men say, God has
been born, reason will be replaced by revelation, idealism will
be replaced by materialism; and justice will be replaced by pity.
Ironically, Herod's predictions are true, but unlike Simeon, the
man of faith, he cannot see them in their true perspective. He
begins to lose his composure in the course of the refutation and
arrives, unintentionally, at a *reductio ad absurdum:* "Why can't
they see that the notion of a finite God is absurd?" His discourse
breaks down at this point and the speech rambles out in an in-
coherent jumble:

> How dare He allow me to decide? I've tried to be good. I
> brush my teeth every night. I haven't had sex for a month.
> I object. I'm a liberal. I want everyone to be happy. I
> wish I had never been born.   (CP, 304)

The parody of a humanist outlook founded wholly on reason
links Auden's Herod to the traditional comic Herod of the me-

dieval Nativity plays. The comic *exordium* even overdoes the caricature and "out-Herods Herod," certainly in the view of some who have felt that in Herod's speech, as in the poem of about the same period, "A Healthy Spot," Auden shows undue disdain for liberal humanist values. But life occasionally imitates art; and Auden's Commonplace Book quotes remarks Hitler made on August 31, 1944 that resemble Herod's peroration written two years earlier: ". . . this war is no pleasure for me. For five years . . . I haven't been to the theater, I haven't heard a concert, I haven't seen a movie." (ACW, 183)

"Advent" proclaimed that the painful crisis of the despairing soul may be the prelude to *kairos*—the restored wholeness and reconciliation that breaks through the anxiety from beyond. Tillich's name for this is "a *Gestalt* of grace"—a concept Auden dramatizes in the second movement of the Oratorio, "The Annunciation." As a prelude to this, he introduces Jung's four faculties as separate personifications—Thought, Feeling, Intuition, and Sensation—to represent the divided psyche seeking "wholeness," and he also incorporates the four classical elements —earth, air, fire, and water—in the imagery of Mary's response to Gabriel:

> What dancing joy would whirl
> My ignorance away?
> Light blazes out of the stone,
> The taciturn water
> Burst into music,
> And warm wings throb within
> The motionless rose:
> What sudden rush of Power
> Commands me to command?   (CP, 278)

Other movements of the Oratorio show Auden equally intent on depicting aspects of the Nativity story from the standpoint of the theologians he was reading. In the third movement, "The Temptation of St. Joseph," for example, he transforms the historical Joseph into a personified abstraction—an archetype—intended to dramatize Kierkegaard's concept of "infinite resignation." The prototype is Kierkegaard's Abraham figure in

Fear and Trembling: A Dialectical Lyric, where Kierkegaard
dwells at length on the difficulty of recognizing a "Knight of
Faith" in the modern world; for he might be any vigorous,
"smartly dressed townsman who walks out to Fresberg on a Sunday afternoon." Some of these characteristics appear in Auden's
St. Joseph, who is accorded such lines as "My shoes were shined,
my pants were clean and pressed" and "The bar was gay, the
lighting well designed."

St. Joseph's trials are represented in three stanzas, each of
which is followed by a brief mocking chorus of disembodied
voices off-stage representing the temptation to doubt Mary's
purity. The verse form then changes for Joseph's direct appeal
to God for consolation. At this point Auden departs from the
scriptural account and follows more closely the Abraham figure
in *Fear and Trembling.* To Joseph's prayer for a sign, Gabriel replies: "No, you must believe; / Be silent, and sit still."
This ignores the assurance given to Joseph in Matthew 1:18-20.
Auden's St. Joseph is intended to present the highest trial of
faith, the acceptance of "the absurd"—as is also Kierkegaard's
Abraham, of whom Theodor Haecker says: "The Abraham of
Fear and Trembling is not the Abraham of the Old Testament
. . . but a philosophic myth, a purely poetic creation . . . to
push the dialectic of faith, obedience, and sacrifice to the fullest
limit."[7] But this intention may not be conveyed convincingly,
possibly because in representing St. Joseph's anguish Auden drew
on his own emotions following Kallman's "betrayal." That he
had his own experience in mind is evident from the solo and
chorus in "The Annunciation" beginning: "Lovers at their betrayal / Weeping alone in the night," and from his use in the
Oratorio of lines from "Love Letter," a poem he wrote to Kallman in 1939, when he was away from New York, fearing such
"betrayal": for example, the line, "The eyes huddle like cattle"
from the opening chorus of "Advent."[8] There is parallel matter
also in the three dreams that comprise a poem of the same period, "The Lesson." (CP, 253)

Auden apparently failed to reconcile two desires when composing *For the Time Being:* one was the desire to write poetry
suitable for setting as an oratorio, and the other was a desire
not merely to philosophize, but to instruct his readers in the

theological theories he had found exciting. In much of the poem, particularly in the choruses, he solved this problem successfully; and some verse in *For the Time Being* stands with his best. The Narrator's speeches in "Advent" and "The Summons," and particularly the concluding Narrator's speech sometimes anthologized as "After Christmas," are accomplished monologues. These, together with the choruses in "Advent" (of which the closing one is reminiscent of Sophocles' chorus on man in *Antigone*), are among his more memorable pieces. The wit in the fugal-chorus "Great Is Caesar," in "The Summons," and in the Soldiers' song in "The Massacre of the Innocents" rates with Auden's best, as does the musical quality of the two short songs in this work: Mary's lullaby in "At the Manger" and the chorale in "The Summons." The final chorus "He Is the Way" was included in *The Cambridge Hymnal* (1967) in a setting by Sir Arthur Bliss and selected for a revised Episcopal *Hymnal* in 1982.

Apart from its technical merit, the Christmas Oratorio may be regarded as a theological work of some distinction, appropriately in keeping with the dedication to the memory of his mother who was a devout Anglican. The epigraph from St. Paul's Letter to the Romans—"What shall we say then? Shall we continue in sin, that grace may abound? God forbid (Romans VI)"—provides a text for the Oratorio as it might for a sermon, and establishes its theological perspective. In this epistle St. Paul recognizes the paradoxical cleavage in human personality—at once destructive and creative—that Tillich calls "the Demonic." The genuine intellectual reach of the Oratorio cautions against explaining it away as simply an emotional response to events in Auden's life—his experience with Kallman and his mother's death—without adequate critical regard for its merits as a work of intellect or as a presence in English literature whose spirit may not be readily accessible to conventional critical vocabularies. While it is true that there are traces in this work of Auden's personal "existential disruption" not altogether transformed in the artistic process, these are few. The Narrator in "The Temptation of St. Joseph," for example, has a stanza that might apply to Auden's relationship with Kallman. It begins: "Without a change in look or word, / You both must act exactly as before; / . . . / Just as if nothing had occurred"; and it ends:

"To choose what is difficult all one's days / As if it were easy, that is faith. Joseph, praise." (CP, 283) For the rest of his life Auden in his relationship with Kallman chose what was difficult. He continued the "family" relationship as if nothing had occurred. He provided Kallman with support, education, and a home; brought him in as a collaborator in the opera libretti—for which Kallman was well qualified; and made him his sole heir.

It is not surprising that Britten found the Christmas Oratorio too diffuse a work to set. His decision not to do so brought an end to their series of collaborations begun in 1936. The one notable work set by Britten after *Paul Bunyan* was Auden's three part "Anthem for St. Cecilia's Day" (sometimes titled "Three Songs for St. Cecilia's Day"), the music for which he wrote on board ship while returning to England in 1942. The festive mood in Auden's anthem (composed for St. Cecilia's Day, 1941) derives some of its joyful overtones from three stimulating aspects of the occasion: first, the impulse to extol music itself on the festival of its patron; second, the opportunity to pay homage to John Dryden by recalling his technique and by continuing his version of the St. Cecilia legend; and third, the happy coincidence that St. Cecilia's Day, November 22, was also Benjamin Britten's birthday.

The quality of Britten's music for the "Anthem for St. Cecilia's Day" makes it regrettable that we do not have a version of the Christmas Oratorio from his hand. Viewed simply as a semi-dramatic work, the Christmas Oratorio is, at best, a substantial, but flawed, achievement which might be placed where Julian Symons placed it: "On the same shelf with the *Essay on Man* and *In Memoriam*."[9] The companion piece, *The Sea and the Mirror: A Commentary on Shakespeare's "The Tempest,"* printed with it in the volume *For the Time Being* (1944), while less profound is a more unified work aesthetically.

XIII

Prospero and Ariel:
The Sea and the Mirror

1

In September 1942 Auden took up a teaching post combined with a Guggenheim Fellowship at Swarthmore College in Pennsylvania. He left Chester Kallman at Ann Arbor to finish his degree at the University of Michigan. While at Swarthmore, he composed the third of his major works in America, *The Sea and the Mirror: A Commentary on Shakespeare's "The Tempest,"* which explores the relation between art and reality in the light of the Christian existentialist theology that informed *For the Time Being*. *The Sea and the Mirror* takes up the theme of Shakespeare's *The Tempest* as the characters embark for the voyage home—as they step from the mirror of art into the sea of life—a moment when they can look backward on the aesthetic world of the play where time could be conjured with, and forward to the future where, until death, time is "a prim magistrate whose court never adjourns." One reason for choosing the end of *The Tempest* as a point of departure was the implication in Prospero's "Epilogue" (sometimes read as Shakespeare's abjuration of art) that the artistic life could be incompatible with spiritual values:

> And my ending is despair,
> Unless I be reliev'd by prayer,
> Which pierces so that it assaults
> Mercy itself, and frees all faults.

As you from crimes would pardoned be,
Let your indulgence set me free.

It is with these lines in mind that the Audience asks of Caliban
in Part Three of *The Sea and the Mirror:* "How *can* we grant the
indulgence for which in his epilogue your personified type of
the creative so lamely, tamely pleaded." (CP, 326)

Auden's point of departure in *The Sea and the Mirror* signifies his intention to respond to questions about the concern of
the Christian artist for the ultimate value of his work which
troubled Chaucer, Tolstoy, and (in some interpretations of *The
Tempest*) Shakespeare. He told Ursula Niebuhr that this work
was "really about the Christian conception of art."[1] While reject-
ing both Tolstoy's call for direct spiritual utility and Romanticism's claim to the autonomy of the imagination, Auden reaf-
firmed the value of art in this technically brilliant work prodigal
with apt lyric forms. *The Sea and the Mirror* has a modern ana-
logue in Eric Gill's sculpture *Prospero and Ariel* (on the BBC
building, with a cast in the Tate Gallery); but whereas Gill's work
implies the sacredness of the imagination by according Ariel the
stigmata of Christ and aligning Prospero with God the Father,
Auden's work denies such sacredness.

The Sea and the Mirror is arranged like a triptych, with
separate panels for the artist, the work of art, and the audience:
Part One, "Prospero to Ariel," is a dramatic monologue in three
movements marked by interpolated lyrics where Ariel ad libs
freely; Part Two, "The Supporting Cast *sotto voce*," is a cycle of
lyrical monologues broken in upon by the voice of Antonio the
would-be regicide in *The Tempest* who stands alone outside the
circle of reconciliation; Part Three, "Caliban to the Audience,"
is an artful prose symposium in which Caliban (representing the
imaginative artist in the flesh) holds a town meeting with the
audience on the meaning of the play they have just seen. A
"Preface" spoken by the "Stage Manager to the Critics," and a
brief "Postscript": "Ariel to Caliban, Echo by the Prompter"
complete the work. This behind-the-scenes trio—the Stage Manager, Ariel, and the Prompter—comprise the three collaborators
in the stage illusion usually invisible to the audience. They

know the world of art is unreal: Ariel can arrange storms or calms, suspend the laws of time and space, or move them about at will; the Prompter knows the words spoken by the actors are not their own; and the Stage Manager is an illusionist who knows that the world behind the proscenium is a left-handed mirror world. His "Preface" addressed to the critics may be an ironic reminder that the three panels in the triptych correspond to *source, form,* and *end*—the three categories of questions that critics perennially ask of art; and by choosing the form of a poetic drama for this work Auden may be reminding the critics of a further irony: that, for poets—as Horace, Boileau, and Pope had shown—prose is not an obligatory medium for criticism; and he adds an imaginative novelty by personifying the abstractions of critical theory, and having them appear on stage like characters in a Morality play. Auden's commentary on *The Tempest* occupies a unique place in twentieth-century literature: it is an existentialist work that is at once joyful, celebratory, and a festival of imagination.

In his "Preface" the Stage Manager raises the problem of art and reality from the viewpoint of someone all too familiar with the world of illusion behind the scenes, particularly in plays like *The Tempest* where skill with mirrors and wire is essential for setting up Ariel's "living drollery" in the banquet scene which is made to "vanish" with "a quaint device." The Stage Manager speaks first of the effect on the spectators of the illusion he manipulates: the innocent and imaginative children accept the aesthetic pretence as essentially play: "How the dear little children laugh / When the drums roll and the lovely / Lady is sawn in half"; but the aged are less capable of forgetting the terror and death which are part of reality: "The aged catch their breath, / For the nonchalant couple go / Waltzing across the tightrope / As if there were no death. . . ." In his second stanza, he comments on the world of reality and ironically suggests that Science, in attempting to account for the surprises of "existence," accords the role of stage manager to the unconscious: "Science is happy to answer / That the ghosts who haunt our lives / Are handy with mirrors and wire." In his third stanza, he declares that art's relation to life is one of analogy, not identity: it represents the *agon* in an ideal form; and he goes on to question the practical effectiveness of art in the real struggle—the existential *agon:*

> . . . but how
> Shall we satisfy when we meet,
> Between Shall-I and I-Will,
> The lion's mouth whose hunger
> No metaphors can fill?

Finally, the Stage Manager alludes to a world which, it seems, the imagination can touch on, but which art cannot adequately represent—a position consistent with Auden's view, adapted from Kierkegaard, that the aesthetic mode cannot directly represent the religious sphere:

> Well, who in his own backyard
> Has not opened his heart to the smiling
> Secret he cannot quote? (CP, 311)

No one can "quote" the secret in question because it is beyond the art of poet or dramatist, but may be revealed in the course of a lone inner journey. The Stage Manager then suggests, through allusions to such lines as "The rest is silence," that Shakespeare was aware of this limitation of art.

This theory of art will be elaborated more fully in Caliban's prose address to the audience which concludes the work. By presenting it at the outset from the Stage Manager's viewpoint, Auden introduces an existentialist motif which is never absent from *The Sea and the Mirror*—the theme of death as a reality that art cannot conjure with. In his opening monologue Prospero even quotes Kierkegaard on existentialist anxiety in the line "Sailing alone out over seventy thousand fathoms" which echoes Kierkegaard's ironic remark about Bishop Mynster in his *Journals:* "Mynster never sailed alone over 70,000 fathoms."[2]

At the point where Auden's poem begins, Prospero has become aware of his misuse of the imaginative faculty—by presuming, like the Romantics, that all its uses are equally good: "All by myself I tempted Antonio into treason" and "Caliban remains my impervious disgrace." He comes to realize that imagination is neither good nor evil and that Ariel should be free to perform his aesthetic duties without demands of prophecy, magic, or redemption from him. But the artist in him finds it difficult to abandon the habit of imaginative projection even while abjuring it. The images that occur to him are startingly concrete, as, for example when he credits Ariel with discovering appropriate settings for comedy and tragedy—and even with having the capacity to imagine the infernal:

> No one but you had sufficient audacity and eyesight
>   To find those clearings where the shy humiliations
> Gambol on sunny afternoons, the waterhole to which
>   The scarred rogue sorrow comes quietly in the small
>   hours:
> And no one but you is reliably informative on hell. (CP, 313)

Prospero has also become aware that the journey really exists which he has only imaginatively dealt with previously, and he wonders if he can face it without relapsing into fantasy:

> If I peg away at it honestly every moment,
>   And have luck, perhaps by the time death pounces
> His stumping question, I shall just be getting to know
>   The difference between moonshine and daylight. . . .
>   (CP, 316)

Deprived of his unique poetic gift, Prospero would be "an old man / Just like other old men, with eyes that water / Easily in the wind." (CP, 315) His ability to distinguish between the mirror and the sea saves him from what Auden has called the fallacy of the romantics: the belief that "the power to conceive of possibility is the divine element in man." (Antonio, on the other hand, affirms this.) This first part of the triptych closes with a lyric encouraging Ariel to sing "Sweetly, dangerously / . . . / With a smoother song / Than this rough world." "Sweetly" because art reflects the possibility of perfect harmony; "dangerously" because its ideal order may become, for some, a refuge from the necessary existential struggle in "this rough world"; and, for others, a temptation to impose on society the arbitrary order which the artist has power to impose on his materials.

2

Except for its special treatment of Antonio, Part Two of *The Sea and the Mirror*, "The Supporting Cast *Sotto Voce*," is a formal pageant like Prospero's wedding masque in *The Tempest*. All the characters in *The Tempest* except Prospero, Ariel, and Caliban appear here as personified types; and each speaks in an appropriate verse form. This group of characters from Ferdinand to Miranda who are "linked as children in a circle dancing" represents the ideal order possible to art. Also, by analogy, it represents a harmonious social and spiritual order, from which the rebel Antonio stands withdrawn.

The arrangement of the group is symbolic. There is first the suggestion of a circle—the symbol of the macrocosm, and of perfection. Within it "courtly" and "low" characters alternate. Auden accorded metrically sophisticated forms to the courtly characters and allotted to the others such conventional folk forms as the ballad of the Master and Boatswain, Stephano's *ballade*, and Trinculo's simple ballad quatrains. The arrangement of the characters also suggests a social order, as Alonso holds the central position, and the courtly and rustic characters are proportioned on either side of him between the lovers in the tableau of the reconciled.

Alonso addresses Ferdinand in a Horatian epistle for which Auden invented an elaborate but tightly constructed stanza in syllabic verse. He warns against the opposing paths to excess arising from the misuse of either feeling or intellect; and in doing so repeatedly employs the antithetical symbols of the sea and the desert to represent primitive potential and actualized triviality. Through this counterpointing of images the letter seeks to convey the double truth that while all persons including kings are responsible for their own choices, they are also mutually responsible for others. Through allusions to *The Winter's Tale* ("having seen the statue move") and *The Tempest* ("the solemn music"), the final stanza implies that the themes of mutual responsibility and forgiveness pervade Shakespeare's last plays in which the sea is a place of purgatorial suffering. (This is also one of Auden's topics in *The Enchafèd Flood*.)

For the lyrics of Sebastian and Miranda Auden chose the highly artificial forms of sestina and villanelle. Sebastian's sestina has attracted some attention as a curiosity, but it has the special merit of drawing attention to his place in the circle of the reconciled from which his tempter, Antonio, has been excluded. Under Antonio's influence, Sebastian came to confuse the imaginative possibility of wearing the crown with the reality of acquiring it by murder. Now, in the sestina, he reflects on the temptation to turn imagined evil into reality—a temptation that has brought him to a clearer recognition of the boundaries between dream and reality. Sebastian's sestina is a successful and beautiful poem, and its formal artificiality goes well with his courtliness, and his deviousness with words and ideas: "Thou dost snore distinctly. / There's meaning in thy snores." (*The Tempest*, II, i, 216-17.)

His fellow plotter, Antonio, assumes greater importance in Part Two of *The Sea and the Mirror* than his role in *The Tempest* would lead one to expect. Antonio, who speaks first, and who also responds to each of the others, is represented as a self-centered egoist who stands withdrawn from the harmonious circle: his world of the *will* is at odds both with their aesthetic world of the *wish* and also with their acceptance of their reconciled state. He will not accord to art "the willing suspension of disbelief" Coleridge called for; and he refuses to play Prospero's aesthetic game and enter the magic circle of the reconciled. The kind of reconciliation art is capable of cannot contain an absolute—especially one evilly disposed; and, lacking his cooperation, the work must fall short of aesthetic perfection. The final stanza of Miranda's villanelle and Antonio's comment on it emphasize the symbolic aspects of this arrangement. Miranda says:

> So, to remember our changing garden, we
> Are linked as children in a circle dancing.

And to this Antonio replies:

> One link is missing, Prospero,
> My magic is my own;

> Happy Miranda does not know
> The figure that Antonio,
> The Only One, Creation's O
>   Dances for Death alone.   (CP, 325)

In the symbolism of *The Sea and the Mirror*—the relation of the actual world of life where deeds are done to the secondary world of art where they are only played with imaginatively—Antonio has a special importance. In *The Tempest*, Antonio tempted Sebastian to act on the imagined possibility of wearing the crown. That is to say, he introduced reality into the sphere of the imagination which, of itself, is neither good nor evil; and his temptation of Sebastian is therefore analogous to Satan's temptation of Eve, of which Auden says in *The Dyer's Hand:* "It is not sinful of Eve to imagine the possibility of being as a god knowing good and evil: her sin lay in desiring to realize that possibility when she knew it was forbidden her, and her desire did not come from her imagination, for imagination is without desire and is, therefore, incapable of distinguishing between permitted and forbidden possibilities; it only knows that they are imaginatively possible." (DH, 133)

In Auden's view, the Romantics failed to understand the neutrality of the imaginative faculty in relation to the true or the good; and their acceptance of the imagination as the divine element in man led them to confound "the identity of the romantic hero with the consciousness of the poet." In discussing the characteristics of the hero of the Romantic imagination—in this instance Baudelaire's "Dandy"—Auden said:

> . . . his ambition is neither to be admired by men nor to
> know God, but simply to become subjectively conscious
> of being uniquely himself, and unlike anyone else. He is
> in fact the religious hero turned upside down—that is,
> Lucifer, the rebel, the defiant one who asserts his freedom
> by disobeying all commands. . . .[3]

Apart from Tom Rakewell in *The Rake's Progress*, Antonio is Auden's only attempt to portray in his poetry a figure who commonly appears in his criticism: the demonic, or "negative religious hero" who, in his self-obsession stakes all on an arbitrary *acte gratuit*. Although he is the inversion of the religious hero, Antonio ironically testifies to the truth about the limitations of the wholly aesthetic mode. It cannot adequately reflect the spiritual even in its negative expression as sin. As Auden says elsewhere quoting Nietzsche: "Art is not enough."

The perfect circle of the reconciled in Part Two of *The Sea and the Mirror* represents the perfected, wholly aesthetic work of art, which, in Auden's view, was capable of reflecting the aesthetic religion of the Greek gods; but the whole of Part Two, with its tensions between Antonio's ethical world of will and the aesthetic circle of the reconciled, represents the duality of Christian art which, in Auden's view, cannot be exclusively aesthetic. One theme of this work, encountered again in "Caliban to the Audience," is that Christian literature is necessarily a mixed bag which must accommodate both the aesthetic and the ethical. Auden developed this part of his theory in detail in several essays in *The Dyer's Hand*, particularly those devoted to the plays of Shakespeare and of Ibsen; and he explored aspects of it in the ironic prose piece that constitutes Part XI of *Collected Poems:* "*Dichtung und Wahrheit* (An Unwritten Poem)," which argues that the "true" love poem cannot be written.

3

In the third panel of Auden's triptych, "Caliban to the Audience," the poet turns critic. Caliban, who responds to the audience's demand for the author, is the natural man who confronts us when we meet the poet in the flesh. Since Caliban as pure nature has no voice of his own, Ariel must speak for him; and with no master to inhibit his freedom to play, he may employ what artistry pleases him—even so elaborate an artistry as Henry James's later style. The thirty pages of Jamesian prose forming Part Three of *The Sea and the Mirror* is a symposium in which Caliban-Auden fills all the roles.

Before replying to his own echo of the audience's question, Caliban reminds any poets present that they *must* reconcile the

demands of Ariel's world with those of the real world despite
the audience's belief—which the poet is in danger of sharing—in
the autonomous spheres of art and reality. Caliban then singles
out two groups in the audience who may insist on making Ariel
or himself their guides: those who wish to escape from life's
problems will approach him—the poet in the flesh—and ask for
wish-fulfillment. A smaller, finer group, he says, "whose *amour
propre* prefers to turn for help to my more spiritual colleague,"
will desire that the ideal order possible in art be imposed upon
reality. These expect the poet to be a teacher—an apostle of the
ideal—not merely an imaginative genius.

The final section of "Caliban to the Audience" puts forward
the view of "the dedicated dramatist": a theory of art differing
from the theories advanced by the audience. (The humor in this
episode implies a measure of correspondence between Caliban
and Auden who had played Caliban in a Gresham's School production of *The Tempest* in 1925. Theoretically also, since this
is Auden's poem, Caliban who here personifies the poet in the
flesh is Auden at moments when he is not being a poet—when he
is sitting down to breakfast, or philosophizing, or presenting a
critical theory as he is doing here. Therefore the theory Caliban
presents on behalf of "the dedicated dramatist" is Auden's theory, not a "feigned" aesthetic performance.) Caliban tells us, in
his conclusion, that in "Beating about for some large loose image
to define the original drama which aroused his imitative passion," the dedicated dramatist is reminded of the Fall which is
"Our performance" and in which "Ariel and I are, you know
this now, just as deeply involved as any of you." It is only at this
point, "when we see ourselves as we are," that we become aware
of the significance of our desire for artistic order:

> . . . our shame, our fear, our incorrigible staginess, all
> wish and no resolve, are still, and more intensely than
> ever, all we have: only now it is not in spite of them but
> with them that we are blessed by that Wholly Other Life
> from which we are separated by an essential emphatic
> gulf of which our contrived fissures of mirror and pro-
> scenium arch—we understand them at last—are feebly figu-
> rative signs, so that all our meanings are reversed and

> . . . it is just here, among the ruins and the bones, that
> we may rejoice in the perfected Work which is not ours.
>
> (CP, 340)

Caliban's final position is that art reflects the state of wholeness we long for, but only by analogy—"feebly figurative signs." In arriving at this view he rejects the extreme Romantic tendency to submerge the real in the imaginative; and he also rejects the propagandist theory of the imaginative as handmaid to the real.

"Caliban to the Audience" contains some of Auden's liveliest writing; and it is not surprising to find that toward the end of his life Auden named "Caliban to the Audience" "as the poem of which he was most proud."[4] Neither is it surprising to read that he listed "Prospero to Ariel" among poems indirectly alluding to his relationship with Chester Kallman.[5]

It is a serious matter to set one's hand on the life of another human being, and Auden, to satisfy his own Romantic longings, had set his hand on the life of Chester Kallman, then aged eighteen; and he made that life, for better or worse, an adjunct to his own:

> We did it, Ariel, between us; you found on me a wish
>   For absolute devotion; result—his wreck
> That sprawls in the weeds and will not be repaired . . .
>
> (CP, 314)

Since he thought seriously of religious questions, Auden thought seriously of guilt and forgiveness in human relationships. In this regard he described Shakespeare as the most "lifelike" of dramatists because he saw him as without peer at conveying "the double truth" that while each person is a unique individual responsible for choices made and not an impotent victim of circumstances, "at the same time we are all members of one another, mutually dependent and mutually responsible. No man is what he is or chooses independently of the nature and choices of those with whom he is associated." And he adds a point directly pertinent to the theme of *The Sea and the Mirror:* "That is why our primary social duty is to forgive our neighbor."[6]

Besides which, as he repeatedly implies in the essays in *The*

Dyer's Hand, all else, including art, is essentially frivolous. Or, as Caliban speaking for Auden on the value of art to the sinner entering on the Pilgrim Way puts it: "what else exactly *is* the artistic gift which he is forbidden to hide, if not to make you unforgettably conscious of the ungarnished offended gap between what you so questionably are and what you are commanded without any question to become." (CP, 339)

The Sea and the Mirror first appeared, as a companion piece to the Christmas Oratorio, in September 1944 in the volume *For the Time Being*. Both were very well received by reviewers and were immediately included in *The Collected Poetry of W. H. Auden*, the most substantial collection of his work to date, published in New York in April 1945, one month before the war in Europe ended. Auden had intended this volume to be an interim collection, and he arranged the shorter poems not chronologically, but in an alphabetical order of first lines, hoping to imply thereby that at age thirty-seven his development as a poet was not yet complete. He also proposed a sentence for the dust jacket: "This volume contains all that Mr. Auden wishes to preserve of the poetry he has written so far." He objected to the publisher's intended title: "As to title, I want *Poems 1928-1945*. The word Collected suggests finality which I *hope*, anyway, is incorrect."[7]

Although the alphabetical arrangement brought some adverse criticism, the *Collected Poetry* was generally well received and it sold in numbers unusual for a book of poetry. (Auden was both puzzled and pleased by a report that the U.S. Navy had purchased 1100 copies.) First printed in April 1945, it was reprinted three times that year, and twenty-one times in all before its replacement by *Collected Shorter Poems* (1966) and *Collected Longer Poems* (1968).

In April 1945 Auden was himself in Germany as a member of the United States Strategic Bombing Survey, a unit that had been formed to report on the effects of bombing on the morale of German civilians. He was assigned to interviewing survivors of bombing attacks in several cities. As had been the case on his return from the Spanish Civil War front in 1937, he refrained from comment on his experiences in Germany; but the extermination camps and the bombed cities moved him deeply, and the

postwar Europe settlement as a whole troubled him. He wrote
no poetic work corresponding to *Spain* or "Sonnets from China"
out of his 1945 experiences. The imagery of his 1949 poem "Memorial for the City," in memory of Charles Williams who died
in April 1945, evokes memories of the camps—"The crow on the
crematorium chimney"—and of the desolation of cities; but the
poem looks deep into Western history as Williams had done for
the sources of Europe's moral crisis. His most significant work
with an explicit wartime setting, *The Age of Anxiety*, looks forward to the healing of the psychic disorder underlying war-
mindedness rather than backward on the events of war. This
work is in some respects a poetic formulation of Jung's *Modern
Man in Search of a Soul*. Auden had begun work on it before he
went to Germany in 1945, but he wrote most of it during 1945-46
following his return. He was then friendly with a young Jewish
woman, Rhoda Jaffe, a friend of Chester Kallman's who was in
the process of separating from her first husband. (She was employed by a New York restaurant chain in personnel management.) Their relationship—which for a time became quite intimate—has some bearing on details of characterization in the last
of Auden's longer works of the 1940s, *The Age of Anxiety: A
Baroque Eclogue*.[8]

XIV

The Age of Anxiety and
The Rake's Progress

1

Reviewing the Swenson-Lowrie translation of Kierkegaard's *Either-Or* (1944) in "A Preface to Kierkegaard," Auden identified the "basic human problem as "man's anxiety in time"; and he categorized three aspects of this: "his present anxiety over himself in relation to his past and his parents (Freud), his present anxiety over himself in relation to his future and his neighbors (Marx), his present anxiety over himself in relation to eternity and God (Kierkegaard)."[1] The phrase "time being" in the title of the Christmas Oratorio, *For the Time Being,* had implied a concern for man's anxiety in time; and this concern remains at the heart of his next major work, *The Age of Anxiety.*

In his early work Auden had symbolically associated man's desire to explore his own psychic depths with mining for lead, a mineral found deep in the fissures of ancient rock formations. But in *The Age of Anxiety* he reached back only to the alliterative beginnings of English verse—to the ur-forms, as it were, of *Beowulf, Deor,* and *Piers Plowman*—for meters fitted to deep exploration of the psyche. Baroque in its reaffirmation of the flesh as well as in its elaborate technique, this work is also properly, if ironically, called an eclogue. It has a precedent in Swift's *A Town Eclogue* (1710), and it has the conventional elements of eclogue: dialogue and song; a setting described by the narrator; and the courtship of a shepherdess. The scenario is both witty and simple.

One Night of All Souls, during World War II, four strangers meet in a Third Avenue bar in New York. They are Malin, a medical intelligence officer in the Canadian air force; Rosetta, a Jewish businesswoman—British by birth; Emble, a college sophomore enlisted in the U.S. Navy; and Quant, an elderly clerk of Irish origin. Led by Malin, the four discuss "the seven ages" of man; then, led by Rosetta, they embark on a surrealist dreamjourney "to Grandmother's House" through seven stages of the unconscious. On awakening, they leave the bar and join Quant in a yearning lament for an archetypal father-figure as they drive through the streets to Rosetta's apartment; later, with Emble as bridegroom in a parodied wedding masque, they seek happiness in sensual love; and finally, at daybreak they go their separate ways wiser and less self-centered than before.

The Four Faculties were separately personified in *For the Time Being* to symbolize the fallen state of the psyche. Here the four strangers in the Third Avenue bar also correspond to Jung's psychic faculties: Thought personified by Malin; Feeling by Rosetta; Intuition by Quant; and Sensation by Emble. Jung's notion of the relations among the faculties is commonly represented by a diagram placing them at the cardinal points. If the two evaluative functions, thought and feeling, are placed north and south respectively (thought high in the conscious sphere and feeling submerged in the unconscious and, therefore, described as feminine because the unconscious is the realm of the primordial Mother); and the two perceptive functions, intuition and sensation, are placed east and west, the resulting figure will serve as a diagram of the psyche of the "Thinking type" which, collectively, the characters in *The Age of Anxiety* constitute.

Auden once described himself as "an intuitive-thinking type," and there is enough of him in Quant and Malin to suggest that the four characters—although they are more than that—are in some degree aspects of himself, as were the characters in his elaborate and amusing self-analysis in the 1933 poem, "The month was April . . ." (EA, 130-32)

Malin, the central character in this work, is clearly characterized as Thought. He habitually makes reasoned deductions and logical inferences, and his speech is sometimes marked by a cryptic wit, and sometimes by a tendency toward abstract speculation not well suited to poetic expression as, for example, the statement: "His pure I / Must give account of and greet his Me / That field of force where he feels he thinks. . . ." The name Malin has interesting symbolic connotations. In association with the direction north and with the head as the seat of the thinking faculty, the place-name Malin Head, the most northerly point on the map of Ireland, comes to mind. In Nordic folklore, and in the European tradition generally, the north is associated with malign forces. The French word *malin,* as an adjective, denotes "clever" in the sense of mischievous; the noun *le Malin* is synonymous with "the devil" in his association with the tree of knowledge. Auden's Mephistopheles in *New Year Letter* is a clever rationalist or dialectician.

Rosetta, representative of the other evaluative function, is clearly defined as Feeling. She evaluates on the basis of likes and dislikes: "why were the men one liked not the sort who proposed marriage and the men who proposed marriage not the sort one liked?" Her character is somewhat more complex than Malin's because of her necessary correlation with an unconscious function; and until the healing process starts we see her mainly through the veil of her habitual day-dream. Rosetta usually expresses her feelings through an imagery of pleasant or unpleasant scenes, and water symbolism frequently accompanies her day-dream of innocence. Her poetic imagery often includes "the big house"—the imaginary mansion of her father; and the changes in Rosetta's attitude to "the big house" (which is also a symbol of the intellect or of thought) parallel the stages of her awakening to her real heritage which she acknowledges in her final speech. Her nostalgia for English Edwardian scenes associates her with Auden's own conception of Eden. The name Rosetta has other symbolic connotations. Its association with one of the mouths of the Nile and with the Rosetta stone—a link between history and pre-history—relates her, like her consistent use of water imagery, to the feminine principle, to the past, and to the unconscious. The fact that Rosetta is represented as Jewish, like Auden's woman friend Rhoda Jaffe, may also point to a deeply personal element in this poem; but by representing her as a highly successful buyer for a department store, Auden is simply following

Jung's view that feeling is concerned with questions of value: "Feeling tells you for instance whether a thing is acceptable or agreeable. It tells you what a thing is *worth* to you."[2]

Of Quant and Emble, the two perceptive functions, Quant, who personifies intuition, is described as "a tired old widower" whose imagination is constantly filled with memories from two sources: his Irish childhood and his random study of books on mythology. Quant is introduced first by the Narrator and is the first to speak. As the drama progresses, the reader realizes that Quant is constantly first to become aware of new situations. (In *For the Time Being,* Intuition had played a similar role.) Quant's mode of apprehension is imaginative and poetic, and, the mirror is his symbol.

The name Quant suggests *quantum,* the perception of things as wholes, perhaps in its specific use by Whitehead in *Process and Reality* to denote anything apprehended as a unity, that is, grasped intuitively. Although he is represented as of Irish origin, Quant appears to speak out of Auden's experience, particularly when he sings a bawdy ballad in which the *double-entendre* draws on the special local vocabulary of Rookehope lead-miners— an unlikely accomplishment in an Irish child who, according to the Narrator, arrived in America at age six. (CP, 357) It also seems out of character that Quant (and not Malin who is a physician-chemist) should wonder about the flavor of the liquor being drunk by his mirror-image: "What flavor has / That liquor you lift with your left hand?" (CP, 346) That is, if Auden intends him to be aware (unless it is simply an intuition) that liquor contains "carbon compounds called *esters* which give it flavor, and most esters are asymmetrical. No one knows what flavor Looking-glass liquor might have, but it is a good bet it would not taste the same as ordinary liquor . . ."[3] The name Emble suggests *emblem,* that which makes concepts manifest to the senses, specifically to the eye. In religious art, the Emblem Books are forerunners of the sensuous element in Baroque art in their reaffirmation of the flesh. Emble who personifies sensation has the additional role of portraying the uncertainty of youth, which adds complexity to his character. His speeches commonly link him to the archetypal Don Juan, through such allusions as "I have pencilled on envelopes / Lists of my loves"—allusions

that also characterize him as an aspect of Auden who kept a list
of his sexual encounters in his Berlin Journal. As a personification of the sensation type he takes note of details, and the Narrator's commentary and his own opening monologue show that
Emble adapts to the world through external perception: "he
looked about him as if he hoped to read in all those faces the
answer to his own disquiet." He is both sensitive and sensual,
and can apprehend the external world almost as poetically or
almost as grossly as Shakespeare's Caliban. In the first of these
qualities, he resembles those who, in his own estimate of an
ideal civilization, "entertained with all their senses / A world of
detail." When this quality is combined with youthful poignancy,
as it sometimes is, his poetic utterances show an unusual sus-
ceptibility to sense impressions. Speaking at one point of the
ruin brought on settled civilizations by barbarian incursions,
Emble says:

> The reticent earth,
> Exposed by the spade, speaks its warning
> With successive layers of sacked temples
> And dead civilians. They dwelt at ease
> In their sown centres, sunny their minds,
> Fine their features; their flesh was carried
> On beautiful bones; they bore themselves
> Lightly through life; they loved their children
> And entertained with all their senses
> A world of detail. Wave and pebble,
> Boar and butterfly, birch and carp, they
> Painted as persons, portraits that seem
> Neighbors with names; one knows from them what
> A leaf must feel. . . .   (CP, 352)

2

The theme of *The Age of Anxiety* is the integration of
personality, and each episode consists of a series of movements
toward "wholeness." The "Prologue," for example, has four
stages corresponding to the stages of awareness through which

an individual becomes fully conscious of a surrounding world and of others. At first all are self-absorbed. Quant is communing with his image in the mirror behind the bar; Malin is thinking about *thinking*. Rosetta is lost in her reveries of innocent landscapes, and Emble is aware of others in a self-conscious way. Then "The radio suddenly breaking in with its banal noises upon their separate senses of themselves . . . began without their knowledge, to draw these four strangers closer to each other." What they hear is a wartime news bulletin of events on many fronts. Their interior monologues turn to thoughts of war, and in the third movement they speak. As the news broadcast concluded, "they could no longer keep these thoughts to themselves, but turning towards each other on their high wooden stools, become acquainted." Their ensuing dialogue becomes a lament for the "City of Man" in which war is the normal condition; and in a brief fourth movement, they take a significant step toward integration by forming a group. Quant (the poet) names the society and their theme; and at Rosetta's suggestion they move from their barstools "to the quieter intimacy of a booth." As their "high wooden stools" had been symbols of their isolation, the booth becomes a symbol of what Jung calls *fourness:* "A perception of the significance of fourness . . . is a first step, a necessary station on the road of inner development."[4]

In Part Two, "The Seven Ages," the newly formed society holds a symposium on the life of man in which the theme is that of Jacques in *As You Like It:* "And each man in his time plays many parts / His acts being seven ages." This philosophic discussion produces no solution to their problems and Quant intuitively chooses Rosetta to lead them further on their quest. Although she wonders what gift of direction is entrusted to her to lead them on the journey homeward "through the Maze of Time, / Seeking its center," Rosetta agrees to seek the "regressive road to Grandmother's House."

The journey into the unconscious in "The Seven Stages" is the focal point of *The Age of Anxiety*. In it the characters make their deepest penetration into the regenerative depths of the psyche, and their actions in subsequent episodes are influenced by their experiences there. It is in this episode, too, that the psychological and spiritual allegories converge. Rosetta's psycho-

logical route to health—"the regressive road to Grandmother's
House"—takes the form of a direct dramatization of Jung's theories on the regenerative powers of the unconscious:

> the libido sinks "into its own depths" . . . and discov-
> ers . . . the world of memories . . . In this subterranean
> kingdom slumber sweet feelings of home and the hopes of
> all that is to be. . . .
>   Yet the danger is great as Mephistopheles says [in
> *Faust,* Part II, the Mothers] for these depths fascinate. . . .
> Whenever some great work is to be accomplished before
> which a man recoils, doubtful of his strength, his libido
> streams back to the fountainhead—and that is the danger-
> ous moment when the issue hangs between annihilation
> and new life. But if the libido manages to tear itself loose
> [from the wonderful inner world] and force its way up
> again, something like a miracle happens: the journey to
> the underworld was a plunge into the fountain of youth,
> and the libido . . . wakes to renewed fruitfulness.[5]

After they make a journey over a landscape symbolically related to the human body, the sixth stage brings all four to the hermetic gardens: the abode of mother nature and the "Grandmother's House" to which Rosetta promised to lead them. This is the
archetypal symbol of the *Magna Mater,* for which generative organs supply the corresponding body imagery. Arrival at this terminus to "the regressive road" of their descent into the collective
unconscious marks the "dangerous moment" Jung speaks of
"when the issue hangs between annihilation and new life." It
is the *temenos* of "New Year Letter"—the garden with the well of
life—a region of taboo from which they must depart immediately.
    After first feeling joy in the Earthly Paradise, the four char-
acters soon find themselves thrown into confusion and "one by
one they plunge into the labyrinthine forest and vanish down
solitary paths, with no guide but their sorrows." Thereafter the
logic of their journey leads to an escape from the region of the
Mothers and a return to consciousness, the region of the Fathers. It is still night when the characters emerge from their
dream and begin the ascent toward consciousness in Part Four,

"The Dirge," in which their minds turn to the recollection of an archetypal father: "Our lost dad, / Our colossal father." Their invocation of a father archetype is appropriate to the ascent into consciousness, for in Jung's view, "Gaining consciousness, formulating ideals—that is the father-principle of the Logos, which in endless struggles extricates itself ever and again from the mother's womb, from the realm of the unconscious."[6] In what seems at first an odd accompaniment to "The Dirge," Auden has set before it the fourth stanza of a simple-minded, anonymous broadsheet ballad, "The Death of King Edward VII," which refers to Edward as "our dear Dad."[7] But if we consider *The Age of Anxiety* as in part, at least, the product of personal exploration, the ballad may seem pertinent to his own Edwardian origins.

In Part Five, "The Masque," the instincts awakened in the hermetic gardens lead the four wanderers to seek erotic happiness at Rosetta's apartment. "The Masque" contrasts ironically with the courtly celebrations of marriage usual in that genre, for it is primitive Eros, not courtly Cupid, who is ceremoniously honored. The tone of "The Masque" is set by the bawdy "prospector's ballad" Quant sings when Emble asks Rosetta to dance:

> When Laura lay on her ledger side
> And nicely threw her north cheek up,
> How pleasing the plight of her promising grove
> And how rich the random I reached with a rise.
>
> (CP, 396)

Here Auden's old imagery from Pennine lead mining appears in an erotic context. Laura is a likely name for a lead vein. Auden lists names of veins in *A Certain World* that include, for example, Dinah's Rake, Barbara Load, Horse-buttock, and Modesty Flat. (ACW, 268) He also quotes from Thomas Sopwith's *A Visit to Alston Moor*, Sopwith's comments on miners' expressions like "improving of the grove," "descending a rise," and so on. "Many a lively song and joke are often added to the entertainment of such an assemblage," says Sopwith, and adds: "It may be here remarked, that the conversation of the miners sometimes has a curious effect from their assuming, as it were, a sort of volition in the mineral world. Thus they speak of a vein being *frighted* to climb the hill, and that she therefore *swings away* to the sun side, (a feminine appellation being generally used). The throw of the strata is attributed, as it were, to an *act* of the vein,—'*she throws* the north cheek up.'" (ACW, 223) "Ledger side" is an obsolete term for the side on which something lies.

The celebration of the love of Emble and Rosetta prepares the way for the final step in their purgatorial ascent: the transformation of Eros into supernatural love. After Malin and Quant leave Rosetta's apartment, the allegory develops rapidly. Rosetta's monologue over the sleeping Emble, who has "passed out" shows her turning from her habitual day-dream to confront reality. She thinks first of the differences in background that would have made their love no more than a casual affair. This leads her to consider her Jewish heritage. She finally faces the truth about her father: "I shan't be at peace / Till I really take your restless hands, / My poor fat father," and concludes with a confession of faith in Hebrew: the *Shema* which proclaims the unity of God. (CP, 404-5)

In the "Epilogue" Malin and Quant take separate ways homeward. Malin is described as traveling southward, that is, toward feeling, and away from the compass point that represents thought as dominant. He first travels underground by subway (in the realm of "the Mothers"). This route brings him to the highly symbolic topographical point where, emerging from the tunnel, he commences his final inner colloquy: "his train came out onto the Manhattan Bridge. The sun had risen. The East River glittered." Malin's traveling south has brought him, in Tillich's terms, to "a *Gestalt* of grace." At this point, the three-stress alliterative line of his speculative musings changes to the four-stress line of his final monologue which affirms that faith in Christ "scorned on a scaffold" is the goal of his quest.

The Age of Anxiety is a profound and ingenious work of art, even though it gives the impression, in places, of having been "roughed out" rather than carefully polished. It pioneers imaginatively in unfamiliar territory; and it was well described by Marianne Moore as "a deep and fearless piece of work matched by a mechanics of consummate virtuosity."[8] Paul Tillich was among those who thought highly of it. Speaking of Tillich's concept, "the courage to be," his biographers say: "Tillich had an answer for those living in a divided world, threatened by meaninglessness and imprisoned in an 'age of anxiety,' as immortalized in Auden's long poem of that title to which Tillich often referred as a perfect mirror of the times. Tillich's answer was 'the courage to be *in spite of*' death, fate, meaninglessness, or despair."⁹

3

No account of *The Age of Anxiety* can ignore the many playful and humorous elements in it that go beyond technical surprise and verbal wit. The dedication to John Betjeman offers a clue to one humorous idea pervading the work as a whole. In the month *The Age of Anxiety* was published, July 1947, a selection of Betjeman's poems came out in New York with an introduction by Auden on "topological poetry." (This introduction appeared that same month in *Town and Country* with the title, "The Practiced Topophile.") In it Auden remarked on Betjeman's genius for translating the surface appearance of cities—including the architectural detail of churches—into a topological poetry differing distinctively from the poetry of rural landscapes. In one of its aspects *The Age of Anxiety* is an extravagant frolic in several kinds of topological verse undreamed of by Betjeman—although one kind resembles his: Each of Auden's characters has an affinity for a particular kind of topophile interest: Emble's is direct and realistic: "The reticent earth, / Exposed by the spade, speaks its warning / With successive layers of sacked temples. . . ." Rosetta's shows a sentimental regard for rural English parishes—the innocent landscape of the detective story; and her forte is toponymy:

> Volatile vault and vagrant buttress
> Showed their shapeliness; with assured ease,
> Proud on that plain, St. Peter Acorn,
> St. Dill-in-the-Deep, St. Dust, St. Alb,
> St. Bee-le-bone, St. Botolph-the-less,
> High gothic growths in a grecian space,
> Lorded over each leafy parish . . .   (CP, 348)

But beyond details of character affinity, the whole allegorical schema of *The Age of Anxiety* relies on what Freud calls "mental topography"—the relations of psychic energies within the mental personality as reflected in his diagrams of the Perceptual-Conscious System; although Auden's scenario draws more immediately on Jung's theory of the four psychic functions through which, as Jung says in *Modern Man in Search of a Soul*, "We can orient ourselves . . . as completely as when we locate a place geographically by latitude and longitude."[10] The four aspects of the psyche orient us in the psychological allegory throughout most of *The Age of Anxiety*, but there are topological variations. The journey in "The Seven Stages," for example, over "a landscape bearing a symbolic resemblance to the human body" is topological in the medical sense of the body's surface, and even though we may recognize the symbolic significance of the parts of the body visited in this sequence, we may miss the underlying jocular reminder that there can be no psyche without a soma—the unconscious we enter cannot be an abstraction, it must be some *body*'s. Even the trivial and intentionally banal verse in "The Masque," like Quant's prospector's ballad, has some topological interest. This includes the otherwise unredeemed love duet between Emble and Rosetta (in which each line in *his* alphabetically arranged alliterative sequence is counterpointed by one of *hers* in reverse alphabetical order). But it is hard to imagine, though, how that particular piece contributes to Auden's more serious purpose.

The Age of Anxiety was awarded a Pulitzer Prize in 1948, and a subsequent German translation received an Austrian literary prize; but the work has generally found little favor with academic critics, although John Bayley's *The Romantic Survival* (1957) judged it Auden's greatest achievement to date, and the one which best showed the true nature of his scope and talent. The psychologist Rollo May drew on its insights in two works: *The Meaning of Anxiety* (1950) and *Man's Search for Himself* (1953). Leonard Bernstein followed the text very closely and sought to produce its musical equivalent in his Symphony No. 2 for Piano and Orchestra, *The Age of Anxiety (After W. H. Auden)*, 1948; and Jerome Robbins based a ballet on Bernstein's music. Even though academic critics were lukewarm about

The Age of Anxiety, other poems of Auden's of the same period gave evidence of the growing popularity of his work on American college campuses—these included "Under Which Lyre" (Phi Beta Kappa poem, Harvard, 1946), destined to become one of his best-known works, and "Music Is International" (Phi Beta Kappa poem, Columbia, 1947).

As *The Orators* had done, *The Age of Anxiety* drew Auden deeply into the labyrinth of self; and as the suggestion of a play for the Group Theatre had drawn him to a more public medium in 1934, so, in 1947, an opportunity to write a libretto for Igor Stravinsky afforded him the chance to turn outward again. Stravinsky saw Hogarth's series of engravings *The Rake's Progress* at the Chicago Art Institute in 1947. The blind beggar playing a one-stringed fiddle in the Bedlam scene stirred his imagination and he conceived the possibility of basing an opera in English on the eighteenth-century story of the Rake. On returning to California he asked Aldous Huxley to suggest a librettist for such a period piece. Huxley told him there was only one choice: Auden. Auden accepted Stravinsky's commission without hesitation, and at an early stage brought in Kallman as a collaborator without consulting Stravinsky in advance. He felt Kallman had greater familiarity than he did with the technical demands of the medium.

So much has been written on the genesis of the libretto for *The Rake's Progress* by the principals that little remains to be added other than to point out that it bears Auden's unmistakable mark of yoking any undertaking of his to contemporary philosophical ideas.[11] His Tom Rakewell is an aesthetic personality who relies on fortune and believes in his own superior destiny—an egoism that makes him capable of the existentialist *acte gratuit:* the arbitrary act that declares his absolute freedom.

To motivate action Auden endowed Hogarth's passive Rake with three wishes: the wish for money and pleasure; the wish for happiness; and the wish for power. In response to his wish for money Nick Shadow appears with news of an inheritance. Later, in response to Rakewell's wish for happiness, Shadow persuades him to marry the fully bearded circus lady, Baba the Turk, purely as a gratuitous act that declares his independence from all constraints:

That man alone his fate fulfils,
    For he alone is free
Who chooses what to will, and wills
    His choice as destiny.   (RP, 25)

As Auden said elsewhere in 1947, this is the act of "Lucifer, the rebel, the defiant one who asserts his freedom by disobeying all commands";[12] and it prepares us for the Messianic theme of the next episode in which Rakewell's dream of doing good for mankind disposes him to accept Nick Shadow's machine for turning stones into bread. At one stage in the collaboration Auden wrote to Stravinsky describing these key scenes: "Have made a few slight alterations in our original plot in order to make each step of the Rake's Progress unique, i.e.:

Bordel   —*Le Plaisir*
Baba   —*L'acte gratuit*
La Machine—*Il désire devenier Dieu.*"[13]

This careful concern for the philosophical perspective suggests that Robert Craft's estimate of the libretto is too facile: "Wystan Auden's devotion to Chester Kallman was the most important fact of the poet's personal life as well as the real subject of the libretto (the fidelity of true love) . . ."[14]

But the opportunity given to Auden and Kallman by Stravinsky did affect their relationship. It made opera the center of their lives. (Auden may have welcomed the work of a librettist partly to give Kallman an occupation.) They arranged to spend their summers within reach of major European opera houses; and they collaborated on many libretti and musical pieces. Their second libretto, *Delia,* was written by arrangement with Stravinsky, but he never composed any music for it. They subsequently collaborated on English versions of *The Magic Flute* and *Don Giovanni.* They derived a libretto from Shakespeare's *Love's Labour's Lost* for Nicolas Nabakov; and in the 1960s, having moved their summer home to Kirchstetten, they collaborated with the German composer, Hans Werner Henze, on *Elegy for Young Lovers* and *The Bassarids* (a modern version of *The Bacchae* of Euripides). Their final collaboration, completed on the eve of Auden's death, was *The Entertainment of the Senses* for John Gardner. (Although fourteen years Auden's junior, Kallman did not long survive him. He died in Greece in 1975.)

Immediately after completing the libretto for *The Rake's Progress* in the spring of 1948, Auden and Kallman went on a holiday to Europe that brought them to Ischia for the first time. Stravinsky took three years to complete the music for the *Rake,* which had its premiere at La Fenice in Venice, in September 1951. Auden and Kallman had meantime found a summer home in Ischia, and it was from there that they went to take part in the rehearsals in Milan and the premiere in Venice.

XV

Ischia: 1948-57
Nature and History

> *I am presently moved*
> *by sun-drenched Parthenopea, my thanks are for you,*
> *Ischia, to whom a fair wind has*
> *brought me rejoicing with dear friends. . . .*
>
> (CP, 416)

1

Auden spent six weeks in May and June 1948 on the island of Ischia in the Bay of Naples, and the following year he
established a permanent summer home there in the fishing village of Forio. Thereafter, until 1958, he divided his working
year seasonally: winters in New York and summers in the Mezzogiorno (as Italians call the southern half of their peninsula,
where the sun seems noon-high all day). His yearly migrations
imposed a pattern on his literary concerns in the decade 1948-57.
New York was his headquarters for work that provided his income: reviewing, poetry readings, and university lecturing. It
was also the place where he kept in touch with friends in the
ecumenical and intellectual group, The Third Hour, to whose
magazine he contributed poems from Ischia. The title of both
group and journal refers to the canonical hours of prayer derived from monastic observance that were to be the subject of Auden's Ischian cycle, "Horae Canonicae."

Auden's secluded house in Forio d'Ischia offered a better atmosphere than New York for writing verse, and most of his poems
and opera libretti of the period were composed there. There are
occasional exceptions to these seasonal rhythms such as the short
periods he spent at Oxford during the four years following his
election as Professor of Poetry in 1956; but his appointments at
American universities were usually in the fall and winter terms.
In 1948, for example, he taught at the New School of Social Research, New York; in 1949 he delivered the Page-Barbour Lectures at the University of Virginia—three penetrating studies of
Romanticism published the following year as *The Enchafèd
Flood;* and in 1953, he was Research Professor at Smith College.
He spent the corresponding spring and summer seasons of these
and other years in Ischia where he wrote verse rich in technical
adaptations from the odes of Horace. Auden's house at Forio is
as intimately present in this verse as the Sabine farm is in Horace's odes; but Auden was his own Maecenas: his working winters in New York supported the house in Ischia and freed him
from the need to defer either to a patron or to critics.

Auden's Ischian poetry may well be his happiest and most
outgoing; and *The Shield of Achilles* (1955), containing the two
major cycles "Bucolics" and "Horae Canonicae," is one of his
best single volumes. The poems in it are distinguished by a sense
of place that sets them apart from his poetry of any other period. Individual poems are frequently meditative. They begin in
the world of the everyday—the thinker's body, house, or garden—
and then move outward in space or in memory.

Auden always required of himself that, whatever its immediate occasion, a poem of his should be informed by general concepts reflecting some intellectual concern of the age. (Hence the
presence in his work of the ideas of Freud, Marx, Kierkegaard,
and Tillich, for example.) The general concepts that inform the
poetry of his Ischian years include the broad spectrum of "existence philosophy"—Kierkegaard, Heidegger, Jaspers, and also
Husserl's phenomenology.

Auden made particular poetic use of Husserl's notion of
"the natural standpoint" of existence summed up in the phrase:
"I-and-my-world-about-me." In defining this concept Husserl says
of the field of perception: "I can let my attention wander from

the writing-table . . . through the unseen portions of the room behind my back to the verandah, into the garden, to the children in the summer-house . . . to all the objects . . . there and yonder . . . in my immediate co-perceived surroundings."[1] Auden's poems present the thinker's "world-about-me" in a similar succession of stages. "Prime," the opening poem in the cycle "Horae Canonicae," begins by charting the process of our daily awakening from the unconscious world of nature into the conscious world of history:

> Recalled from the shades to be a seeing being,
>> From absence to be on display,
> Without a name or history I wake
>> Between my body and the day. (CP, 475)

This awakening, in which the thinker realizes that he is "not alone, but with a world," is not taking place in imagination—in New York, say, or London—but in the actual world of Ischia, as the details of the second stanza's imagery reveal:

> . . . next
> As a sheet, near as a wall,
> Out there as a mountain's poise of stone,
> The world is present, about,
> And I know that I am, here, not alone
> But with a world . . .

The images in the sequence "sheet," "wall," "mountain," "world . . . about," and "with a world" come in a phenomenological succession of stages of awareness. The "mountain's poise of stone" beyond his garden wall was Epomeo, an ever-present part of Auden's everyday world in Ischia. Also, looking down from his house in Piazza Santa Lucia (there was an even better view from his second house) he could see "The flat roofs of the fishing village / Still asleep in its bunny," of a later stanza in this poem. Auden's philosophical orientation at the time demanded that the poems he wrote in Ischia should reflect his immediate "world-about-me"; but when he moves to the outer margins of his "world-about-me" he moves quickly from his immediate surroundings into the world of mind—to the world of books, for example; and in Ischia in the 1950s this world would include the works of classical authors like Virgil and Horace.

Touched by a long succession of civilizations, Ischia offers more varied associations than New York for such poetry. Its own history allows an almost unlimited perspective on the past; for the island has strong links with Mediterranean literary tradition and the mythological past. Lying off the Cumaean promontory where Virgil had Aeneas visit the Sybil's Cave, Ischia has been identified by some as the rock of the Sirens. It formed part of the early Greek settlement of Parthenopea, named for the Siren, Parthenope, who drowned herself, as did her companions, after Odysseus outwitted them. It was occupied by the early Romans, and in the period of the Empire it was valued for its sulphur springs like neighboring Baiae on the Cumaean peninsula—a resort of the Caesars and familiar also to the Augustan poets Virgil and Horace. Among Ischia's occupiers in the course of later history, as Auden's Horatian ode "Ischia" recalls, were the Aragonians who brought its characteristic grapes to the vineyards on the slopes of Epomeo and fortified its ports. This ode also addresses the spirit of the place directly. (The word "lean" in these lines carries the same kind of association with the term "anaclitic" in Freud's theory of infant sexuality—"leaning-up-against" the mother for safety and nutrition—as it did in the 1929 poem "Venus Will Now Say a Few Words"):

> . . . What design could have washed
>   with such delicate yellows
> and pinks and greens your fishing ports
>
> that lean against ample Epomeo, holding on
> to the rigid folds of her skirts? The boiling springs
>   which betray her secret fever,
>   make limber the gout-stiffened joint
>
> and improve the venereal act . . .   (CP, 416)

When Auden first went there in 1948, Forio d'Ischia was a rural backwater, not a tourist Mecca; but the nucleus of a colony of artists lived there, and it fairly rapidly attracted a small international musical and literary set among whom Auden and Chester Kallman could find congenial company. The English composer Sir William Walton already lived there; and Hans Werner Henze, the German composer with whom Auden and Kallman later collaborated, came there also. So did friends of Auden from earlier years, like Brian Howard to whom the poem "Ischia" is dedicated, and a variety of literary and theater people including playwright Terrance Rattigan and actress Elizabeth Taylor. Part of Ischia's attraction for Auden—that perhaps lent color to the mood of his poems—was that Kallman found the place very congenial. Ischia certainly had great advantages as a summer place of residence for opera lovers far from New York and the Metropolitan Opera. Naples was close by; Rome not too far off; and even Venice, where Stravinsky's *The Rake's Progress* had its premiere in September 1951, was within fairly easy reach.

A local sense of Ischia begins to enter into Auden's work almost from the moment of his arrival there. The references to "the shady side of a square at midday" and to "steep stone gennels" in "In Praise of Limestone" allude to Forio; and the puzzling lines, seeming to lack context, in the same poem: "and these gamins / Pursuing the scientist down the tiled colonnade / With such lively offers, . . ." may derive from an experience he described in one of his first letters from Ischia: "Kids of 5 years old appear on the beach and shove their arses at you giggling."[2] A libretto he worked on in 1948 shows Ischian influence more clearly. There are two prose sketches in the New York Public Library's Berg Collection for an Auden-Kallman opera libretto, *On the Way,* possibly begun in New York in the hope of further collaboration with Stravinsky. The subject of the libretto is that of the inspired Bard or nineteenth-century artist-genius that they were eventually to incorporate into *Elegy for Young Lovers.* The principal characters in the first draft are the Muse and three European composers of the post-Napoleonic period who appear under their own names: Berlioz, Rossini, and Mendelssohn. In the second draft, a typescript with annotations in Auden's hand, the three composers now identified as "Bards," are named Vergile Mousson, Gregor Schöngeist, and Giocondo Pollicini; and a prefatory note says that they should remind the audience of Berlioz, Mendelssohn, and Rossini, respectively. The Muse, in her three manifestations, is named Stella, Maria, and Laura; and other characters include Giorgio Sbuffone and Gisella Saltimbocca. (This second sketch borrows names from Foriani known to Auden and Kallman: Giocondo Sachetti served as factotum in Auden's first house. Maria Senese owned "Il Bar Internationale" and had a companion named Gisella.) *On the Way,* for which the librettists prepared a full outline, is the work referred to by Robert Craft (in addition to *Delia,* on the main outline of which Auden and Stravinsky had agreed in New York in the winter of 1951-52): "Regretably, plans for two further collaborations come to nothing. A second libretto, whose protagonists were to be 'Rossini (the man of heart), Berlioz (the man of intellect), and Mendelssohn (the man of sensibility)' did not develop beyond the talking stage. But the text of *Delia,* the masque written especially for Stravinsky, is complete, awaiting a composer with some of the same gifts of a Stravinsky—or a Mozart."[3]

Some of Auden's less serious verse reflects the more frivolous and convivial side of life in Ischia—wryly recognizing that he keeps homosexual company. "The Love Feast," for example, a memento of his first summer there in 1948, is an ironic poem—in its manner very like "Pleasure Island" of a year before. It introduces allusions to "an upper room at midnight," to "catechumens," and to "The Love that made her out of nothing," that imply an uncomfortable tension between the pleasures of Eros and the demands of Agape in the Ischian setting.

It was in Forio that perhaps for the first time in his life Auden acquired a sense of belonging to a community. He even became embroiled in village politics, particularly the battle between those Foriani who wanted to preserve historic houses and those who wanted them replaced by modern tourist accommodations. During his years in Ischia Auden rented two "historic" houses. For the first seven years he had a very old house in the Piazza Santa Lucia at Monterone on the slopes of Epomeo above Forio. In the period 1956-58 he leased a house built in the sixteenth century. The first house had a wonderfully quiet and private walled garden with flowers and shade trees that appear in a number of poems including "Their Lonely Betters":

> As I listened from a beach-chair in the shade
> To all the noises that my garden made,
> It seemed to me only proper that words
> Should be withheld from vegetables and birds.
>
> (CP, 444)

Auden's garden offered a particularly fine prospect of "steep Epomeo": beyond the garden wall were the terraced vineyards above Monterone; above them, mountain tracks, sparse vegetation, and yellow furze; further up, the bare rock of the ancient crater's serrated edge that appears in "Nocturne":

> Appearing unannounced, the moon
> Avoids a mountain's jagged prongs
> And sweeps into the open sky
> Like one who knows where she belongs.   (CP, 446)

Auden liked to walk down the half-mile or so from Piazza Santa Lucia through steep narrow streets—that then had gardens and open spaces—to Forio's main piazza where Maria Senese's "Bar Internationale" and the café tables outside it were the center of social life. The narrow streets, the square, and the Foriani merge into the background of "In Praise of Limestone" (which incorporates glimpses of other remembered limestone landscapes also):

> Watch, then, the band of rivals as they climb up and down
>   Their steep stone gennels in twos and threes, at times
> Arm in arm, but never, thank God, in step; or engaged
>   On the shady side of a square at midday in
> Voluble discourse, knowing each other too well to think
>   There are any important secrets, . . .   (CP, 414)

Auden himself enjoyed the voluble discourse. The first chair to the right outside "Bar Maria" became recognized as his place of privilege, and he "held forth" there over the café tables—a note caught in the poem "Islands" in his cycle "Bucolics": "Sappho, Tiberius and I / Hold forth beside the sea." In September 1953 he wrote some verse for Maria Senese's autograph book. It is, of course "autograph" verse intended as a simple compliment to

Maria and her co-workers; but its three Sapphic stanzas give some sense of the place and the company it attracted:

Il Bar Internationale

How serene and jolly it is to sit here
Round a table under the stars of summer
Laugh and gossip over wine or stregas
    Brought you by Vito.

But when Beauty passes, remember Stranger,
In a corner there, inescapable as
Death or taxes, noting your goings on, the
    Eyes of Gisella.

Yankee, Limey, Kraut, Foriano, Roman,
Ladies, Gentlemen, and the third sex, join me,
Raise your glass, drink to our hostess, crying
    "Viva Maria!"[4]

2

Typically, Auden's more serious Ischian poems treat of nature and of history—the latter no longer seen as an impersonal force—and the ode is their characteristic form. Among the more notable of those on nature are "In Praise of Limestone" and "Ode to Gaea"; and of those on history, "The Shield of Achilles"—an account of the despair of the aesthetic mode in the face of the realities of history—and "Homage to Clio." This last has intentional echoes of Horace. Its opening stanza not only imitates the form of "Diffugere Nives" (c.4:7), but paraphrases its matter. Horace had written:

Diffugere nives, redeunt iam gramina campis
    arboribusque comae;
mutat terra vices, et decrescentia ripas
    flumina praetereunt . . .

(The snow has gone, and green returns again to fields and trees; the earth changes, and torrents subside within the margins of the river banks.)

Auden's ode begins:

> Our hill has made its submission and the green
>   Swept on into the north: around me,
> From morning to night, flowers duel incessantly,
>   Color against color . . .   (CP, 463)

Auden's purpose, however, was not to paraphrase Horace, but to imply a contrasting view. His ode to the Muse of History sees her, although silent, encouraging a sense of individual responsibility, while Horace sees only a sad promise of emptiness beyond the seasonal round. For him, and for the aesthetic outlook—Yeats is an example—nature and history appear to coin-here. For Auden, the great matter is their difference. His two Ischian cycles "Bucolics" and "Horae Canonicae" dwell on this difference.

"In Praise of Limestone" offers a good introduction to the theme and spirit of the cycle "Bucolics." With the earlier "Venus Will Now Say a Few Words" (1929) and the later "Dame Kind" (1959), "In Praise of Limestone" is one of three humorous poems that show a remarkable consistency in Auden's views on man's relationship with Mother Nature. Since the limestone poem is a family portrait of Mother Nature and the band of little rivals for her attention, the humor is indulgent; and the theme of our relationship with Mother turns on the supposition that all works of the human imagination—art, architecture, and cultivation—derive from sibling rivalry for Mother's attention:

> . . . From weathered outcrop
>   To hill-top temple, from appearing waters to
> Conspicuous fountains, from a wild to a formal vineyard,
>   Are ingenious but short steps that a child's wish
> To receive more attention than his brothers, whether
>   By pleasing or teasing, can easily take.   (CP, 414)

Henry Moore, who in 1974 produced a series of lithographs related to Auden's poems ("The Shield of Achilles," for example, is the source of Moore's "Multitude"), has noted something akin to this in his own experience: "Perhaps what influenced me most over wanting to do sculpture in the open air and to relate my sculpture to landscape comes from my youth in Yorkshire . . . seeing a huge natural outcrop of stone at a place near Leeds which as a young boy impressed me tremendously—it has a powerful stone, something like Stonehenge has . . . ."[5]

Auden's poem ascribes such insights to all of us as members of the "band of rivals" vying for Mother's attention in various ways: some by shaping an object for her praise, some by outrageous behavior: "Intendant Caesars rose and / Left slamming the door." (Goebbels had boasted that the Nazis would "slam the door of history.") The poem implies certain psychological affinities with landscape: "Immoderate soils" like granite wastes attract solitary exceptions; limestone valleys "Where everything can be touched or reached by walking" lend themselves to communities where all are neighbors with names. Since marble is but limestone transformed by heat, it is no surprise to find sculptured works as symbols of perfection in this poem: "These modifications of matter into / Innocent athletes" may remind us that "The blessed will not care what angle they are regarded from, / Having nothing to hide"; and the natural sculpture of the limestone invites a corresponding analogy:

> Dear, I know nothing of
> Either, but when I try to imagine a faultless love
>   Or the life to come, what I hear is the murmur
> Of underground streams, what I see is a limestone landscape.
>
>   (CP, 415)

Various limestone landscapes contribute to the specifics of this poem, but its chief inspiration appears to come from Anthony Collett's description of Yorkshire limestone which Auden quotes in *A Certain World*: ". . . Mountain limestone has almost as much scenery within it as without . . . the chief limestone districts are full of streams that dive into swillets or swallow-holes, to emerge again, in putative identity, miles away. . . . Through all the mountain limestone country the interest of its surface moulding and the attraction of its plant and insect life is heightened by the sense of the unknown sculpture in the roots of the rocks. . . ." (ACW, 216-17)

The poems in the cycle "Bucolics" combine the virtues of "In Praise of Limestone" in various ways. All seven of them: "Winds," "Woods," "Mountains," "Lakes," "Islands," "Plains," and "Streams" are humorous, and they have in common "the theme of the relation of man as a history-making person to nature."[6] Auden's method in this cycle may owe something to the example of Alexis Léger (St.-John Perse) whose works include *"Pluies," "Neiges,"* and *"Vents,"* and to whom "Winds," is dedicated.

"Winds," the first poem in the cycle, takes up the notion of the *pneuma*—the breath of the spirit—and puns on its literal sense of being blown into by a divinity. Written after the exposé of the Piltdown Man fraud in 1953, the poem begins with a series of playful variations on theories of creation—combining, in particular, the most recent theories on the evolution of the human "bubble-brain" with the Genesis story of creation. Its opening also includes a playful query about the possible consequences of the Creator's having chosen a different species to endow with consciousness:

> Deep, deep below our violences,
> Quite still, lie our First Dad, his watch
>   And many little maids,
> But the boneless winds that blow
>   Round law-court and temple
> Recall to Metropolis
>   That Pliocene Friday when,
> At His holy insufflation
>   (Had He picked a teleost
> Or an arthropod to inspire,
>   Would our death also have come?)
> One bubble-brained creature said—
>   "I am loved, therefore I am"—:
> And well by now might the lion
>   Be lying down with the kid,
> Had he stuck to that logic.   (CP, 426)

To suggest correspondences between the biblical sixth day of creation and the final stage of human evolution, Auden

makes the work-week for both enterprises end on Friday. Geologically, the end of the Pliocene "week" was the eve of the
Pleistocene—the epoch when traces of man are first apparent.
Two other bony kinds, the fish-boned teleost and the exoskele-
tal arthropod, flourished during that Pliocene week-end. The
"boneless" winds, representing the non-material force of the
creative power, might have been moved to inspire either species,
rather than the equally undeserving upright vertebrate whose
brain was so rapidly inflated. "Winds" ends in the poet's prayer
for inspiration (since his function is aesthetic, he can pray to a
divinity of the aesthetic Greek pantheon):

> Goddess of winds and wisdom
>
> .   .   .
>
> Let him feel You present,
> That every verbal rite
>   May be fittingly done,
> And done in anamnesis
>   Of what is excellent
> Yet a visible creature,
>   Earth, Sky, a few dear names.   (CP, 427)

The cycle as a whole implies that as the creative personality
has an affinity for winds, so other types of personality find
different natural elements congenial. In "Bucolics," mountains
and plains attract the greater desperados: "perfect monsters—
remember Dracula— / Are bred on crags in castles" (CP, 429);
plains, monotonous to most people, attract militarists: "Caesar
with all his They" who strike swiftly: "How swift to the point
of protest strides the crown" (CP, 433); but woods hide lesser
peccadillos; "Guilty intention still looks for a hotel / That wants
no details and surrenders none; / A wood is that, and throws in
charm as well." Small lakes are, essentially, innocent and
"comfy"; islands attract saints, pirates, prison-builders, and
tourists; the flow of streams brings us back to unconscious innocence. "Streams," the final poem in the sequence, is remarkable
for the complexity of its bubbling and swirling internal rhymes
and assonances while, at the same time, remaining appropriately
fluent. In imposing a strict form on it, Auden may have felt that

since water leads quickly to the unconscious, and it does in this poem, he needed a highly conscious form to keep a tight rein on the instinctive.

3

It seems probable that the cycle "Horae Canonicae," Auden's major work in the Ischian years, had a longer period of gestation than almost any other work of his. During the 1940s—at least occasionally—he attended meetings of an ecumenical group in New York called The Third Hour which included among its members Reinhold and Ursula Niebuhr, Denis de Rougemont, V. S. Vanovsky, William Lynch, S.J., editor of *Thought,* and Anne Fremantle; and he contributed a number of poems from Ischia, including "One Circumlocution" and "Hunting Season" to their journal *The Third Hour.*

As early as the summer of 1947, having finished *The Age of Anxiety,* Auden appears to have had in mind a cycle of poems on the canonical hours; and he started on it in a preliminary way that summer at the Long Island resort, Fire Island, where he had spent summer holidays before going to Ischia. (This is the "Pleasure Island" of the volume *Nones.*) Ursula Niebuhr recalled that Auden then wanted to know all about church offices and their historical origins. Given some information, she says, "he wanted more and more; he needed exact texts, not only their history."[7] Conventional schedules placing the night hours, for example, at 6 p.m., 9 p.m., midnight, and 3 a.m. would be unlikely to satisfy him since he commonly associated daylight with the time-space world of consciousness and darkness with the undifferentiated and myth-making world of the unconscious. Therefore the day and night divisions of the cycle would interest him for their psychological as well as liturgical significances.

The daytime hours, Prime, Terce, Sext, and Nones are named for the first, third, sixth, and ninth hours of the Roman day that correspond in modern chronology to 6 a.m., 9 a.m., noon, and 3 p.m. The night vigils, not measured by sundials, have less precise formulation. Vespers, the hour of evening prayer, takes its name from *hesperos*—toward the west—the realm of the "west-ering" star and of those departed beyond the sunset. Compline, the final prayer at nightfall, marks the "completion" of the day and the approach of sleep. Matins and Lauds are morning songs. Their observance is commonly combined with Compline or with Prime, except in monasteries of strict observance.

Auden may have been drawn to the canonical hours as a subject for poetry by Charles Williams's *The Descent of the Dove;* but since he had a more than common interest in punc-tuality and the keeping of exact hours and schedules—he was a compulsive clock-watcher—his interest may have been sparked years earlier by a passage in *Psychology of the Unconscious* where Jung finds the ground and condition of the Western con-ception of time rooted in monastic observance. He may have had either Jung or Williams in mind in his remark in *The Dyer's Hand:* "I have heard it suggested that the first punctual people in history were the monks—at their office hours. It is certain at least that the first serious analysis of the human experience of time was undertaken by St. Augustine, and that the notion of punctuality, of action at an exact moment, depends on drawing a distinction between natural and historical time which Chris-tianity encouraged if it did not invent." (DH, 140)

The seven poems in Auden's cycle (there is no separate poem for Matins) unfold as a daily round recollecting the events of Good Friday. In the first half of the cycle there is a thematic progression toward increasing responsibility for the act of crucifixion accompanied by the ironic implication that the human qualities of conscious decision, judgment, and effective action necessary for such a deed are also qualities necessary to civilized life. In the second half of the cycle there is a regression toward sleep and the innocence of nature.

The cycle opens with the poet in "Prime" awakening into consciousness and thereby sharing in the historical world where deeds are done—including the deed of crucifixion. "Prime" sup-poses an instant of suspension in time—a momentary state of innocence or perfection—between total absence from the con-scious world in the unconsciousness of sleep and the full state of wakefulness leading to self-awareness. This is the moment

Auden spoke of in his review of Reinhold Niebuhr's *The Nature and Destiny of Man*, where, expanding on the point that
"no Christian doctrine is more unwelcome to the modern liberal
than Original Sin," Auden said: "The Church is not altogether
blameless for this hostility because it has sometimes spoken of
the Fall as if it were a literal historical event, as if each man's
sin were related to Adam's sin in terms of seminal identity,
instead of its being 'a symbol of an aspect of every historical
moment in the life of man . . . Perfection before the Fall, is in
other words, perfection before the act,' though act must here
be taken to include thought."[8] This notion of perfection before
the act is expressed in "Prime":

> And smiling to me is this instant while
> Still the day is intact, and I
> The Adam sinless in our beginning,
> Adam still previous to any act.   (CP, 475)

Niebuhr's conception of the Fall as an element in each historical moment of choice pervades much of Auden's poetry. To
act consciously—to will—is to depart from the natural compact
that binds Mother Nature's other children—bird, beast, or
flower—to her. With the gift of consciousness comes a potential
for guilt. Having no conscious will, bird, beast, and flower cannot harm Nature; conscious man can. Only he can also act as an
agent of the crucifixion. "Prime" concludes by considering the
cost of awakened consciousness of self: "I draw breath; / . . .
and the cost, / . . . is Paradise / Lost." This cost includes separation from the innocent and unanxious world of mountain, sea,
and sleeping village which are now merely *zuhanden*—"things-
to-hand":

> The eager ridge, the steady sea,
> The flat roofs of the fishing village
> Still asleep in its bunny,
> Though as fresh and sunny still, are not friends
> But things to hand, this ready flesh
> No honest equal, but my accomplice now,
> My assassin to be, and my name

> Stands for my historical share of care
>   For a lying self-made city,
> Afraid of our living task, the dying
>   Which the coming day will ask.   (CP, 476)

The verse form with its counterpointed internal rhymes having an element of chance association—*cost, lost; bunny, sunny; share, care; lying, dying; task, ask*—points up the paradoxical co-presence of chance (natural) and choice (historical) in the human situation.

"Prime" is a complex poem and its language is highly symbolic and associational. "Terce" by contrast is almost directly narrative, and its syntax has a clarity and fluency befitting wakefulness. "Terce" corresponds in time to 9 a.m., the opening of the secular daily round. It introduces three characters about to enter on their working day: hangman, judge, and poet; and it alludes to a fourth, uneasy presence: their victim. The hangman, kind to his dog, is the agent of justice, and the judge, loving to his wife, is its authority. The poet, ambiguously related to them and to their victim (they are all good poetic copy), "Does not know whose Truth he will tell."

The theme of human responsibility is more fully developed in the noon poem, "Sext." This significant three-part poem introduces the civilized agencies of justice, and also "the public" in whose behalf they act. Its first part is about those dedicated to a vocation who have the qualities required for the deed: the will and skill to kill. The second part is devoted to those who get things done on a larger scale—generals, bacteriologists, prosecutors—without whom "there would be no authority / to command this death." Both types are also necessary instruments of civilization. Without the former we would be "wandering through forests without / a consonant to our names"; and as for the latter:

> You may not like them much
> (who does?) but we owe them
>
> basilicas, divas,
> dictionaries, pastoral verse,
>
> the courtesies of the city . . .   (CP, 478)

The third part of "Sext" distinguishes those moments when an individual is fully a unique person conscious of a vocation from those other moments when his individuality is submerged in "the crowd"; "the crowd rejects no one, joining the crowd / is the only thing all men can do." "The Crowd" as represented in "Sext" is a Kierkegaardian concept corresponding to Auden's symbol for unconscious mindlessness: the Dynamo. His essay "The Poet and the City" in *The Dyer's Hand* explores the philosophical theme of "Sext" at length—including "the metaphysics of the Crowd"; and may therefore be looked on as a companion piece to this poem.

"Nones" is the climactic poem in "Horae Canonicae." It is also the most resonant in its themes, and perhaps the most successful poetic accomplishment. It brings the unthinkable—"It is barely three / Mid-afternoon, yet the blood of our sacrifice is already / Dry on the grass"—into full proximity with the customary and everyday (for it is siesta time in Forio: "The shops will re-open at four, / The empty blue bus in the empty pink square / Fill up and depart"). Those who then lie sprawled, calmly sleeping, if challenged about their part in the event would reply: "—'It was a monster with one red eye / A crowd who saw him die, not I.' " Participation in the crowd, the world of the Dynamo, brings separation from the individual world of the Virgin:

> The Madonna with the green woodpecker,
>   The Madonna of the fig-tree,
> The Madonna beside the yellow dam,
>   Turn their kind faces from us . . .   (CP, 480)

and the poem implies that none of our chosen routes of escape, fanciful or romantic, can altogether free us from a sense of guilt: "behind the wonder / Of tow-paths and sunken lanes, / Behind the rapture on the spiral stair, / We shall always now be aware / Of the deed into which they lead."

Paradoxically, siesta time—by nourishing the natural and instinctive body—may show the road to restoration. It was consciousness, not the flesh itself (or the surrounding instinctive

world of hens, bugs, and deer) that consented to the deed of
crucifixion; and sleep may lead us back to unconscious springs
of innocence:

> That, while we are thus away, our own wronged flesh
>> May work undisturbed, restoring
> The order we try to destroy, the rhythm
>> We spoil out of spite . . .   (CP, 482)

This note of restoration will be picked up again in "Compline" at nightfall, but meanwhile "Vespers" introduces personifications of our two typical conscious modes of evading
present responsibility: the Arcadian personality seeking escape
in the past and the Utopian seeking it in the future. "Vespers"
is a *tour de force* in both manner and matter. It is a prose poem
in which a protagonist and antagonist engage in a *danse
macabre*—their opposing routes to death crossing as each "goes
west" in his own way. Besides its classical association, the term
vespers in Oxford tradition applies to the public disputation on
the eve of the conferral of degrees—so named because originally
held in the west end of a church which is that opposite to the
altar. So Auden adds implications of dispute and opposition to
what we ordinarily think of as calm evening prayer. Stylistically,
Auden's "Vespers" is built on opposition. It employs counterpointed and chiastic constructions to develop a theme of the
intersecting paths "between my Eden and his New Jerusalem"
as the two anti-types take afternoon walks: "Passing a slum
child with rickets, I look the other way: He looks the other way
if he passes a chubby one." The crossing of paths, however,
forces "both, for a fraction of a second, to remember our victim
(but for him I could forget the blood, but for me he could forget the innocence")." Each of the anti-types in this poem has some
measure of the truth; but each is single-minded like "The
either-ors, the mongrel halves / Who find truth in a mirror," in
New Year Letter.

"Compline" concludes the cycle thematically. ("Lauds," following it, is a transitional poem that is prelude to the cycle's
beginning again.) Commonly related to the hour before sleep,

"Compline" reverses the stages of awakening in "Prime" to signify the return to the closed world of the unconscious at one with Mother Nature:

> As, seizing its chance, the body escapes,
>   Section by section, to join
> Plants in their chaster peace which is more
>   To its real taste . . .   (CP, 484)

Although the stanza form is the same as in "Prime," the rhythms move more easily and without the sharply counterpointed rhymes that accompanied the shock of awakening in "Prime." Indeed, as the conscious ego rejoins the natural round: "A heart's rhythm, a sense of stars / . . . / I can measure but not read . . . ," the rhythms take on the ease and movement of a lullaby. As the body takes over, a sense of humor asserts itself, there is a sleepy confession—in response to the canonical requirement of confession at Compline:

> . . . *libera*
> *Me, libera* C (dear C)
> And all poor s-o-b's who never
> Do anything properly . . . ;

and there is incomprehension:

> . . . what comes to be
> Must go back into non-being
> For the sake of the equity, the rhythm
> Past measure or comprehending.   (CP, 485)

Auden's "Lauds" is an *aubade* or morning song (specifically, the form of *aubade* known as a Spanish *cossante*); and since *matin* is an old synonym for *aubade,* this tactic combines Matins and Lauds as liturgical observance commonly does. As a musical interlude suspended rhythmically between sleep and waking, "Lauds" completes the cycle and prepares for the re-emergence of the awakened individual into the world of the many:

> The crow of the cock commands awaking;
> Already the mass-bell goes dong-ding:
>> *In solitude, for company.*   (CP, 486)

"Lauds" was not written specifically for this cycle, but is a slightly modified version of the final chorus of *Delia: or a Masque of Night* (after George Peele's *Old Wives' Tale*) that Auden and Kallman wrote for Stravinsky, but which the composer did not set. "Lauds" itself was set by Lennox Berkeley.[9]

XVI

Kirchstetten:
About the House

1

Not all of the memorable poems written in Auden's house in the Piazza Santa Lucia, Forio, were his. Auden was best man at Theodore Roethke's wedding in New York in January 1953. They had been friends since they first met at Penn State University in 1941, and Auden offered his house to Roethke and his wife, Beatrice, for their honeymoon, which they spent there between March and May of 1953, looked after by Giocondo Sachetti, who was Auden's factotum in Forio. Roethke completed "Words for the Wind," "The Dream," and "I Waited" at Auden's house; his terrifying little poem "The Thing" is set in Ischia on the slopes of Epomeo; the house in Forio is the setting for "The Storm"; and Allan Seager has recorded that the line: "A witch who sleeps with her horse" in the second poem of "Meditations of an Old Woman" ("I'm Here") was supplied him by Giocondo who pointed out an old hag in the village and said she was such a woman.[1]

When Auden's poem "Islands," which was written in Ischia in the late summer of 1953, first appeared in *The Shield of Achilles* (1955), it was dedicated to Giocondo Sachetti. In all subsequent printings the dedication of this poem reads: "for Giovanni Maresca"—an expression of regard for the Forian barber who was Auden's confidant and adviser on charitable disbursements. The circumstances that led to the change were among those that led to Auden's leaving Ischia. During the winter of 1955 Auden sent Giocondo a check for salary and household expenses. He had intended to write it for 60,000 lire, but added an extra zero. The mistake was discovered and rectified but the episode led to enduring ill-will.

When Auden moved in 1956 from the house in the Piazza Santa Lucia to the Via San Giovanni he had some extensive remodeling done to enclose the walled garden. This seemed to imply an intention to stay; but the village was changing. Historic houses were being torn down to accommodate expanded tourism, and there was an official plan to install a fountain in the square outside the Bar Internationale from which a segment had been surrendered to automobile traffic. The Foriani had been divided in their attitudes toward the plan; and Auden had sided with those seeking to preserve the historic houses. This group also opposed the fountain, which became the focus of contention. On the day the fountain was installed Auden told Giovanni Maresca: "I promise you, Giovanni, that fountain will bring the end of Forio."[2]

Nevertheless when he received a major Italian literary award, the Feltrinelli Prize of the *Accademia Nazionale dei Lincei* (amounting to more than $30,000) in 1957, Auden first thought of using the money to buy the house he was leasing; but the owner, hearing of the prize, raised the price significantly and Auden decided to look elsewhere. He wanted a place near a city with a major opera house, preferably in wine country. This made the vicinity of Vienna a likely choice; and with the aid of an Austrian acquaintance, Hedwig Petzold, he found a suitably secluded house in the lower Austrian village of Kirchstetten on the edge of the Vienna woods. When these arrangements were made in the late summer of 1958 Auden wrote his farewell to Ischia, "Good-Bye to the Mezzogiorno," which reveals that he had begun to equate the effect of life in Ischia on his own development with the effect on himself that Goethe recorded in *Italian Journey*. The poem alludes to Goethe's *Roman Elegies*, V, in the lines:

> . . . Goethe,
> Tapping homeric hexameters

> On the shoulder-blade of a Roman girl, is
> (I wish it were someone else) the figure
>
> Of all our stamp . . .   (CP, 487)

In his foreword to *Collected Shorter Poems, 1927-57* (1967), Auden said: "This collection stops at the year nineteen-fifty-seven. In the following year I transferred my summer residence from Italy to Austria, so starting a new chapter in my life." The idea of beginning a new chapter to prevent the mortal danger of inertia is central to the poem, "Good-Bye to the Mezzogiorno," and it therefore concludes by thanking a certain Monte (the landlord who asked an exorbitant price for the house) while expressing gratitude for the wine-harvests and the cultural tradition:

> Go I must, but I go grateful (even
> To a certain *Monte*) and invoking
> My sacred meridian names, *Vico, Verga,*
> *Pirandello, Bernini, Bellini,*
>
> To bless this region, its vendages, and those
> Who call it home: though one cannot always
> Remember exactly why one has been happy,
> There is no forgetting that one was.   (CP, 488)

Although the Autobahn from Vienna to Slazburg runs by Kirchstetten on an overpass, it has neither exit nor entrance there and the village must still be approached as in the past by a country road or from the railroad halt. Auden's house on what is now Audenstrasse was an unpretentious farmhouse on the village outskirts; and in addition to being itself isolated it had an upper room reached by an outside staircase which gave him a place to write cut off from chance interruption. The work Auden produced there in the years that remained to him after moving in the autumn of 1958—reviews, lectures, introductions, the opera libretti with Kallman, as well as the five books of verse: *Homage to Clio* (1960), *About the House* (1966), *City Without Walls* (1969), *Epistle to a Godson* (1972), and the posthumous *Thank You, Fog* (1974)—compare with the total lifetime accomplishment of some notable poets. The house itself is his subject in the lyric cycle, "Thanksgiving for a Habitat," in the 1966 volume *About the House.*

2

The cycle "Thanksgiving for a Habitat" consists of twelve poems celebrating the Kirchstetten house and its rooms—kitchen, living room, dining room, bathroom, toilet, cellar, attic, and so on. The house and rooms serve practical functions, but as the occasion for a poem in the cycle each room provides a locus for expanding circles of analogy reaching ultimately toward some spiritual horizon. In celebrating the artist in the bath, at stool, in bed, presiding at a feast, or composing an elegy on a friend, Auden is engaged in the quite unromantic pursuit that Martin Buber calls "the hallowing of the everyday." An alternative title for this cycle might be "Against the Manichees"; for it provides a poetic counterpart for the thesis against the Manichean-Gnostic imagination that pervades his criticism including *The Enchafèd Flood* and his collection of critical essays *The Dyer's Hand.*

The house at Kirchstetten—the only "home" he ever owned—with its appurtenances within and without provides the poet with a symbolic center for celebrating, like the Psalmist, his providential circumstances: his heritage in nature, history, art, and belief. In this regard the epigraph from Psalm XVI is pointed: *Funes ceciderunt mihi in praeclaris: etenim hereditas mea praeclara est mihi.* (The lines are fallen unto me in pleasant places: Yea, I have a goodly heritage.)

The providential inheritance that Auden celebrates in "Thanksgiving for a Habitat" is twofold. There is first the natural gift of Dame Kind, "the flesh Mum formulated"—not altogether perfect, perhaps, even though it can boast a "stalwart digestion," but without which there would be no habitat for the imagination to play in. There are sundry other inheritances from the historical world like the English language and, of course, "the dictionaries (the very/best money can buy)." Regarding this useful heritage he confides to the shade of Louis

MacNeice: "For Grammar we both inherited / good mongrel barbarian English / which never completely succumbed to the Roman rhetoric / or the Roman gravity, that nonsense / which stood none . . ." (CP, 521) To extend the list could be misleading; for Auden's Thanksgiving is a carnival rite rather than a solemn memorial, and the poems in the cycle achieve much of their impact through humor and ironic understatement. The language has an astonishing lexical range and evocative overtones reflecting Auden's aspiration that every poem of his should be a hymn in praise of the English language.

The twelve self-reflective poems of the cycle permit a complex view of the world-about-me contained within the horizon of the self—not a morbidly confessional self; but one capable of affirming the potentialities of the imagination, the intellect, and the flesh. The poet at the center is *Homo viator,* preferring the Pilgrim's Way to the War Path, reflecting on his relationship to space and time, to things given by nature, and to things that are man-made, and taking particular delight in contemplating the shell man constructs for himself as an expression of what he imagines his ideal *self* to be. As an Austro-American, Auden draws his instances from both countries: Schönbrunn, the palace of the Austrian emperors in Vienna, and William Randolph Hearst's rococo mansion in California, San Simeon. Schönbrunn, a reflection of the "divinity that hedges kings," is "someone's idea of the body / that should have been his, as the flesh / Mum formulated shouldn't." And "Only a press lord / could have built San Simeon" in an age when "no unearned income / can buy us back the gait and gestures / to manage a baroque staircase . . ." Such projections of the ideal self as San Simeon that ignore the realities of time and place are a product of fantasy rather than of truly creative imagination. An equally false counterpart is produced by those earnest city planners who imagine that "a pen for a rational animal" is a "fitting habitat for Adam's sovereign clone." (CP, 520)

The cycle's Prologue, "The Birth of Architecture," places the poet in his own historical setting with a rapid sweep through time from gallery-grave (Hetty Pegler's Tump is named in the next poem) to his own first bicycle at about age seven—the traditional "age of reason":

> From gallery-grave and the hunt of a wren-king
>   to Low Mass and trailer camp
> is hardly a tick by the carbon clock, but I
>   don't count that way nor do you:
> already it is millions of heartbeats ago
>   back to the Bicycle Age,
> before which is no *After* for me to measure,
>   just a still prehistoric *Once*
> where anything could happen.   (CP, 518)

This Prologue touches in small space on all the major concerns of the cycle: the human imagination, its products, and their relation to time and to nature. Architecture, whose changing styles embody a changing human vision of the self, provides the appropriate instances of the human faculty, the realistic imagination that distinguishes man from other creatures in Mother Nature's Commonwealth:

> Among its populations
>   are masons and carpenters
> who build the most exquisite shelters and safes,
>   but no architects, any more
> than there are heretics or bounders: to take
>   umbrage at death, to construct
> a second nature of tomb and temple, lives
>   must know the meaning of *If*.   (CP, 518)

To emphasize the significance of the final phrase—that each life must exercise its own imaginative powers—Auden added a blunt, disenchanting "Postscript" in octosyllabic couplets, deflating the contemplative mood of this poem through an unpleasant contrast in both style and attitude. This "Postscript," like the voice of Caliban in Ariel's domain, warns against the Romantic tendency to regard the poet in the flesh as the heroic possessor of a creative imagination.

The Romantic tendency to idealize either art or the artist is a target that Auden frequently belabors with his later vocabulary of heresies, particularly his characterization of outlooks or attitudes as Manichaean or Gnostic. *About the House* constantly warns against the undervaluing of the creaturely and mocks at a fastidiousness that seeks detachment from material things. His poem celebrating the water-closet, while attacking such fastidiousness exuberantly, finds room for an aside on its heretical roots:

> (Orthodoxy ought to
> Bless our modern plumbing:
> Swift and St. Augustine
> Lived in centuries
> When a stench of sewage
> Ever in the nostrils
> Made a strong debating
> Point for Manichees.)   (CP, 527)

Auden's mockery of those who prefer their humanity idealized is aimed ultimately at the misuse of imagination by political systems idealizing a class or a race, or proposing to build future Utopias on the sufferings of those living now. In the realm of imagination he is more tolerant of Edens than of Utopias. Both are imaginatively possible; but while Edens are immediately recognizable as fanciful and are therefore innocent or harmless fun, Utopias can cause endless suffering if their agents attempt to impose them on present reality.

Auden celebrates Eden in his poem on the modern bathroom, "Encomium Balnei," where he asks "what Eden is there for the lapsed but hot water?" Eden is a state free from the anxiety arising from the conflict between freedom and necessity, and a notable characteristic of the poem is the analogous appropriateness of its form to its subject. The verse appears to float free of the demands of form, and the syntax flows on ignoring the conventions of capitalization and punctuation. The modern sage, relaxing in a warm bath presenting a "Lieder Abend / to a captive audience of his toes" may experience a momentary Eden—an ideal state of perfect concord, "as if Von Hügel's hoggers and lumpers were extinct / thinking the same as thanking / all military hardware / already slighted and submerged." This reference to Baron Von Hügel whom Yeats in "Vacillation" dismissed with "So get you gone, Von Hügel, though with blessings on your head," is a reminder that Auden shared the antipathy for over-fine refinement that Von Hügel defined as modern Gnosticism. The phrase "hoggers and lumpers" he attributes to Von Hügel may be derived from a letter of Von Hügel to his niece in which, in discussing discrimination, the art of "discerning jewel eyes in a toad's head," requisite to reading Tertullian, he exclaims: "I want my niece to end by becoming such a discriminator; how weary I am of the *lumpers, the whole-hoggers!*" The intention of Auden's cycle, as a whole, might well be described by another passage in this letter reminding his niece of how vulgar, lumpy clumps of camphor produce an ethereal smell, and also of how a solid breakfast and its digestion contribute to the joy of a morning on horseback: "Yet . . . a person who would both enjoy camphor scent *and* disdain camphor lumps; a person who would revel in that liberal open air *and* contemn porridge and digestion . . . would have an unreal, a superfine refinement."[3]

If "Encomium Balnei" offers a fanciful Eden to be enjoyed as a respite from the daily tensions of the Pilgrim's Way, "Up There" suggests that the attic, with its motley souvenirs, may be visited safely only by children "who conjure in its plenum, / . . . / Now a schooner on which a lonely only / Boy sails north or approaches coral islands." For adults it encourages the false day-dream of innocence, and that sentimentality of disoriented feeling of which Rosetta in *The Age of Anxiety* supplies the representative Jungian type. It is in this Jungian context, which distinguishes consciousness as masculine and the unconscious as feminine, that the words *men* and *women* are used in the opening stanza of "Up There":

> Men would never have come to need an attic.
> Keen collectors of glass or Roman coins build
> Special cabinets for them, dote on, index
> Each new specimen: only women cling to
> Items out of their past they have no use for,
> Can't name now what they couldn't bear to part with.
>
> (CP, 525)

The cellar on the other hand, "deep in Mother Earth beneath her key-cold cloak," leads through the more difficult route

of the instinctive and the natural to the core of the unconscious—a route which, if braved, can be realistically fruitful:

> sometimes, to test their male courage,
> A father sends the younger boys to fetch something
> For Mother from down there; ashamed to whimper, hearts
>   pounding,
> They dare the dank steps, re-emerge with proud faces.
>
> (CP, 525)

Approached solely at the psychological level "Up There" and
"Down There" may be seen as minor pieces helping to fill out
the cycle while permitting oblique glances at the imagination
feeding on useless daydream, or manfully accepting the realities
of flesh and instinct. But their humor is more readily apparent
when they are read in the light of contemporary theological discussion. The titles "Up There" and "Down There" are drawn
from the technical vocabulary of existentialist theologians (as
was the term "out there" in "Prime") and reflect ideas to be
found in Heidegger and Tillich that were given popular cur-
rency in Bishop John Robinson's *Honest to God* (1963) at about
the time Auden was composing the cycle. One theme of Robinson's book was that the traditional image of God as "up there"
or "out there" must be abandoned in favor of a concept of God
"down there" as the depth and ground of being. *Honest to God*
caused an immediate flurry of controversy in England in both
press and television that drew in even the Archbishop of Canterbury.[4] Auden, who shared Tillich's view that religious thought
should recognize depth psychology, would have enjoyed the controversy both for its serious and humorous aspects—so much so
that if his house lacked either cellar or attic he would have felt
the need to invent them to accommodate a contemporary concern. In the light of these theological concerns the final stanza
of "Down There" culminates in a parable of human and divine
love:

> . . . a cellar never takes umbrage;
> It takes us as we are, explorers, homebodies,
> Who seldom visit others when we don't need them.
>
> (CP, 525)

But however close to God, a cellar may not be an ideal place for the work of the imagination in transforming insights into lasting objects. For this a "Cave of Making," designed to shut out the attic's daydream and the cellar's natural life and so to heighten consciousness, is essential:

> from the Olivetti portable,
>   the dictionaries (the very
> best money can buy), the heaps of paper, it is evident
>   what must go on. Devoid of
> flowers and family photographs, all is subordinate
>   here to a function, designed to
> discourage daydreams—hence windows averted from plausible
>   videnda but admitting a light one
> could mend a watch by. . . .   (CP, 521)

"The Cave of Making" becomes an elegiac monologue addressed to the shade of Louis MacNeice, with confidential asides on the present status of the poet's craft: "This unpopular art which cannot be turned into / background noise for study / or hung as a status trophy by rising executives." In tone, it preserves a fine balance between the understatement that characterizes all the poems in the cycle and an elegiac strain tinged with nostalgia. The movement of rhythm and syntax is masterful, except for one passage where the involutions of the syntax become too much for the speaking voice to carry effectively, and the tone, in "re the Cross," skirts bathos—possibly for the sake of strict syllable count:

> I should like to become, if possible,
>   a minor atlantic Goethe,
> with his passion for weather and stones but without his silliness
>   re the Cross: at times a bore, but,
> while knowing Speech can at best, a shadow echoing
>   the silent light, bear witness
> to the Truth it is not, he wished it were, as the Francophile
>   gaggle of pure songsters
> are too vain to.   (CP, 522-23)

No such awkwardness mars "Tonight at Seven-Thirty," the
poem most successful in combining the themes of the flesh, the
imagination, and the spirit. As an artistic object this poem consists of six fourteen-line stanzas with lines of varying lengths recurring exactly and conforming to an exact rhyme scheme. To
repeat so complex a pattern six times seems an almost impossible undertaking. Yet, Auden's syntax vaults the hurdles without breaking stride. Although its overtones imply the ritual of a
sacred meal, the literal subject of "Tonight at Seven-Thirty" is
a dinner party of our times. The poem begins with a typical
sweep through evolutionary time to reach man who shares a
common need for food with other creatures but who differs from
them in his potentiality for gratuitous acts. Food may be necessary, but a feast is gratuitous, and is, like art, an expression of
man's uniqueness. Immediately after the first reference to a
"feast," the poem glances beyond the temporal order to a mystic
meal in Paradise "when at God's board the saints chew pickled
Leviathan"—a humorous reference to God's taking the symbol of
evil, the great Leviathan, and dividing its flesh among the elect
(an image that may invite the additional humorous possibility
of Hobbes's bureaucratic state, pickled). There follows a rapid
résumé of the status accorded guests through the ages to today's
necessarily limited guest list. "Six," we are told, "is now a Perfect
Social Number." (The six stanzas of the poem therefore correspond analogously to the perfect number.) The middle stanzas
dwell on the problem of selection—or election: whom to exclude
and whom to include; and the final stanza outlines the qualities
desirable in a perfect set of guests.

Quite evidently, it is impermissible to read the poem on this
literal level and ignore the spiritual analogy to a mystic meal.
We may note, too, that the guests are chosen, essentially, on the
basis of the gifts they can bring to the feast—each according to
his kind. Finally the analogy to the olamic Sabbath—God's order
as it existed before the Fall and as it continues after the Judgment—is explicitly stated. The guests are ". . . men / and women
who enjoy the cloop of corks, appreciate / dapatical fare, yet can
see in swallowing / a sign act of reverence, / in speech a work of
re-presenting / the true olamic silence." (CP, 534) The poem it-

self becomes a work of re-presenting this vision of order. As an object it represents a playful order composed by *Homo Ludens,* related by analogy to the social harmony of the dinner party which is a microcosm of the ideal society, and related allegorically to the harmony of the olamic Sabbath "when at God's board / the saints chew pickled Leviathan." Apart from its spiritual analogies, this poem draws much of its detail from M. F. K. Fisher's "The Perfect Dinner" in *The Art of Eating* (for which Auden provided an introduction in 1963), and it is appropriately dedicated to her.[5]

Few poets would risk "the hallowing of the everyday" on so extensive a scale as Auden does in this cycle. Simply to carry such a scheme through without pratfall would be an accomplishment. But Auden does not merely squeeze by. He invents a style that is formally appropriate and musically compelling and that can bear repeated reading.

Beneath their carnival air the poems in *About the House* are concerned with inner human freedom and with the imagination as a key to such freedom. Reflecting in *The Dyer's Hand* on what he calls the "Curious statement in the Preamble to the Constitution about the self-evident right of all men to 'the pursuit of happiness,'" Auden remarks that "To be happy means to be free, not from pain or fear, but from care or anxiety." And he says a man is free in this sense when he knows what he desires and when what he desires is real and not fantastic. He glosses the word *desire* in a manner pertinent to his poems on the imagination in *About the House*. "A desire is real" he says, "when the possibility of satisfaction exists . . . and the existence of such a possibility for any man depends, first, on his present historical and social situation . . . and, secondly, on his natural endowment as an individual." (DH, 327-28)

The poems in *About the House* presuppose that the realistic imagination is similarly circumscribed by the poet's historical situation and natural endowment. Given autonomy from the flesh that it inhabits, the imagination tends to devolve into the delusions of day-dream or fantasy: "Even the stoutest dreamer / can fly without wings." To say that the realistic imagination is circumscribed by the limitations of the flesh is no disparagement

of its works. It has, after all, given us "basilicas, divas, dictionaries," the modern American kitchen, and other aids to "the
pursuit of happiness."

3

In a number of poems of the 1930s, and in his plays of
that period in collaboration with Isherwood, Auden had personified two types of personality as the Truly Weak and the
Truly Strong. The Truly Weak felt compelled to undertake
difficult tasks in order to prove himself. The Truly Strong, by
contrast, was self-assured and aware of his strength. Auden as we
saw identified T. E. Lawrence as one of the few living examples of
self-transformation from the Truly Weak doer of extraordinary
deeds as Lawrence of Arabia to the Truly Strong who sought
anonymity under an adopted name in the ranks of the Air Force
as Aircraftsman Shaw. Lawrence was the model for Michael
Ransom in *The Ascent of F6,* and he was also the model for the
two opposing types in the sonnet "Who's Who." The sonnet's
ostensible topic is the surface biography that records deeds of
prowess while remaining blind to the subject's psychological mo-
tivation. The octave tells of such a figure:

> A shilling life will give you all the facts:
> How Father beat him, how he ran away,
> What were the struggles of his youth, what acts
> Made him the greatest figure of his day . . .

The self-assured anti-type in the sestet has no need to leave home
to prove himself:

> With all his honours on, he sighed for one
> Who, say astonished critics, lived at home;
> Did little jobs about the house with skill
> And nothing else . . .   (CP, 109)

The sonnet "Who's Who"—its theme encapsuled in the phrase
"explorers, homebodies" in "Down There"—is alluded to in the

title *About the House,* implying that Auden himself had come home to everyday tasks. Does it also imply that like T. E. Lawrence he had effected a self-transformation from Truly Weak to Truly Strong? To feeling at home in life and no longer estranged?

There are a number of concealed allusions to this in *About the House.* Besides the cycle "Thanksgiving for a Habitat"—of which the title poem concludes with thanks for "a place / I may go both in and out of"—this volume contained a group of unrelated poems headed "In and Out." Like the titles "Up There" and "Down There," and the "hoggers and lumpers" of "Encomium Balnei," the phrase "in and out" alludes to a work Auden felt at home with. It is a quotation from the advice of the Raven to Mr. Vane in George Macdonald's novel *Lilith,* to which Auden wrote an introduction in 1954:

"The only way to begin to know what you are is to begin to make yourself a home."

"How am I to begin that when everything is so strange?"

"By doing something."

"What?"

"Anything; and the sooner you begin the better! For until you are at home, you will find it as difficult to get out as it is to get in. . . . Home, as you may or may not know, is the only place where you can go out and in. There are places you can go into, and places you can go out of; but the one place, if you do but find it, where you may go out and in both, is home."[6]

XVII

The Post-Romantic Hero:
Horace, Hammarskjöld, Isaiah

1

Beginning with "Sonnets from China" in 1938, and thereafter in the poetry and criticism of his middle years, Auden
toned down the Byronism of his early work and began to represent the ideal heroic figure as one who is primarily a restorer
and renewer; whose creativity thrives on limitations; and who
might take for a motto Goethe's lines that Auden liked to quote:

> A master shows his powers in limitations
> And freedom follows from the rule of law.

One of his lecture topics as Professor of Poetry at Oxford in
1960 was "The Hero in Modern Poetry," and a subsequent essay, "The Poet and The City," defines this hero in capsule terms:
"The characteristic style of 'Modern' poetry is an intimate tone
of voice. . . . And its characteristic hero is neither the 'Great
Man' nor the romantic rebel, both doers of extraordinary deeds,
but the man or woman in any walk of life who, despite all the
impersonal pressures of modern society, manages to acquire and
preserve a face of his own." (DH, 84) There are heroes of this
kind in his own later poems, including, for example, the memorial poems for his housekeeper at Kirchstetten, Emma Eiermann,
and for his physician in New York, David Protetch. But however
much the notion of the hero in literature may differ from one
age to another, Auden's definition in *The Enchaféd Flood* ac-

cords him the same characteristic marks at all times: "The exceptional individual is one who possesses authority over the average. This authority can be of three kinds, aesthetic, ethical and religious." (EF, 93) Auden rejects the doers of extraordinary deeds as having authentic authority in our time, but he accords this authority—in its three kinds—to less flamboyant models. His 1969 poem "Moon Landing" satirizes that space-age achievement as "a phallic triumph"—"a grand gesture" by "our apparatniks," and he prays on history's behalf that "artists, / chefs and saints"— representing the aesthetic, ethical, and religious modes—"may still appear to blithe it." (CP, 633) Kierkegaard's triad remains his touchstone, and it is no surprise to find that his heroic ideal for our time combines in some degree qualities of imagination, reason, and belief corresponding to the three spheres of authority. Among the exemplary figures whose authority his later poems invoked, are, in the aesthetic sphere, Horace and Goethe—both of whom restored Greek meters; in the ethical sphere, Dag Hammarskjöld—a man confronted with the practical task of finding more workable solutions to international problems than the "big" answers offered by nuclear stockpiles; and Isaiah, the prophet of renewal, whose image for society's malaise is fallen city walls that need rebuilding: "Look, I am laying a stone in Zion, a block of granite, a precious cornerstone for a firm foundation . . ." (28:16 NEB)

His two exemplars in the aesthetic sphere, Horace and Goethe, were skilled in the craft of verse. Horace transformed Aeolian lyric meters (especially those of Sappho and Alcaeus) into equally musical Latin rhythms; and Goethe, in turn, fitted these meters to German, as Auden did to English. For some sixteen years before he died—the period of his summer residence at Kirchstetten—Auden's work became increasingly Horatian in style and attitude. He caught the Horatian tone and spirit to greatest perfection in such poems as "The Horatians" and "Ode to Terminus" in *City Without Walls* (1969), and in many of the poems in *Epistle to a Godson* (1972).

While the example of Horace, and at times, of Goethe dominates these poems technically, their intellectual cutting edge is honed on the ideas of such modern thinkers as Karl Jaspers, Martin Buber, and Dag Hammarskjöld. Auden's later poems are commonly about man's situation in the present; and, in particular about the need for an *authentic* response to life in the sense that Karl Jaspers uses the term. Jaspers defined *authenticity* as the determination to affirm life again and again; the willingness to persist in creative activity in spite of seeming futility. One could describe Dag Hammarskjöld's diary, *Markings,* as a search for such authentic existence; and Martin Buber—whose phrase "the hallowing of the everyday" to some extent summed up its essence—advocated this authentic response to life. Hammarskjöld admired Buber's thought and volunteered to translate *I and Thou* into Swedish even while burdened by his immediate duties as Secretary General of the United Nations. He was working at this translation on board the plane that carried him to his death during a mission to the Congo in 1961. Hammarskjöld left behind the private diary which Auden—with the help of Leif Sjöberg—translated into English and published under the title *Markings.* Auden alludes to it in a stanza of "The Horatians":

> Some of you have written poems, usually
> short ones, and some kept diaries, seldom published
>   till after your deaths, but most
>   make no memorable impact . . .   (CP, 580)

Few modern lives are lived at Hammarskjöld's level of intensity. Consequently the closing lines of "The Horatians" assert that those who create in minor forms, who "hymn the small but journal wonders"—live no less authentically than the great masters or the "authentic martyrs." This category of "authentic martyrs," which could include such dedicated men as Dag Hammarskjöld, is represented in "The Horatians" by Regulus, the Roman hostage of the Carthaginians who, sent by his captors as an emissary to Rome to arrange a truce, returned (having advised to the contrary) and submitted to their death sentence as he had promised:

> You thought well of your Odes, Flaccus, and believed they
> would live, but knew, and have taught your descendants to
>   say with you: "As makers go,
>   compared with Pindar or any

of the great foudroyant masters who don't ever
amend, we are, for all our polish, of little
    stature, and, as human lives,
      compared with authentic martyrs

like Regulus, of no account. We can only
do what it seems to us we were made for, look at
    this world with a happy eye
      but from a sober perspective."   (CP, 580-81)

In general, Auden's representative Horatians are busy creative spirits who heal the sick, tend libraries, or enjoy the art of
cooking. (The phrase about the "happy eye" alludes to an apho-
rism of Wittgenstein's that Auden and Louis Kronenberger included in *The Viking Book of Aphorisms:* "Is it the essence
of the artistic way of looking at things that it looks at the world
with a happy eye?") Absorbed in a vocation, Horatians escape
the prevailing malaise: the boredom and sense of estrangement
that obsesses those for whom work is a meaningless function
divorced from life. When the language of the city is infected
with chronic vagueness, the Horatians heal it; when the Bar-
barians destroy its walls, the Horatians rebuild them. In the face
of unending violence and fashionable excess, they pay their duti-
ful devotion to Terminus the Mentor, god of limits and boundaries, as Auden does in "Ode to Terminus," where the strict
syllabic stanzas are an appropriate offering to the god of meter:

God of walls, doors and reticence, nemesis
overtakes the sacrilegious technocrat,
    but blessed is the City that thanks you
    for giving us games and grammar and meters.
                              (CP, 609)

For citizens not blessed with a capacity for "games and grammar
and meters" these stanzas may serve to show that just as Horace
renewed and transformed Greek lyric measures to suit contemporary Roman speech, so Auden in turn has renewed them and
fitted them to twentieth-century themes. It was Marianne Moore
who taught him the first step: a form of verse based on strict

syllable count which he used, for example, in his ode "In Praise
of Limestone." His own contribution was, in part, to endow
syntax with taut muscles. Syntax thus quickened demands more
vital language; and tired words must make way for livelier forms,
as in these closing lines of "Old People's Home" where Auden
recounts a visit to an aged friend, Elizabeth Mayer:

> . . . we all know what to expect, but their generation
> is the first to fade like this, not at home but assigned
> 　　to a numbered frequent ward, stowed out of conscience
> as unpopular luggage.
> 　　　　　As I ride the subway
> 　　to spend half-an-hour with one, I revisage
> who she was in the pomp and sumpture of her hey-day,
> 　　when week-end visits were a presumptive joy,
> not a good work. Am I cold to wish for a speedy
> 　　painless dormition, pray, as I know she prays,
> 　　that God or Nature will abrupt her earthly function? (CP, 646)

These lines from "Old People's Home" have the same syllabic
base as "In Praise of Limestone": that is, alternatively eleven
and thirteen syllables with elision of contiguous vowels. Obviously, the demands of this pattern spurred the use of some un-
common words or forms. None of these unusual words are new
coinages. They are survivals, not new arrivals; and the attempt
to restore their authenticity lost through misuse or neglect is
linked by analogy, in the artistic context, to Horace's revitalized
forms, and in the moral context to Isaiah's vision of restoring
the walls of the city.

　　That this present age is the first in which ordinary people
commonly find themselves in situations without precedent is a
frequent theme in Auden's Horatian poems. Even the aged in
"Old People's Home" must absorb the bewildering knowledge
that their generation "is the first to fade like this." In the poem
"Epistle to a Godson" addressed to young Philip Spender who
can't remember "when everyone travelled by railway," Auden
reflects that only yesterday, when inherited ways, trades, and
tools were still useful

the old could still be helpful

when they could nicely envisage the future
as a named and settled landscape their children
would make the same sense of as they did, . . .

(CP, 624)

Now that change is too rapid for such accurate foresight, morbid speculation on the uncertain future may conjure up nightmare visions:

the Muses scuttering,
smelly, from eutrophied Helicon,

. . .

Herod's genetic engineers commanded
to modify the Innocents . . .   (CP, 625)

The title poem in *City Without Walls*—a brief allegorical Morality play with aspects of a divided self for characters—piles up a series of such images of a civilization in dissolution. By contrast "Epistle to a Godson" is a sane and serious vision of the unique responsibilities facing the young:

in elite lands your generation
may be called, to opt for a discipline

that out-peers the monks, a Way of obedience,
poverty and—good grief!—perhaps chastity . . . (CP, 626)

Other poems in *Epistle to a Godson,* like the "Ode to the Medieval Poets" and "An Encounter" (on the meetings between Attila the Hun and Pope Leo), recall historical moments of great uncertainty which mankind endured and survived. Their general tenor is that the Horatians in any age respond creatively to the stimulus of pressures—frequently in the face of the opposing bias of those who, aspiring like Faust to unfettered freedom, seek a city without walls.

Auden did not include the noisy 1960s' devotees of uninhibited freedom in his hopeful expectancy that the young might heal our ailing universe. His poem, "Circe," on the enchantress who turned Odysseus' men into pigs, warns against the then fashionable myth of Circe's garden as a haven of universal peace, gentleness, and love:

> Her Garden is easy to find. In no time
> one reaches the gate over which is written
>   large: MAKE LOVE NOT WAR.   (CP, 646)

Faced by a meaningless life, Circe's children seek an unreal world to replace or destroy the old. The Horatian response to Nothingness, by contrast, is the way of affirmation in Carnival mood. Auden, paraphrasing Thoreau, once characterized the poet as "someone who having nothing to do finds something to do" and he caught the spirit of this affirmation very effectively in his "Ballad of Barnaby"—his version of the medieval story of the Jongleur of Paris, who, knowing no prayers, tumbled before the statue of the Virgin. The Jongleur, like the aged in "Old People's Home" and the young in "Epistle to a Godson," is faced with a situation without precedent. He responds—by choosing to do a technically perfect thing; and in this respect he is a Horatian too:

> The French Vault, the Vault of Champagne,
> The Vault of Metz and the Vault of Lorraine,
> He did them all till he sank to the ground,
> His body asweat and his head in a swound.
>
> Unmarked by him, our Lady now
> Steps down from her niche and wipes his brow.
> "Thank you, Barnaby," She said and smiled;
> "Well have you tumbled for me, my child." (CP, 619-20)

There is a subtle implication in a number of these poems of Auden's last years that, because each life is unique, *all* human situations are, in effect, situations without precedent. And since every human perplexity provides an opportunity for creative response, this present age of rapid change is, in a special sense, the age Horatian man was made for. Auden puts it this way in

"Lines to Dr. Walter Birk on His Retiring from General Practice":

> For nothing can happen to birds that has not
> happened before: we though are beasts with a sense of
> real occasion, of beginnings and endings, . . .   (CP, 578)

In Auden's view, what is called for even when words fail in the face of the unprecedented, is an affirmative gesture. Hence his 1962 "Whitsunday at Kirchstetten"—a serio-comic poem about the gifts of language and communication—concludes:

> There is no Queen's English
> in any context for *Geist* or *Esprit:* about
> catastrophe or how to behave in one
> what do I know, except what everyone knows—
> if there when Grace dances, I should dance.
> (CP, 560)

These references to catastrophe and affirmation echo Hammarskjöld's diary entry "Whitsunday 1961":

> I don't know Who—or what—put the question . . . But at some moment I did answer *Yes* to Someone—or Something—and from that moment I was certain that existence is meaningful, and that, therefore, my life, in self-surrender, had a goal. . . . Led by the Ariadne's thread of my answer through the labyrinth of Life, I came to a time and place where I realized that the Way leads to a triumph which is a catastrophe, and to a catastrophe which is a triumph . . .[1]

Hammarskjöld's saying "yes" to the meaningfulness of existence marks him as a true Horatian. But as the passage unfolds he is disposed to view himself as a sacrificial victim—a proclivity the carnival tone of Auden's poem disavows. Nevertheless Hammarskjöld had a significant direct influence on Auden and his work. Auden testifies to this in his Foreword to *Markings:*

> Brief and infrequent as our meetings were, I loved the
> man from the moment I saw him. His knowledge and
> understanding of poetry . . . were extraordinary, and pre-
> sumptuous as it sounds, I felt certain of a mutual sym-
> pathy between us, of an unexpressed dialogue beneath
> our casual conversation.[2]

There are frequent suggestions of Hammarskjöld's influence in
Auden's later poems. For example Hammarskjöld used the haiku
form extensively in his diaries as a frame for personal reminiscence. After editing the diaries Auden began to use the haiku
form, partly in imitation of Hammarskjöld's manner of casting
autobiographical allusions in the third person, and partly as a
recreational form on which he imposed new prosodic constraints
in addition to the limitation of seventeen syllables in three lines.
("Archaeology," Auden's last poem, August 1973, is his most
elaborate development of the form: a pair of syllables within
each line rhyme; two vowels in each line find assonances in the
other two lines of the tercet; and a vowel in each final line
rhymes with one in the first line of the next tercet. The poem's
twenty-three tercets come as close as counting in threes will
permit to three-score-and-ten lines. It will yield pleasure only to
those willing to dig.)

But, beyond his adoption of the haiku, there is a much more
pervasive sense of Hammarskjöld's influence in the many poems
about friends and personal acquaintances in Auden's last volumes. Hammarskjöld speaks, at times, in his diaries of what he
calls "the 'great' commitment": "The 'great' commitment all too
easily obscures the 'little' one. But without the humility and
warmth which you have to develop in your relations to the few
with whom you are personally involved you will never be able
to do anything for the many."[3]

Long before reading Hammarskjöld, Auden had spoken of a
version of the "great" commitment—which he called "some great
suffering"—in the concluding Narrator speech in *For the Time
Being:*

> We look round for something, no matter what, to
>   inhibit

Our self-reflection, and the obvious thing for that
    purpose
Would be some great suffering. So, once we have met
    the Son,
We are tempted ever after to pray to the Father:
"Lead us into temptation and evil for our sake." (CP, 308)

Writing in his introduction to *Markings* of two themes that preoccupied Hammarskjöld's thoughts, Auden identified these as,
first, his conviction "that no man can do properly what he is
called upon to do in this life unless he can learn to forget his
ego and act as an instrument of God," and, second, "that for
him personally, the way to which he was called would lead to
the Cross, i.e., to suffering, worldly humiliation, and the physical sacrifice of his life." And Auden added: "Both notions are,
of course, highly perilous. The man who says 'not I, but God in
me' is always in danger of imagining he *is* God."[4] Commenting
on this passage Edward Mendelson remarks that Auden had first-
hand knowledge of a Messianic temptation and that "this allowed him to write about Hammarskjöld's experience with insight and force."[5] If so, Auden's insight had ironic consequences
in his own life. As a member of the Swedish Academy, Hammarskjöld had supported Auden as a candidate for the Nobel Prize
for literature. The process began in connection with an earlier
candidate of Hammarskjöld's, St.-John Perse (Alexis Léger).
Hammarskjöld sponsored a translation of Perse's works into
Swedish in the mid-1950s, and himself translated, and circulated
to the Academy, Perse's 1959 work *Chronique*. When Perse was
awarded the 1960 Nobel Prize, Hammarskjöld persuaded Auden
to make an English translation of his acceptance address.[6] Auden was Hammarskjöld's next candidate; but, after Hammarskjöld's death, Auden's candidacy was put in jeopardy by his remarks on Messianic temptation in his introduction to *Markings*.
His remarks offended influential members of the Swedish Academy which awards the Nobel Prize. (Humphrey Carpenter specifically names Leif Belfrage then Swedish Permanent Under-
Secretary for Foreign Affairs.)[7] It was conveyed to Auden that
unless he modified the offending passage, the 1964 Nobel Prize
for which he was a nominee would be offered elsewhere. But

Auden felt Hammarskjöld would approve of what he wrote and he refused to change the passage. Although he later lectured at a Nobel symposium in Stockholm, he did not receive the Nobel Prize in 1964, or in his nine remaining years.

A significant number of poems in Auden's last volumes are poems—to use Hammarskjöld's phrase—about "the few with whom he was personally involved." Some are about friends and acquaintances at Kirchstetten, including the housekeeper and her brother. There are other poems of this period about relatives and friends in England and in memory of his father. The most public of these later poems, "The United Nations Hymn" composed for music by Pablo Casals, aims not only to blend words with Casals's music, but to celebrate music itself as an analogy for peace:

> Let mortals beware
> Of words, for
> With words we lie,
>
> . . .
>
> Let music for peace
> Be the paradigm,
> For peace means to change
> At the right time, . . .   (CP, 621)

These lines have interesting correspondences with Martin Buber's reminiscence of Dag Hammasrkjöld. Buber says of Hammarskjöld: "We were both pained in the same way by the pseudo-speaking representatives of states and groups of states who, permeated by a fundamental reciprocal mistrust, talked past one another out the windows. We both hoped, we both believed that still in sufficient time before the catastrophe, faithful representatives of the people . . . would enter into a genuine dialogue."[8]

When Buber was asked to join a society whose declared purpose was "to create words of spiritual value for the speech of Western Peoples," he responded by saying that what was needed was "not the use of new words, but fighting the misuse of the great old words."[9] Readers hounded to dictionaries by unfamiliar words in Auden's poetry may notice that these, as already remarked, are almost always survivals, not new arrivals. Even so strange a collection as *hirple, blouts, stolchy, glunch, sloomy, snudge,* and *snoachy,* in "A Bad Night (A Lexical Exercise)," contains no new inventions. These are dialect words. *Hirple,* for example, means to walk with a limp or to drag a leg; and *stolchy* describes wet mud trampled with sliding hoof marks. The *Oxford English Dictionary* will readily yield the others, for the poem is, after all, a lexical exercise; but behind the carnival mood of this lexical exercise lies a more serious purpose: to restore links to an older tradition and thereby to accord the dead a continuing voice in our affairs. Auden liked to quote a remark of Chesterton's to the effect that "tradition is the democracy of the dead," and in "The Garrison" he says "personal song and language" make it possible for "the breathing / still to break bread with the dead." (CP, 633)

However much the spirits of Horace, Hammarskjöld, and Isaiah brood over Auden's later poems, they are not the sole influences. Many of these poems have affinities with the later work of Goethe, who himself adapted classical forms to German verse. When Auden wrote "I should like to become, if possible, / a minor atlantic Goethe / with his passion for weather and stones but without his silliness / re the Cross" (CP, 522), he was not expressing a simple wish to be knowledgeable in matters of climate or geology. The word "passion" implies that he has in mind the anecdote he remarked on in his review of *Goethe: Conversations and Encounters* (1967): "Goethe suddenly got out of the carriage to examine a stone, and I heard him say: 'Well, Well! how did *you* get here?'—a question which he repeated. . . ." (F&A, 151) Despite his quip in *Academic Graffiti:* "Martin Buber / Never said 'Thou' to a tuber," Auden admired Goethe's saying "Thou" to a stone. What his later poetry most approves of is a sense of sacred awe in the presence of nature—an awareness that compelled Goethe, like St. Francis of Assisi, to recognize "brother stone." (Auden himself drew the line at insects. He had a phobia about spiders.)

Several poems in *Epistle to a Godson* that "hymn the small but journal wonders" have, as a common perspective, the limited horizon of a man seated in a familiar garden observing the natural world around him with gratitude and awe. Some of these, like "Talking to Dogs" or "Talking to Mice," are verse essays in a conversational manner resembling both Horace and Goethe. Others, like "Natural Linguistics" and "The Aliens," are philosophical meditations on the selfhood of natural things and altogether Goethean. The languages of the non-human things as Auden interprets them bespeak their calm presence—neither alien nor alienated—in the natural community. One amusing *tour de force,* "Natural Linguistics," speaks wittily in fluent rhythms, of the expressive languages of minerals, flowers, and animals. In it we are told that "Verbs first appear with flowers who utter imperative odors"—a line that seems to echo Goethe's "The Metamorphosis of Plants" (ll, 66-67):

> Every flower speaks out bravely,
> The mystic language of the Goddess Nature.

Auden's flowers, however, have a more individual selfhood—they speak for themselves rather than for the goddess.

A companion poem, "The Aliens," is more directly indebted to Goethe for its form. Speaking of this poem in a late interview affirming the significance of form for his art, Auden said: "For example, a few years ago, I was preoccupied with the, to us, strange and repellant ways of the Insects. At the same time under the influence of Goethe in his middle 'classical' period, I was wondering whether it would be possible to write an English poem in accentual hexameters."[10] The outcome was "The Aliens," a poem in hexameters about insects, which begins as a meditation on the selfhood of plants, animals, and birds: our "neighbours," "cognates," and "cousins," admitted to degrees of kinship we are reluctant to extend to the insects. To account for our lack of empathy with insects, Auden invents a fable of an earlier Fall in which the insects chosen to replace the fallen angels lost Eden when seduced by Satan's offer: "If I programme your ganglia for you, you shall inherit the earth."

Many poems of Auden's later years—like "Winds," "Tonight at Seven-Thirty," and "The Aliens"—sweep through evolutionary time to the point where the works of consciousness have now brought us, particularly in our relationships with birds, beasts, and flowers—Dame Kind's children of lesser endowment. These poems imply that consciousness and its works have brought us to the threshold of a new age in which we must recognize that the scientific tasks begun at the Renaissance have been done—that the exploitive character of Renaissance science (summed-up in Bacon's definition: "Putting nature to the question") and of the Western colonial episode released by its energies must now be replaced by a mutual bond of partnership between man and nature demanded by the logic of the Quantum Age. "The Aliens" is a transparent fable intended to put a humorous emphasis on this notion of our bonds with nature.

The oddness of the experimental hexameter lines makes "The Aliens" less appealing than a popular late poem of Auden's in more conventional rhythms first published in *Scientific American*, "A New Year Greeting": a poem on the micro-organisms inhabiting the human skin. He found the idea for this poem in the article "Life on the Human Skin" by Mary J. Marples in *Scientific American*, January 1969. In this case he had little more to do than to versify, with zest and obvious delight, what was already there. Miss Marples had provided the rest: not only passages such as "even the gentle exercise involved in dressing and undressing is accompanied by the shedding of . . . bacteria-bearing rafts," but some expressions that seem to belong peculiarly to Auden's cast of mind, such as "The micro-organisms live as Adam and Eve did, in a paradise where all their needs are supplied." But Auden, predictably, balked at this last analogy:

> I should like to think that I make
>   a not impossible world,
> but an Eden it cannot be:
>   my games, my purposive acts,
>   may turn to catastrophes there.   (CP, 629)

And he wondered how drama, in such a society, would account for unmerited suffering. Yet he took up Miss Marples's philosophizing on their man-inspired catastrophies directly:

> By what myths would your priests account
>   for the hurricanes that come
> twice every twenty-four hours,
>   each time I dress or undress,

        when, clinging to keratin rafts,
            whole cities are swept away
        to perish in space, or the Flood
            that scalds to death when I bathe?

    Auden rejects Miss Marples's notion of the human skin as
an Eden for micro-organisms; and he does so on the basis of the
blunt fact that we die—making the Eden short-lived:

        Then, sooner or later, will dawn
            A Day of Apocalypse,
        when my mantle sudenly turns
            too cold, too rancid, for you,
        appetising to predators
            of a fiercer sort, . . .   (CP, 629)

But his denial of the possibilities of an Eden for yeasts and bac-
teria is a reminder of his suspicion of all Edens and Utopias,
and it is also a reminder that however perilous he judged our
present circumstances—the only time we have to exist in—he had
no wish to undo the scientific work begun at the Renaissance or
to turn the clock all the way back to an Eden where there were
no clocks. He would be lost there without his watch: and, of
course, he recognized that every creative discovery in art or
science, like every acquisition of knowledge, involves a loss of
innocence, and that we are now farther from Eden than ever.
The question is, "How far?" And the answer his poems give is
quite specific. His Ischia and Kirchstetten poems on our relationships with our mother, Dame Kind, remind us, "She mayn't
be all she might be, / But she *is* our Mum." We therefore bear
responsibility for her condition. He says in his Commonplace
Book: "We have to realize that every time we make an ugly
lampstand, we are torturing helpless metal, every time we make
a nuclear bomb we are corrupting the morals of a host of innocent neutrons below the age of consent." (ACW, 282) That is,
we are where consciousness has brought us, and our mother, reduced at times to a drab, is now our responsibility. From this,
the greatest revolution, there is no turning back.
    As there is no way back to lost innocence in science, so there

is no way back in art; not even in the particular case of Auden's art. He was not simply a poet of the thirties. The significance of his work, early and late, transcends local loyalties. His perennial themes were consciousness and the human condition; and no other writer has so consistently chosen for theme the gap between the world of consciousness where the responsibilities of freedom begin and the unconscious natural world where necessity rules. His works in prose explore this theme also; and a measure of the qualities of mind he brought to criticism was his capacity for turning such occasional pieces as reviews and introductions into essays of permanent value. But his reputation as an artist rests, ultimately, on the poetry; and—apart from a Romantic emphasis on the spirit where Auden would include the flesh—what Sir Herbert Grierson said of seventeenth-century metaphysical poetry—that it was a poetry inspired by a philosophical conception of "the role assigned to the human spirit in the great drama of existence"—applies to Auden's poetry three centuries on.

Appendix A

List of "Books To Read"
appended to "Psychology and Art To-Day" (1935)

The presence of works by Blake, D. H. Lawrence, Homer Lane, Rivers, Groddeck, Heard, and Klages on this list shows it to be idiosyncratically Auden's and not that of a compiler or editor. The list, omitted when "Psychology and Art To-Day" was re-printed in *The English Auden*, gives evidence of his acquaintance with Jung's *Psychology of the Unconscious* and *Two Essays in Analytical Psychology* before 1935 when "Psychology and Art To-Day," appeared in Geoffrey Grigson, ed., *The Arts To-Day* (London: John Lane The Bodley Head, 1935), pp. 1-21.

Freud. *Collected Works.* International Library of Psychoanalysis.
Jung. *Psychology of the Unconscious. Two Essays in Analytical Psychology.*
Klages. *The Science of Character.*
Prinzhorn. *Psychotherapy.*
Rivers. *Conflict and Dream.*
Nicoll. *Dream Psychology.*
Burrow. *The Social Basis of Consciousness.*
Heard. *Social Substance of Religion.*
Thomas Mann. *Essays.*
Blake. *Collected Works.*
D. H. Lawrence. *Psycho-analysis and the Unconscious. Fantasia of the Unconscious. Studies in Classical American Literature.*
Homer Lane. *Talks to Parents and Teachers.*
Lord Lytton. *New Treasure.*
Mathias Alexander. *The Use of the Self.*

Groeddeck. [sic] *Exploring the Unconscious. The World of Man.*
Herbert Read. *Form in Modern Poetry. Art Now.*
I. A. Richards. *Principles of Literary Criticism,* etc.
Bodkin. *Archetypal Patterns in Poetry.*
Robert Graves. *Poetic Unreason.*
Bergson. *The Two Sources of Morality and Religion.*
Benedict. *Patterns of Culture.*

Appendix B

List of "Modern Sources"
appended to *The Double Man* (1941)

The following list appeared only in the first New York printing of two thousand copies of *The Double Man* (1941), pp. 161-62, and not in any subsequent printing of this work under the title *New Year Letter:*

Anton Tchekov. *Letters* (Translated by Tomlinson and Koteliansky)

Hans Spemann. *Embryonic Development and Induction*

Henry James. *The Spoils of Poynton*
          The American Scene

Margaret Meade. *From the South Seas*

Soren Kierkegaard. *Journals* (Translated by Alexander Dru)

Franz Kafka. *The Great Wall of China* (Translated by Edwin Muir)

R. M. Rilke. *The Duino Elegies* (Translated by Leishman and Spender)

          Letters to a Young Poet (Translated by H. D. Norton)

Werner Jaeger. *Paideia*

Nietzsche. *The Case of Wagner* (Translated by Thomas Common)

F. L. Wells, & C. M. Child. *The Unconscious: a Symposium*

Hyman Levy. *Modern Science*

Wolfgang Koehler. *The Place of Value in a World of Facts*

Thucydides. *History of the Peloponnesian War* (Translated by Crawley)

R. G. Collingwood. *Metaphysics*

Francis Steegmüller. *Flaubert and Madame Bovary*
Carl Jung. *The Integration of Personality*
T. S. Eliot. *Collected Poems*
Georg Groddeck. *The Book of the It*
R. S. & H. M. Lynd. *Middletown in Transition*
Vaslav Nijinsky. *Diary*
C. S. Lewis. *The Allegory of Love*
Thomas Mann. *Stories of Three Decades*
A. N. Whitehead. *Process and Reality*
Henry Adams. *The Education of Henry Adams*
Vachel Lindsay. *Collected Poems*
Paul Tillich. *The Interpretation of History*

Notes

Chapter I: A Flaker of Flints

1. Sigmund Freud, *The Ego and the Id,* trans. Joan Riviere (London: The Hogarth Press, 1927); quoted here from the revised standard version newly edited by James Strachey (New York: Norton, 1962), p. 49. The quotation in the next paragraph describing the ego as a "frontier-creature" comes from the same work, p. 46.

2. Sir Christopher Wren's *Parentalia,* quoted in the Introduction to W. H. Auden and Norman Holmes Pearson, eds., *Poets of the English Language,* III (New York: Viking, 1950), xxiii-xxiv.

3. Caedmon Record TC-1019, *W. H. Auden Reading* (New York, 1954).

4. Igor Stravinsky, *Memories and Commentaries* (London: Faber, 1960), p. 154.

5. *Anchor Review: Number Two* (New York, 1957), p. 276. (Not DH but an article first pub. in 3 parts in *The Listener,* June 16, 23, 30, 1955.)

6. "On 'A Change of Air'," in A. Ostroff, ed. *The Contemporary Poet as Artist and Critic* (Boston: Little, Brown, 1964), p. 186.

7. "Writers of Today," Television Interview with Walter Kerr, NET, New York, January 1957.

8. Ostroff, p. 186.

9. This dream of Wordsworth's in *The Prelude* provides the springboard for the discussion of Romanticism in Auden's *The Enchafèd Flood: The Romantic Iconography of the Sea* (New York, London, 1950).

Chapter II: Three Grateful Memories

1. John Auden, "A Brother's Viewpoint," in Stephen Spender, ed., *W. H. Auden: A Tribute* (New York: Macmillan, 1975), p. 26.

2. *Ibid.*

3. For Dr. G. A. Auden's letters to *The Times:* on Kier Hardie, see *The Times,* January 31, 1935, 10d; and on Darwin, *The Times,* January 2, 1935, 6c.

4. These were *Historical and Scientific Survey of York and District,* for the seventy-fifth annual meeting of the British Association, 1906; and *A Handbook to Birmingham and the Neighbourhood,* for the eighty-third annual meeting, 1913.

5. Christopher Isherwood, *Lions and Shadows* (London: Methuen, 1953), pp. 181-82.

6. John Auden, "A Brother's Viewpoint," p. 26.

7. Auden discusses his childhood imaginary world in "Freedom and Necessity in Poetry," in Arne Tiselius, ed., *Nobel Symposium 14: The Place of Value in a World of Facts.* (Stockholm, 1970), pp. 135-42; in *A Certain World: A Commonplace Book.* (New York: Viking Press, 1970); and in "Making Knowing and Judging," *The Dyer's Hand* (New York: Random House, 1962), p. 34. His most specific rejection of Platonism, and of Greek aesthetics appears in "Lecture Notes," *Commonweal,* 37 (November 13, 1942), 84-85. His fullest statement of the significance for the imagination of the doctrine of the Word made Flesh may be found in "Words and the Word," the fourth of his T. S. Eliot Memorial Lectures in *Secondary Worlds* (London: Faber, 1968).

8. P. H. Salus and P. B. Taylor, eds., *For W. H. Auden, February 21, 1972* (New York: Random House, 1972), p. 35.

9. Dacre Baldson, *Oxford Now and Then* (New York: St. Martin's Press, 1970), p. 56.

10. Louis MacNeice, *The Strings Are False* (New York: Oxford University Press, 1966), p. 103.

11. Christopher Isherwood, *Christopher and His Kind* (New York: Farrar, Straus & Giroux, 1976), p. 18.

12. *Ibid.,* p. 334.

13. *Ibid.,* p. 335.

14. In *W. H. Auden: A Tribute,* p. 79. Reprinted by permission of the Estate of W. H. Auden.

15. See Humphrey Carpenter, *W. H. Auden: A Biography* (London: Allen and Unwin, 1981), p. 83.

16. Postscript by Simon Nowell-Smith, *The Autobiography of William Plomer* (New York: Taplinger, 1976), p. 447.

17. Michael Davidson, *The World, the Flesh, and Myself* (Washington, D.C.: The Guild Press, 1962; London: Bruce & Watson, 1962), p. 129.

18. Auden included two works by Jung in the list of "Books to Read" appended to his 1935 essay "Psychology and Art Today" (see

Appendix A, above, p. 269), and during the 1950s he emerged as something of an expert reviewer of books on and by Sigmund Freud. He wrote the essay "Sigmund Freud," occasioned by the re-issue of a group of Freud's works, for *The New Republic* in 1952, followed in 1953 by "The Greatness of Freud," a review for *The Listener* of the first volume of Ernest Jones's biography. In 1954 and 1955 he reviewed the second volume of Ernest Jones's biography of Freud, under the title "The History of an Historian" in *The Griffin*, 4 (November 1955), 4-10, and "The Freud-Fliess Letters," on *Sigmund Freud's Letters: The Origin of Psychoanalysis*, in *The Griffin*, 3 (June 1952), 4-10. In the course of this last review, before going on to detail the causes of Fliess's break with Freud, he quite properly made the revealing claim: "Fliess's side of the correspondence is missing and few people—this reviewer is not among them—have read his books. . . ."

CHAPTER III: OXFORD POEMS

1. Robert Medley, "Gresham's School, Holt," in *W. H. Auden: A Tribute*, p. 40.

2. B. C. Bloomfield, *W. H. Auden: A Bibliography, The Early Years Through 1955* (Charlottesville: The University of Virginia Press, 1964), "Foreword" by W. H. Auden, p. ix.

3. Although "Storm's" in this stanza has reappeared unchanged in successive editions since 1937, it may have originated as "Storr's" and may imply a veiled reference to a series on English authors and literature: *English School Classics* by Francis Storr. The alteration rhymes with "swarms."

4. Auden quotes a key passage from Heisenberg in *A Certain World*, p. 333.

5. John Betjeman, "Oxford," in *W. H. Auden: A Tribute*, p. 44.

6. Stephen Spender, *World Within World* (London: Hamish Hamilton, 1951), p. 116. Spender's context, however, pp. 107-16, seems to imply the summer of 1929. See also the account of *Poems*, 1928, in B. C. Bloomfield, *W. H. Auden: A Bibliography* which identifies the vacation as 1928.

7. Anthony Storr, *C. G. Jung* (New York: Viking, 1973), p. 31.

8. Nicholas Blake (C. Day Lewis), *A Question of Proof* (London: Collins, 1935), p. 108.

9. Sigmund Freud, *The Ego and the Id* (quoted more fully in Chapter I, above). Auden printed a version of "Wulf and Eadwacer" trans. Michael Alexander in *A Certain World*, p. 230.

CHAPTER IV: BERLIN AND POEMS, 1930

1. See Humphrey Carpenter, *W. H. Auden: A Biography*, p. 84.
2. "Letter to the Intelligentsia," in Michael Roberts, ed., *New Country* (London: Hogarth, 1933), p. 9.
3. *Lions and Shadows*, p. 299.
4. See Carpenter, p. 100.
5. W. H. Auden, "A Saint-Simon for Our Time," a review of *In the Twenties: The Diaries of Harry Kessler* (New York: Holt, 1972) in *New York Review of Books*, 19 (August 31, 1972), 4.
6. The list of names is given by Carpenter, p. 97.
7. André Gide, *Fruits of the Earth* (London: Secker & Warburg, 1949), p. 151f; quoted in Carpenter, *W. H. Auden*, p. 87.
8. *Oxford German Studies*, 1 (1966), 166. Quoted in Carpenter, p. 85.
9. D. E. S. Maxwell, "Time's Strange Excuse: W. B. Yeats and the Poets of the Thirties," *Journal of Modern Literature*, 4 (Yeats Issue, February 1975), 718.

CHAPTER V: THE CHARADE OF THE LOVING AND TERRIBLE MOTHER

1. Edward Mendelson notes that Lawrence Heyworth identified the source, *Beowulf*, line 1305, "possibly adapted from John R. Clark Hall's 1901 prose translation"; *Early Auden* (New York: Viking, 1982), p. 42.
2. B. C. Bloomfield and E. Mendelson, *W. H. Auden: A Bibliography*, 2nd ed., lists productions at Briarcliff College, New York (1931) and the Festival Theatre, Cambridge (1934).
3. Jung, *Psychology of the Unconsicous*, trans. Beatrice M. Hinkle (New York: Moffit, Yard & Co., 1916), p. 554n. See Appendix A above.
4. Jung, *Symbols of Transformation*, Bollingen Series XX, trans. R. F. C. Hull (New York: Pantheon Books, 1956), p. 182. This excerpt also glosses the lines on Hitler: "Find . . . / What huge imago made / A psychopathic God," in the now discarded poem "September 1, 1939" (*Collected Poetry*, 1945, p. 57).
5. Quoted in B. C. Bloomfield, *W. H. Auden: A Bibliography*, p. 3.
6. Sir James Frazer, *The Golden Bough*, abridged ed. (London: Macmillan, 1922), p. 393.
7. Darwin, *The Descent of Man*, Chapter X; Jung, *Symbols of Transformation*, p. 160n. Edward Mendelson's account of *Paid* does not comment on Bo or Po but includes this in a note on the Man-Woman: ". . . it is clear that the Man-Woman in the charade em-

CHAPTER IV: BERLIN AND POEMS, 1930

1. See Humphrey Carpenter, *W. H. Auden: A Biography,* p. 84.

2. "Letter to the Intelligentsia," in Michael Roberts, ed., *New Country* (London: Hogarth, 1933), p. 9.

3. *Lions and Shadows,* p. 299.

4. See Carpenter, p. 100.

5. W. H. Auden, "A Saint-Simon for Our Time," a review of *In the Twenties: The Diaries of Harry Kessler* (New York: Holt, 1972) in *New York Review of Books,* 19 (August 31, 1972), 4.

6. The list of names is given by Carpenter, p. 97.

7. André Gide, *Fruits of the Earth* (London: Secker & Warburg, 1949), p. 151f; quoted in Carpenter, *W. H. Auden,* p. 87.

8. *Oxford German Studies,* 1 (1966), 166. Quoted in Carpenter, p. 85.

9. D. E. S. Maxwell, "Time's Strange Excuse: W. B. Yeats and the Poets of the Thirties," *Journal of Modern Literature,* 4 (Yeats Issue, February 1975), 718.

CHAPTER V: THE CHARADE OF THE LOVING AND TERRIBLE MOTHER

1. Edward Mendelson notes that Lawrence Heyworth identified the source, *Beowulf,* line 1305, "possibly adapted from John R. Clark Hall's 1901 prose translation"; *Early Auden* (New York: Viking, 1982), p. 42.

2. B. C. Bloomfield and E. Mendelson, *W. H. Auden: A Bibliography,* 2nd ed., lists productions at Briarcliff College, New York (1931) and the Festival Theatre, Cambridge (1934).

3. Jung, *Psychology of the Unconscious,* trans. Beatrice M. Hinkle (New York: Moffit, Yard & Co., 1916), p. 554n. See Appendix A above.

4. Jung, *Symbols of Transformation,* Bollingen Series XX, trans. R. F. C. Hull (New York: Pantheon Books, 1956), p. 182. This excerpt also glosses the lines on Hitler: "Find . . . / What huge imago made / A psychopathic God," in the now discarded poem "September 1, 1939" (*Collected Poetry,* 1945, p. 57).

5. Quoted in B. C. Bloomfield, *W. H. Auden: A Bibliography,* p. 3.

6. Sir James Frazer, *The Golden Bough,* abridged ed. (London: Macmillan, 1922), p. 393.

7. Darwin, *The Descent of Man,* Chapter X; Jung, *Symbols of Transformation,* p. 160n. Edward Mendelson's account of *Paid* does not comment on Bo or Po but includes this in a note on the Man-Woman: ". . . it is clear that the Man-Woman in the charade em-

Notes

CHAPTER I: A FLAKER OF FLINTS

1. Sigmund Freud, *The Ego and the Id,* trans. Joan Riviere (London: The Hogarth Press, 1927); quoted here from the revised standard version newly edited by James Strachey (New York: Norton, 1962), p. 49. The quotation in the next paragraph describing the ego as a "frontier-creature" comes from the same work, p. 46.

2. Sir Christopher Wren's *Parentalia,* quoted in the Introduction to W. H. Auden and Norman Holmes Pearson, eds., *Poets of the English Language,* III (New York: Viking, 1950), xxiii-xxiv.

3. Caedmon Record TC-1019, *W. H. Auden Reading* (New York, 1954).

4. Igor Stravinsky, *Memories and Commentaries* (London: Faber, 1960), p. 154.

5. *Anchor Review: Number Two* (New York, 1957), p. 276. (Not DH but an article first pub. in 3 parts in *The Listener,* June 16, 23, 30, 1955.)

6. "On 'A Change of Air'," in A. Ostroff, ed. *The Contemporary Poet as Artist and Critic* (Boston: Little, Brown, 1964), p. 186.

7. "Writers of Today," Television Interview with Walter Kerr, NET, New York, January 1957.

8. Ostroff, p. 186.

9. This dream of Wordsworth's in *The Prelude* provides the springboard for the discussion of Romanticism in Auden's *The Enchafèd Flood: The Romantic Iconography of the Sea* (New York, London, 1950).

CHAPTER II: THREE GRATEFUL MEMORIES

1. John Auden, "A Brother's Viewpoint," in Stephen Spender, ed., *W. H. Auden: A Tribute* (New York: Macmillan, 1975), p. 26.

2. *Ibid.*

3. For Dr. G. A. Auden's letters to *The Times:* on Kier Hardie, see *The Times,* January 31, 1935, 10d; and on Darwin, *The Times,* January 2, 1935, 6c.

4. These were *Historical and Scientific Survey of York and District,* for the seventy-fifth annual meeting of the British Association, 1906; and *A Handbook to Birmingham and the Neighbourhood,* for the eighty-third annual meeting, 1913.

5. Christopher Isherwood, *Lions and Shadows* (London: Methuen, 1953), pp. 181-82.

6. John Auden, "A Brother's Viewpoint," p. 26.

7. Auden discusses his childhood imaginary world in "Freedom and Necessity in Poetry," in Arne Tiselius, ed., *Nobel Symposium 14: The Place of Value in a World of Facts.* (Stockholm, 1970), pp. 135-42; in *A Certain World: A Commonplace Book.* (New York: Viking Press, 1970); and in "Making Knowing and Judging," *The Dyer's Hand* (New York: Random House, 1962), p. 34. His most specific rejection of Platonism, and of Greek aesthetics appears in "Lecture Notes," *Commonweal,* 37 (November 13, 1942), 84-85. His fullest statement of the significance for the imagination of the doctrine of the Word made Flesh may be found in "Words and the Word," the fourth of his T. S. Eliot Memorial Lectures in *Secondary Worlds* (London: Faber, 1968).

8. P. H. Salus and P. B. Taylor, eds., *For W. H. Auden, February 21, 1972* (New York: Random House, 1972), p. 35.

9. Dacre Baldson, *Oxford Now and Then* (New York: St. Martin's Press, 1970), p. 56.

10. Louis MacNeice, *The Strings Are False* (New York: Oxford University Press, 1966), p. 103.

11. Christopher Isherwood, *Christopher and His Kind* (New York: Farrar, Straus & Giroux, 1976), p. 18.

12. *Ibid.,* p. 334.

13. *Ibid.,* p. 335.

14. In *W. H. Auden: A Tribute,* p. 79. Reprinted by permission of the Estate of W. H. Auden.

15. See Humphrey Carpenter, *W. H. Auden: A Biography* (London: Allen and Unwin, 1981), p. 83.

16. Postscript by Simon Nowell-Smith, *The Autobiography of William Plomer* (New York: Taplinger, 1976), p. 447.

17. Michael Davidson, *The World, the Flesh, and Myself* (Washington, D.C.: The Guild Press, 1962; London: Bruce & Watson, 1962), p. 129.

18. Auden included two works by Jung in the list of "Books to Read" appended to his 1935 essay "Psychology and Art Today" (see

Appendix A, above, p. 269), and during the 1950s he emerge thing of an expert reviewer of books on and by Sigmund wrote the essay "Sigmund Freud," occasioned by the re-issue of Freud's works, for *The New Republic* in 1952, followed i "The Greatness of Freud," a review for *The Listener* of the fi of Ernest Jones's biography. In 1954 and 1955 he reviewed volume of Ernest Jones's biography of Freud, under the History of an Historian" in *The Griffin,* 4 (November 1955), "The Freud-Fliess Letters," on *Sigmund Freud's Letters: The Psychoanalysis,* in *The Griffin,* 3 (June 1952), 4-10. In the cou last review, before going on to detail the causes of Fliess's b Freud, he quite properly made the revealing claim: "Fliess's s correspondence is missing and few people—this reviewer is n them—have read his books. . . ."

CHAPTER III: OXFORD POEMS

1. Robert Medley, "Gresham's School, Holt," in *W. H.* Tribute, p. 40.

2. B. C. Bloomfield, *W. H. Auden: A Bibliography, The Ea Through 1955* (Charlottesville: The University of Virginia Pre "Foreword" by W. H. Auden, p. ix.

3. Although "Storm's" in this stanza has reappeared unch successive editions since 1937, it may have originated as "Stor may imply a veiled reference to a series on English authors an ture: *English School Classics* by Francis Storr. The alteration with "swarms."

4. Auden quotes a key passage from Heisenberg in *A Certair* p. 333.

5. John Betjeman, "Oxford," in *W. H. Auden: A Tribute,*

6. Stephen Spender, *World Within World* (London: Hamish ton, 1951), p. 116. Spender's context, however, pp. 107-16, s imply the summer of 1929. See also the account of *Poems,* B. C. Bloomfield, *W. H. Auden: A Bibliography* which identi vacation as 1928.

7. Anthony Storr, *C. G. Jung* (New York: Viking, 1973), p. 31.

8. Nicholas Blake (C. Day Lewis), *A Question of Proof* (L Collins, 1935), p. 108.

9. Sigmund Freud, *The Ego and the Id* (quoted more fully i ter I, above). Auden printed a version of "Wulf and Eadwacer" Michael Alexander in *A Certain World,* p. 230.

bodies a hidden reference to Auden's sexuality . . . soon after writing *Paid on Both Sides* he told Stephen Spender, 'I am the Man-Woman.' Presumably he was alluding not only to his homosexuality but also to the role he imagined for himself as an agent of the healing impulse . . ." (*Early Auden*, p. 51)

8. Georg Groddeck, *The Book of the It* (New York: Mentor Books, 1961), pp. 28-29.

9. Louis MacNeice, "Poetry To-Day," in G. Grigson ed., *The Arts To-Day,* p. 57.

CHAPTER VI: THE ORATORS

1. The last title in this list is invented.

2. John W. Layard, "Degree-Taking Rites in the South-West Bay of Malekula," *Journal of the Royal Anthopological Institute,* 58 (January-June 1928), 139-233, and "Malekula: Flying Tricksters, Ghosts, Gods and Epileptics," *JRAI,* 60 (July-December 1930), 501-24. Quotation from the latter article from p. 515. Professor John Blacking, Queens University Belfast, brought Layard's articles to my attention in 1970.

3. Interview in *Isis,* November 8, 1967, p. 14. Quoted in Carpenter, p. 230.

4. James Stephens, "The James Joyce I Knew," in Lloyd Frankenberg, ed., *James, Seumas and Jacques* (New York: Macmillan, 1964), p. 154.

5. Frank O'Connor, *A Short History of Irish Literature* (New York: Putnam's, 1967), p. 211.

6. Gertrude Stein, "Picasso" (1909) in E. Burns, ed., *Gertrude Stein on Picasso* (New York, 1970), p. 80.

7. Isherwood, *Christopher and His Kind,* p. 39.

8. Jung, *Psychology of the Unconscious,* p. 186.

9. "Auden and Politics," *New Verse,* 26-27 (November 1937), 21-22.

10. Louis MacNeice, "Poetry Today," pp. 56-57.

11. J. Hayward, *Criterion,* 12 (October 1932), 131-34.

CHAPTER VII: PLAYS FOR THE GROUP THEATRE, 1933-37

1. See H. Carpenter, *W. H. Auden: A Biography,* p. 139.

2. Isherwood has identified the Francis of the title as an English homosexual acquaintance of his and Auden's in Berlin, Francis Turville-Petre. He says that Francis, who appears in some of Auden's poems as Fronny, is a character also present, though unnamed, in *The*

Dance of Death. "He is one of the roles mimed by the Dancer. As the paralyzed patron of a boy bar, he is wheeled onto the stage, makes his will, orders drinks all round, and dies." *Christopher and His Kind,* p. 28. The history of the series of Auden-Isherwood collaborations is given in detail in Edward Mendelson's *Early Auden,* 272-80.

3. Edward Mendelson draws attention to this and other correspondences in *Early Auden,* p. 336.

4. Joseph Warren Beach, *The Making of the Auden Canon* (Minneapolis: University of Minnesota Press, 1957), pp. 174-80.

5. T. S. Eliot, typewritten letter to Rupert Doone, March 5, 1936, in the Berg Collection, New York Public Library. This and the item mentioned in the note following were on display in the Berg Collection Auden Exhibit, 1981. See Edward Mendelson, *W. H. Auden, 1907-1973: An Exhibition from the Berg Collection* (New York Public Library and Readex Books, 1981).

6. W. B. Yeats, holograph letter to Rupert Doone, March 18, 1937 in the Berg Collection.

7. Eleanor Terry Lincoln, *Through the Grecourt Gates: Distinguished Visitors to Smith College 1875-1975* (Northampton: Smith College, 1978), p. 98.

8. Carpenter, p. 85.

9. *Christopher and His Kind,* p. 258.

10. "Democracy's Reply to the Challenge of Dictators." *New Era in Home and School,* 20 (January 1939), 6.

11. Freeman Dyson, *Disturbing the Universe* (New York: Harper and Row, 1979). Quotations in this and the preceding paragraph are from Chapter 7, "The Ascent of F6," pp. 69-81.

12. Bentley S. Gilbert, *Britain Since 1918* (New York: Harper & Row, 1967), p. 88.

13. "W. H. Auden," in James A. Pike, ed., *Modern Canterbury Pilgrims* (New York: Morehouse-Gorham, 1956), p. 41.

CHAPTER VIII: POEMS OF THE THIRTIES

1. Harold Nicolson, *Diaries and Letters, 1930-1939* (London: Collins, 1966), I, 153. For an account of the unpublished work Nicolson heard Auden read from see Lucy MacDiarmid's "W. H. Auden's 'In the Year of My Youth . . .'" in *Review of English Studies,* August 1978.

2. See W. S. Baring-Gould, *The Annotated Mother Goose* (1967), no. 548, p. 221. Paul Fussell identified Christopher Smart's "A Song of David" as the source of the stanza in a review of E. Mendelson's *Early Auden,* in the *New Republic* (August 4 & 11, 1981, p. 35). Auden in-

cluded "A Song of David" in *Poets of the English Language*, III, pp. 567-83. The "White Paternoster" supplies a basic device for *Finnegans Wake* (which includes Auden in its cast of characters, p. 279).

3. *Modern Canterbury Pilgrims*, p. 41.

4. Charles Williams, *The Descent of the Dove: A History of the Holy Spirit in the Church* (New York: Meridian Books, 1956), "Introduction" by W. H. Auden, p. v.

5. See Bernard Crick, *George Orwell: A Life* (Boston: Little, Brown, 1980), note to Chapter 10, "Spain and 'Necessary Murder' (1937)," p. 435. Orwell criticized "Spain" and the offending phrase at greater length in *Inside the Whale* (1940).

6. *Early Auden*, p. 320.

CHAPTER IX: CHINA AND AMERICA

1. "The Means of Grace," *New Republic*, 104 (June 1941), 756-57.

2. Quoted by Christopher Isherwood in *Christopher and His Kind*, pp. 315-16.

3. John Auden, "A Brother's Viewpoint" in *W. H. Auden: A Tribute*, p. 28.

4. Quoted in Carpenter, *W. H. Auden*, p. 259.

5. *Ibid.*, p. 266.

6. Vera Stravinsky and Robert Craft, *Stravinsky in Pictures* (New York: Simon and Schuster, 1978), p. 490.

7. *Modern Canterbury Pilgrims*, p. 41.

8. Carpenter, p. 263.

9. *The Observer*, November 27, 1966. Quoted in Carpenter, p. 418. Editors of anthologies used in American colleges who still commonly include "Spain" and "September 1, 1939," as well as the unrevised version of the elegy on Yeats, seem to approve the Alvarez view. *W. H. Auden: Selected Poems, New Edition*, ed., E. Mendelson (Vintage Books, 1980) also prints the elegy unrevised on grounds of its historical importance.

10. "Young Auden" in *Shenandoah*, 18 (Winter 1967), 15.

11. Draft in the Berg Collection, quoted by Carpenter, p. 418.

CHAPTER X: DISENCHANTMENT WITH YEATS

1. G. Handley-Taylor and Timothy d'Arch Smith, comp., *C. Day Lewis, The Poet Laureate: A Bibliography*, with a Letter of Introduction by W. H. Auden (London: St. James Press, 1968), pp. v-vi.

2. The Yeats quotations are from *The Collected Poems of W. B. Yeats* (New York: Macmillan, 1956).

3. "Yeats as an Example," *Kenyon Review*, 10 (Spring 1948), 194.

4. "Craft Interview: W. H. Auden," *New York Quarterly*, 1 (Winter 1970), 13.

5. Auden appears familiar with *A Vision*—he echoes a phrase of Blake's quoted in it later in this poem; and he would know such typical statements as "At death consciousness passes from *Husk* to *Spirit; Husk* and *Passionate Body* are said to *disappear*" and "Spirits can have neither past nor present because *Husk* and *Passionate Body* have *disappeared*" in *A Vision* (New York: Macmillan, 1956), pp. 188 and 192.

6. The Steinach procedure sought to increase vigor and mentality by tying off the duct through which spermatozoa leave the testicle. It was not a transplant employing animal glands.

7. W. H. Auden, "The Public *vs.* the Late Mr. William Butler Yeats," *Partisan Review*, 6 (Spring 1939), 46-51.

8. "Yeats as an Example," 188.

9. For a reproduction of Miss Horniman's letter offering to subsidize the Abbey Theatre and her diagram of the tarot cards she read as a good omen, see Liam Miller, *The Noble Drama of W. B. Yeats* (Dublin: Dolmen, 1976), p. 330.

10. "A Great Democrat," *Nation*, 147 (March 1939), 352-53. Reprinted in E. Mendelson ed., *The English Auden*, pp. 387-88.

11. Charles Williams, *The Descent of the Dove*, p. 232.

12. I recall his comments on this in the course of a reading at Loyola University, Chicago, in 1956.

13. B. C. Bloomfield, *W. H. Auden: A Bibliography, The Early Years Through 1955* (Charlottesville: University of Virginia Press, 1964), p. viii.

14. W. H. Auden, "Two Ways of Poetry," *The Mid-Century*, No. 18 (October 1960), p. 16.

15. [Reply by] W. H. Auden in A. Ostroff, ed. *The Contemporary Poet as Artist and Critic* (Boston: Little, Brown, 1964), p. 185.

16. W. H. Auden, "Heretics," *New Republic*, 100 (November 1, 1939), 374.

17. W. H. Auden, "Yeats Master of Diction," a review of *Last Poems and Plays* by W. B. Yeats, *Saturday Review*, 22 (June 1940), 14; reprinted in Jon Stallworthy, ed., *Yeats: Last Poems* (Macmillan, 1968), pp. 47-49, from which all quotations in this paragraph are taken.

18. Cyril Connolly, *The Evening Colonnade* (New York: Harcourt Brace, 1975), p. 203. Connolly may be partly right; but he was unaware

that twelve years before Henze gave them a chance to portray the nineteenth-century artist-hero Mittenhofer, they had already sketched a libretto, *On the Way,* in which three "Bards" (representing Berlioz, Mendelssohn, and Rossini) in love with the Muse personify the artist-hero. They had hoped Stravinsky would collaborate with them in a follow-up to *The Rake's Progress.*

19. From "Yeats's Lecture Notes for 'Friends of My Youth,' " ed. Joseph Ronsley, first published in Robert O'Driscoll and Lorna Reynolds, eds., *Yeats and the Theatre* (Toronto: Macmillan of Canada, 1975), p. 74.

<h3 style="text-align:center">CHAPTER XI: AMERICA, 1939-41</h3>

1. Alan Levy, "On Audenstrasse: In the Autumn of the Age of Anxiety," *New York Times Magazine,* August 8, 1971, p. 42.

2. Excerpts from "The Prolific and the Devourer" written in July 1939 have been published posthumously in *The English Auden,* pp. 394-406, and it is apparent from these that Auden incorporated some of its axiomatic statements into the "Prologue" of *The Dyer's Hand:* "Reading" and "Writing." H. Carpenter gives an informative summary of its three parts in *W. H. Auden: A Biography,* pp. 267-71.

3. *New Yorker,* May 2, 1977, pp. 131-32.

4. This letter of 1.1.40 is substantially quoted in Carpenter, p. 286.

5. See Appendix B, above. NYL has "Notes to Letter"; DM has "Notes."

6. Monroe K. Spears, *The Poetry of W. H. Auden* (New York, Oxford University Press, 1963), p. 138.

7. Charles Williams, *The Descent of the Dove,* p. 55. The title is not derived from the epigraph from Montaigne as Carpenter surmises.

8. *Ibid.,* Introduction by W. H. Auden, p. v. For elaboration of this theme see Williams's novel *Descent into Hell.*

9. Carpenter, p. 303.

10. Williams, *The Descent of the Dove,* p. 22.

11. *Ibid.,* p. 16.

12. An ingenious set of nineteen artificial names each containing a combination of three vowels giving a clue to the arrangement of premises in all 24 valid modes beginning:

> *Barbara, Celarent, Darii, Ferioque,* prioris.
> *Cesare, Camestres, Festino, Baroco,* secundae:
> Tertia *Darapti, Disamis, Datisi, Felapton,*
> *Bocardo, Ferison,* habet: quarta insuper addit
> *Bramantip, Camenes, Dimaris, Fesapo, Fresison.*

13. *Common Sense,* March 1940, p. 25. Quoted in Carpenter, p. 287.

14. First published in *Thought,* 29 (Summer 1954), 237-70, and re-printed in *The Dyer's Hand. Thought,* a philosophical quarterly which had earlier published Auden's "Nature, History, and Poetry" (1950) and "Notes on the Comic" (1952) was then edited by the Rev. William Lynch, S.J., who was associated with the New York ecumenical group "The Third Hour."

CHAPTER XII: KAIROS AND LOGOS

1. "Memories of the 1940" in *W. H. Auden: A Tribute,* p. 106.

2. Sören Kierkegaard, *Concluding Unscientific Postscript,* trans. David Swensen and Walter Lowrie (New York: Oxford University Press, 1941), p. 208. Auden, like Kierkegaard, commonly uses this meta-phor of "the peril of sailing on the deep" to symbolize the existentialist anxiety in contrast to unexamined assumptions of bourgeois compla-cency. It appears, for example, with slightly varied phrasing in Kierke-gaard's *Concluding Unscientific Postscript,* p. 182: "Without risk there is no faith . . . I must constantly . . . remain upon the deep, over seventy thousand fathoms of water, still preserving my faith"; and p. 208: "the martyrdom of believing against the understanding, the peril of lying upon the deep, the seventy thousand fathoms, in order to find God"; and again in Kierkegaard's *Journals,* trans., A. Dru (New York: Oxford University Press, 1939; Harper Torchbooks, 1959), p. 115: "If I refuse to deify the established order *à la* Mynster . . . and out of zeal for morality end by confusing it with the bourgeois spirit . . . Mynster has never been out over 70,000 fathoms . . . he has always clung to the established order of things. . . ."

3. *Modern Canterbury Pilgrims,* p. 41.

4. Letter to Alan Ansen, October 1947 (Berg Collection). Quoted by Carpenter, p. 313.

5. The date of his mother's birth is wrong. It was 1869.

6. Auden omitted the "Shepherd's Carol" from the printed version. For an account of the sequence of events that led Britten to abandon the collaboration, see Carpenter, pp. 322-324.

7. Theodore Haecker, *Soren Kierkegaard,* trans. A. Dru (London, 1947), p. 16.

8. Auden wrote this personal "Love Letter" to Chester Kallman in May 1939 to express his anxiety about leaving Chester in New York while he taught for a month at St. Mark's School, Southborough, Massachusetts. The portion containing the line "The senses huddle like

cattle observing nothing" is reproduced in Carpenter, p. 266. The variation in "Advent" is "The eyes huddle like cattle." "Love Letter" was published in *Hika* (Kenyon College), 8 June 1939, but not collected.

9. Julian Symons, "The Double Man," in *Focus II*, ed. B. Rajan (London: Dobson, 1946), p. 137.

CHAPTER XIII: PROSPERO AND ARIEL

1. *W. H. Auden: A Tribute*, p. 111.
2. See Chapter XII, note 2, above.
3. W. H. Auden, Introduction to *Charles Baudelaire: Intimate Journals*, ed. Christopher Isherwood (Hollywood: Marcel Rodd, 1947).
4. Carpenter, *W. H. Auden*, p. 328.
5. *Ibid.* p. 325. But the widely dispersed lines from the beginning, middle, and end of Prospero's Farewell of which Carpenter makes an amalgam to support this view are insensitively wrenched from context. *The Tempest*, where Prospero is reluctant to let Ariel go (he keeps finding new tasks for him), gives ample warrant for the first and third elements in this composite. The middle one expresses Heidegger's view of existence as *zum-Tode-sein* (Being towards death). The aspects of the poem touching on his relationship with Kallman are more likely subsumed in the Shakespearean themes of innocence, guilt, forgiveness, and reconciliation.
6. "Two Sides to a Thorny Problem: Exploring Below the Surface of Shakespeare's *Merchant*," *New York Times*, March 1, 1953, sec. 2, p. 1.
7. *W. H. Auden: A Bibliography, 1924-1969*, p. 59.
8. Rhoda Jaffe remarried and had children. According to Carpenter she died by suicide.

CHAPTER XIV: THE AGE OF ANXIETY

1. *New Republic*, 90 (May 15, 1944), 683.
2. Anthony Storr, *C. G. Jung* (New York: Viking, 1973), p. 70.
3. Martin Gardner, *The Ambidextrous Universe: Left, Right and the Fall of Parity* (New York: Mentor, 1969), p. 120, quoted in Richard Johnson, *Man's Place: An Essay on Auden* (Ithaca: Cornell University Press, 1973), p. 34n. Auden quotes an extract from Gardner's *The Ambidextrous Universe* in *A Certain World*, p. 334.
4. C. G. Jung, *The Integration of the Personality* (New York: 1939), p. 41.

5. C. G. Jung, *Symbols of Transformation,* pp. 292-293.

6. Jolan Jocobi, *The Psychology of Jung,* trans. K. W. Bash (New Haven: Yale University Press, 1943), p. 41.

7. Auden quotes only the fourth stanza of the ballad. The phrase "our dear Dad" is from the third: "Greatest sorrow England ever had / When death took away our dear Dad; / A king was he from head to sole, / Loved by his people one and all."

8. *New York Times Book Review,* July 27, 1947, p. 5.

9. Wilhelm and Marion Pauck, *Paul Tillich: His Life and Thought* (New York: Harper and Row, 1974), p. 224.

10. *Modern Man in Search of a Soul* (New York: Harvest Books, 1962), p. 108.

11. Accounts of the progress of the work appeared in *Memories and Commentaries* (1960) by Igor Stravinsky and Robert Craft, and in the related Penguin Book, *Stravinsky in Conversations with Robert Craft* (1962). There is even greater detail in Vera Stravinsky's and Robert Craft's *Stravinsky in Pictures and Documents* (1978). Auden wrote on it in *Harper's Bazaar* (February 1953), and he gave his final summing up in "The World of Opera" in *Secondary Worlds* (1968). Other accounts by Kallman, Stravinsky, and Vera Stravinsky may be found in the booklet distributed with the Columbia recording, *Stravinsky Conducts "The Rake's Progress"* (1964).

12. Introduction to *Charles Baudelaire: Intimate Journals,* p. 20.

13. Igor Stravinsky and Robert Craft, *Memories and Commentaries,* p. 158.

14. Vera Stravinsky and Robert Craft, *Stravinsky in Pictures and Documents,* p. 413.

Chapter XV: Ischia

1. Edmund Husserl, *Ideas,* trans. W. R. Boyce Gibson (New York: Collier Books, 1962), p. 91. First published 1931.

2. To Rhoda Jaffe, May 30, 1948. Quoted by Carpenter, pp. 357-58.

3. Vera Stravinsky and Robert Craft, *Stravinsky in Pictures and Documents,* p. 415.

4. From the autograph book of Maria Senese, Bar Internationale, Forio d'Ischia. Printed here for the first time by permission of Edward Mendelson and the Estate of W. H. Auden.

5. Quoted in Ionel Jianou, "The Artistic Universe of Henry Moore" in Ionel Jianou, ed., *Henry Moore* (New York: Tudor, 1968; Arted Editions, Paris), p. 9. See also British Museum Publication, *An Exhibition*

of a Book Dedicated by Henry Moore to W. H. Auden with Related Drawings: Auden, Poems—Moore, Lithographs (Catalogue of an exhibition held at the British Museum April 24 to June 30, 1974), with Introductions by Henry Moore. "The nucleus of this exhibition is an advance copy, presented to the department of prints and drawings by the artist, of a selection of poems by W. H. Auden illustrated—or, it would perhaps be truer to say, interpreted by Henry Moore." (From "Preface" by John Gere, Keeper of Prints and Drawings.)

6. Auden's "Note" on record sleeve, *W. H. Auden Reading His Poems,* Caedmon Record Album, TC-1019 (New York, 1953).

7. "Memories of the 1940s," in *W. H. Auden: A Tribute,* p. 116.

8. "The Means of Grace," *New Republic,* 104 (June 2, 1941), 765-66.

9. For a more complete account of the libretto for *Delia* and of settings of Auden's poems by Lennox Berkeley see Monroe K. Spears, *The Poetry of W. H. Auden* (New York: Oxford University Press, 1963), pp. 278-79 and *passim.*

CHAPTER XVI: KIRCHSTETTEN

1. Allan Seager, *The Glass House: A Life of Theodore Roethke* (New York: McGraw-Hill, 1968), p. 210.

2. Giovanni Maresca, conversation with Edward Callan, June 1974.

3. Friedrich von Hügel, *Selected Letters, 1896-1926,* ed. Bernard Holland (London: Dent, 1933), pp. 271-77.

4. See David A. Palin, "Theology," in C. B. Cox and A. E. Dyson, eds., *The Twentieth-Century Mind,* III (Oxford University Press, 1972), pp. 142-43.

5. Auden reviewed the 1958 American edition of *The Art of Eating* in "The Kitchen of Life," *Griffin,* 6 (June 1958), 4-11, and he revised this for his introduction to the Faber edition (London, 1963).

6. Quoted from Auden's Introduction to *The Visionary Novels of George Macdonald,* ed. Anne Fremantle (New York: Noonday Press, 1954). This volume contained Macdonald's *Lilith* and *Phantastes.* The Introduction is reprinted in *Forewords and Afterwords.*

CHAPTER XVII: THE POST-ROMANTIC HERO

1. Dag Hammarskjöld, *Markings,* trans. by Leif Sjöberg and W. H. Auden, with a Foreword by W. H. Auden (New York, Knopf, 1964), p. 205.

2. *Ibid.*, p. xi.

3. *Ibid.*, p. 131.

4. *Ibid.*, p. xiv.

5. *Early Auden,* p. 255n.

6. Brian Urquhart, *Hammarskjöld* (New York: Knopf, 1973), p. 39.

7. Carpenter, p. 405.

8. Martin Buber, *A Believing Humanism: My Testament, 1902-1965,* trans. and with Introduction by Maurice Friedman (New York, Simon and Schuster, 1967), p. 57.

9. *Ibid.*, p. 31.

10. *Agenda* (Autumn-Winter 1972-73).

Index

    CHRONOLOGY: (*Cont.*)
        214; period of summer resi-
        dence in Ischia (1948–57), 218–
        39; Professor of Poetry, Ox-
        ford (1956–61), 28, 219; period
        of summer residence at Kirch-
        stetten, Austria (1950–73), 239–
        67; death, 3, 21; burial, 21;
        Westminster Abbey Poets'
        Corner Memorial, 143, 162
    LONGER WORKS: POETRY AND PROSE
    About the House, 238, 241–51
    Academic Graffiti, 263
    Address Unknown, 168
    Age of Anxiety, The, 4, 37, 71,
        151, 162, 203, 204–15, 230, 245
    Another Time, 121, 127, 129,
        135, 139–42
    Ascent of F6, The, 40, 75, 105–
        11, 127, 130, 250
    Bassarids, The, 216
    Bucolics, 11, 219, 224, 226, 228–
        30
    Calendar of the Year (film), 64
    Certain World, A (Commonplace
        Book), 19, 30, 31, 169, 211, 227,
        266
    Chase, The, 101
    City Without Walls, 27, 240
    Collected Longer Poems (1969),
        171, 202
    Collected Poems (1976), 49, 72,
        116, 120, 121, 162, 168, 171, 172
    Collected Poetry (1945), 92, 103,
        120, 155, 202
    Collected Shorter Poems (1957),
        141, 202
    Dance of Death, The, 64, 74, 97–
        101, 103, 115, 119
    Delia, 216, 237
    Dichtung und Wahrheit, 199
    Dog Beneath the Skin, The, 64,
        101–4
    Double Man, The, 161, 167–71,
        173; see also *New Year Letter*
    Dyer's Hand, The, 12, 16, 24, 25,

        28, 174, 180, 198, 199, 202, 234,
        241, 249, 252
    English Auden, The, 72
    Elegy for Young Lovers, 14, 49,
        96, 125, 146, 150, 157–60, 216,
        222
    Enchafèd Flood, The, 18, 135,
        197, 219, 241, 252
    Enemies of a Bishop, 101
    Entertainment of the Senses, An,
        21, 155, 217
    Epistle to a Godson, 10, 240,
        256–66
    Forewords & Afterwords, 16
    *For the Time Being: A Christ-
        mas Oratorio*, 6, 18, 102, 109,
        113, 161, 162, 178, 180–90, 191,
        202, 204, 205, 207, 260–61
    Fronny, The, 101
    Homage to Clio, 240
    Horae Canonicae, 218, 220, 226,
        230–37
    In Time of War (sonnet se-
        quence), 131–36; see also
        Sonnets from China
    Journey to a War, 15, 22, 111,
        113, 128–35, 168
    Letters from Iceland, 10, 27, 124–
        25, 127, 130, 136, 168
    Letter to Lord Byron, 10, 25, 33,
        41, 124, 130
    *Living Thoughts of Kierkegaard,
        The*, 181
    Look, Stranger, 139; see also *On
        This Island*
    Magic Flute, The, 216
    New Year Letter (see also *The
        Double Man*), 7, 10, 16, 55, 68,
        75, 76, 120, 152, 161, 164, 165,
        168–79, 180, 206, 210, 235
    Night Mail (film), 64
    Nones, 230
    On the Frontier, 111–12, 127, 136
    On the Way, 222
    On This Island, 121–23; see also
        Look, Stranger
    Orators, The, 34, 71, 80, 85–96,

World War I, 14, 23, 29, 71, 94, 96
World War II, 68, 71, 96, 165, 167, 169, 177, 183, 202–3
Wren, Christopher, 8, 9
"Wulf and Eadwacer," 50, 275n9
Wuthering Heights, 78

Yeats, Georgie (Mrs. W. B. Yeats), 149, 157, 162
Yeats, W. B., 7, 15, 16, 20, 45, 63, 101, 104, 125, 143–62; *A Vision,* 148, 149, 152, 156, 161–62
York, 23, 26, 27